# CHURCH ARCHITECTURE
## IN NEW FRANCE

# CHURCH ARCHITECTURE IN NEW FRANCE

ALAN GOWANS

UNIVERSITY OF TORONTO PRESS : 1955
TORONTO                                    CANADA

Copyright, Canada, 1955
University of Toronto Press
Printed in Canada

Published in the United States by
Rutgers University Press, New Brunswick, New Jersey

Distributed in Great Britain by
Geoffrey Cumberlege
Oxford University Press

# PREFACE

IT WOULD BE DIFFICULT TO CITE EVERYONE TO WHOM I AM INDEBTED for help in preparing this study. But there are two persons without whose help it certainly never would have been written—Professor Donald Drew Egbert of the Department of Art and Archaeology of Princeton University, and M. Gérard Morisset of the Musée de le Province de Québec. In his capacity as director of the Inventaire des Œuvres d'Art de la Province de Québec, M. Morisset has been unfailingly helpful and courteous in providing me with documentary and illustrative material. The number of photographs reproduced from the Inventaire—many of them representing the work of M. Morisset himself—is ample witness to M. Morisset's generosity. To Professor Egbert I am deeply grateful for the time he has taken out of a busy schedule to read earlier drafts of this study; the advice and suggestions he has given me have been invaluable, and I should like to record my most sincere thanks to him.

I also wish to thank the American Council of Learned Societies, the Humanities Research Council of Canada, and the Research Council of Rutgers University for grants which made research for this study possible; Messrs. W. Kaye Lamb and Norman Fee of the Public Archives of Canada, for the many reproductions they have supplied; Professor Ramsay Traquair, for useful advice and photographs; Professor Richard Stillwell for suggestions regarding the interpretation of certain points in the church of Armenonville; Mr. George H. Moffatt for help in preparing the drawings; the Redpath Library of McGill University for photographs supplied from the file there.

To the curés of various parishes in Quebec I am grateful for unfailing courtesy on the many occasions I have asked for information and photographs from them. To the Editorial Office of the University of Toronto Press I am particularly grateful for painstaking care in the reading of the manuscript. And to all the many other persons who have contributed in various ways to this work, may I express my deep appreciation.

A. G.

*The Fleming Museum*
*University of Vermont*
*July, 1954*

# CONTENTS

# ILLUSTRATIONS

# ABBREVIATIONS

THE FOLLOWING ARE THE ABBREVIATIONS USED FOR THE WORKS MOST frequently cited in the bibliography. Each abbreviation has been noted in the text at the time of its first appearance.

*A.N.F.*   Gérard Morisset, *L'Architecture en Nouvelle-France,* Quebec, 1949.

*A.V.M.*   L.-A. Huguet-Latour, *Annuaire de Ville-Marie,* Montreal, 1863–1877, 2 vols. and supplements.

*B.R.H.*   *Bulletin des recherches historiques,* published at Lévis from 1895 on.

*C.O.A.*   Gérard Morisset, *Coup d'Œil sur les arts en Nouvelle-France,* Quebec, 1941.

*D.G.F.C.*   Cyprien Tanguay, *Dictionnaire généalogique des familles canadiennes,* I, Quebec, 1871. The reference is always to volume I unless otherwise noted.

*L.S.A.*   Antoine Roy, *Les Lettres, les sciences et les arts au Canada sous le régime français,* Paris, 1930.

*M.E.A.*   E.-Z. Massicotte, "Maçons, entrepreneurs, architectes," *B.R.H.,* XXXV, 1929, pp. 129 f.

*McG.U.P.*   *McGill University Publications,* Series XIII (Art and Architecture).

*M.H.:M.*   Olivier Maurault, *Marges d'histoire: Montréal,* Montreal, 1929.

*M.H.:S.-S.*   Olivier Maurault, *Marges d'histoire: Saint-Sulpice,* Montreal, 1930.

*P.G.M.*   *Plan général de l'état présent des missions du Canada fait en l'année 1683,* found in H. Têtu and C.-O. Gagnon, *Mandements des évêques de Québec,* I, Quebec, 1887, p. 115 f.

*P.K.T.*   A. B. Benson (ed.), *Peter Kalm's Travels in North America, from the English Version of 1770,* II, New York, 1937. The reference is always to volume II unless otherwise indicated.

*V.d.Q.*   Pierre-Georges Roy, *La Ville de Québec,* Quebec, 1930, 2 vols.

*V.E.*   Pierre-Georges Roy, *Les Vieilles Eglises de la Province de Québec,* published by the Commission des Monuments Historiques de la Province de Québec, Quebec, 1925. There is also available an English translation of this book.

# CHURCH ARCHITECTURE
# IN NEW FRANCE

# I

# INTRODUCTION

"IN QUEBEC, OLD FRANCE STILL LIVES." EVERYONE HAS MET THIS phrase, the theme of innumerable romantic writings, guide-books, and popular articles about the Province of Quebec. And while not strictly accurate in many respects, there is one real sense in which it is true—Old France does survive in a certain distinctive and characteristically French spirit which runs throughout the historical culture of Quebec. That is Quebec's real heritage from Old France; and in this volume I propose to study one of its finest manifestations, church architecture during the period of French rule in Canada.

Contrary to popular belief, there are extant in the Province of Quebec today very few monuments which antedate 1760. Antoine Roy, the present Provincial Archivist, writes that "eighteenth-century Canadian archaeology seems a much more hazardous science than French archaeology of the Middle Ages."[1] It is a statement even truer for the seventeenth century, of course. In 1925 the Commission des Monuments Historiques de la Province de Québec came to the conclusion that not more than fifteen churches went back to the French régime, and of these, practically all had been heavily restored.[2] Subsequently, even this handful has been reduced in number.

The major part of this destruction occurred during the Seven Years' War, at the end of the French régime. A letter written in 1759 to the King of France by Mgr de Pontbriand, sixth Bishop of Quebec, declares that "Quebec has been bombarded and shelled for two months. . . . The cathedral church has been entirely consumed by fire. . . . The church in Lower Town is completely destroyed; those of the Récollets, of the Jesuits, and of the Seminary are not fit for use without extensive repairs. . . ."[3] He goes on to say that "the whole Beaupré coast and the Ile d'Orléans have been ravaged. . . . The churches, to the number of ten, have been saved; but the windows, doors, altars, statues, and tabernacles have been ruined. . . . On the other side of the river . . . there are . . . nineteen parishes, of which the greater number have been wiped out. . . ." The subsequent campaign of 1760 laid waste the Sainte-Foy area. Montreal, while not

[1]Antoine Roy, *Les Lettres, les sciences et les arts au Canada sous le régime français,* Paris, 1930, p. 175. Hereafter referred to as *L.S.A.*

[2]P.-G. Roy, *Les Vieilles Eglises de la Province de Québec, 1647–1800,* Quebec, 1925. Hereafter referred to as *V.E.*

[3]H. Têtu and C.-O. Gagnon, *Mandements des évêques de Québec,* II, Quebec, 1888, p. 6 f.

suffering so heavily in the war, had experienced a series of devastating fires in the first half of the eighteenth century, and had not recovered from the latest of them when the Seven Years' War broke out.[4] Only Trois-Rivières survived the Cession of New France to Great Britain in any way intact; the old quarter of that city, including the splendid parish church begun in 1710, was preserved until its total destruction in the great fire of 1908, and photographs of the church are extant.

Some churches in rural parishes survived into the nineteenth century, most of them to be replaced by more "modern" buildings at later dates; the very few that still exist are all altered on the interior, and nearly all of them on the exterior as well.

Thus, a study of church architecture in the Province of Quebec under the French régime must depend almost entirely on documentary evidence for reconstruction. There has been very little archaeological research in the Province.

Documentary evidence for reconstructing the vanished churches of the *ancien régime* in Canada is fairly satisfactory. There are, first of all, various engravings, of which those made from Richard Short's drawings are the most important. Short was a naval officer who accompanied the armada led by General Wolfe against the city of Quebec in 1759. He entered the city with the occupying forces, and made a series of drawings depicting the most important landmarks of the conquered capital "on the SPOT," a fact which he carefully noted on each. Engraved in London and published in 1761, they constitute the most valuable single record of the eighteenth-century architecture of New France.[5]

Short was a careful draughtsman of no little skill; while his figures may display a somewhat Hogarthian tendency towards the satirical, there is no good reason to doubt the accuracy of his representations as a whole. The same cannot be said for the engraved views of Quebec which we find adorning the pages of various treatises that expounded the attractions of the New World to eighteenth-century sophisticates in Europe. Like the text accompanying them, these engravings present a general picture of some value, but the details are usually quite distorted. Of main interest here are the books by Lahontan, Lapotherie, and Charlevoix.[6] The remarks of the Swedish traveller Peter Kalm in 1749 are also of significance.[7]

[4]Cf. E.-Z. Massicotte, "Les Incendies à Montréal sous le régime français," *Bulletin des recherches historiques,* XXV, 1919, p. 216 f. This periodical will hereafter be referred to as *B.R.H.*

[5]Photostats of these engravings may be obtained from the Public Archives of Canada, Ottawa.

[6]R. G. Thwaites (ed.), *Lahontan's New Voyages to North-America,* Chicago, 1905. Note especially plate 14. Lahontan's works were first published in Holland in 1703; an English translation appeared in the same year. M. de Bacqueville de Lapotherie, *Histoire de l'Amérique septentrionale,* Paris, 1722, 4 vols. Note especially vol. I, facing p. 23. Père F.-X. de Charlevoix, *Histoire et description générale de la Nouvelle France,* Paris, 1744, 3 vols. Note especially vol. III, facing p. 14.

[7]A. B. Benson (ed.), *Peter Kalm's Travels in North America, from the English Version*

I *Carte générale des paroisses et missions établies des deux côtés du fleuve Saint-Laurent; c.* 1750. (Public Archives of Canada)

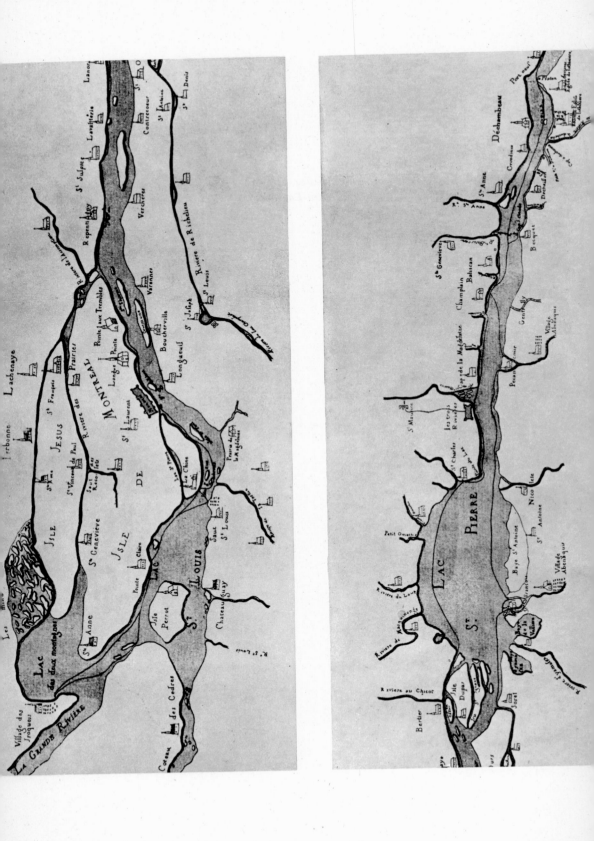

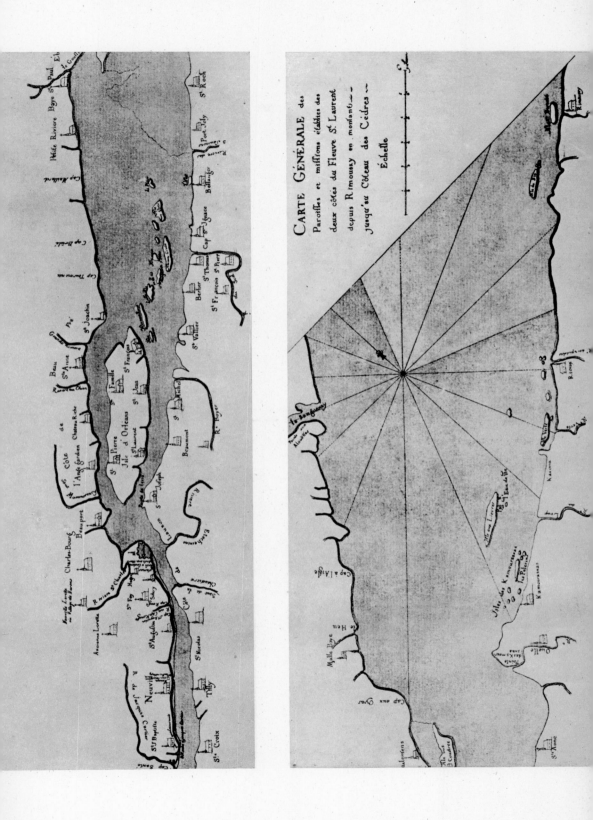

CARTE GÉNÉRALE des
Paroisses et missions établies des
deux côtes du Fleuve St Laurent
depuis Rimousy en montant
Jusqu'au Côteau des Cèdres
Échelle

In addition, information may be gleaned from miscellaneous maps, plans, and drawings preserved in various archival deposits in the Province.[8] There are also several instructive reports and letters sent back to France by authorities in the colony. The most important of these are the *Plan général de l'état présent des missions du Canada fait en l'année 1683,*[9] and the *Lettre de Monseigneur l'Evêque de Québec où il rend compte à un de ses amis de son premier voyage de Canada, et de l'état où il a laissé l'Eglise et la colonie.*[10]

The *Plan général* is an objective and careful record. It was made up, probably by the local curés and missionaries, as the basis for a memoir which Bishop Laval presented to King Louis XIV in 1684.[11] Although it represents only the mission churches, it is the most reliable check-list we have from contemporary sources, certainly much more so than the lists of churches contained in the highly erratic censuses taken in New France.[12] The *Lettre de Monseigneur l'Evêque,* which was written by Bishop Saint-Vallier about 1687, is broader in scope, but is much less objective; it seems to have been intended to arouse sympathy and support in influential French circles for the impoverished missions of New France.

A vast amount of documentary information has been preserved in the *Livres de Comptes,* or parish record-books, kept by succeeding generations of curés at the various parochial charges. Supplementing these is an immense number of minor works relative to *Québécois* culture and history which have been appearing since about 1875. This body of literature constitutes not only a storehouse of miscellaneous facts, but a record of the history of criticism in Quebec as well, and represents the third major source for the reconstruction of the church architecture of New France.

In the church architecture of Quebec, the high tide of Victorian eclecticism reached its peak at about the time artistic thought in other parts of the Western world had begun to reject it, that is, about 1890. And so, when other countries were beginning to investigate and appreciate their own native artistic heritages, the peculiarly long-lived and tenacious cultural traditions of Quebec, which had

*of 1770,* New York, 1937, 2 vols. Hereafter referred to as *P.K.T.* Peter Kalm, born in 1716, travelled in North America during the years 1747 to 1751, as a member of the Royal Academy of Sweden. He spent most of his time in the American colonies, but was in Canada for several months of 1749. His journal is primarily concerned with scientific observations, but there are many remarks of general interest, especially as regards architecture. Cf. P.-G. Roy, "Pierre Kalm au Canada," *B.R.H.,* V, 1899.

[8]The main archival deposits here are the Archives de la Province de Québec, Quebec, Que.; Archives de l'Evêché de Québec, Quebec, Que.; Public Archives of Canada, Ottawa.

[9]The text of this document is found in H. Têtu and C.-O. Gagnon, *Mandements des évêques de Québec,* I, Quebec, 1887, p. 115 f. It will hereafter be referred to by the abbreviation *P.G.M.,* with page numbers referring to the above work.

[10]Têtu and Gagnon, *Mandements des évêques de Québec,* I, p. 191 f.

[11]The *Plan général* is sometimes found attributed to Bishop Saint-Vallier, without apparent reason, since Laval's successor did not come to Canada until 1685.

[12]*Statistics of Canada,* IV, *Censuses of Canada,* Ottawa, 1876. Of the numerous censuses recorded here, only that of 1734 is credited with any reliability.

survived far into the nineteenth century, seemed destined to be completely ignored and forgotten, considered unworthy of serious attention. This was especially true in the case of churches. Everywhere, at the beginning of the twentieth century, the older churches of Quebec were being ruthlessly demolished or rebuilt. In their stead, the landscape was dotted with as bizarre an assemblage of edifices as could be found anywhere; in a burst of enthusiasm, one *canadien* editor dubbed them "gorgeous Byzantine castles, such as are found on the banks of the Rhine."

But here and there were found individuals who, while welcoming the new splendours which marked French Canada's coming of age, rather regretted to see the older buildings disappear. One such man was Jesuit Father L. Lalande, who in 1890 was writing the history of *Une Vieille Seigneurie—Boucherville: Chroniques, portraits, et souvenirs*.[13] The old church of Boucherville had just been redecorated on the exterior and interior in a garish version of the French Beaux-Arts style considered especially appropriate to ecclesiastical architecture. The new ornament, thought Father Lalande, considerably improved the simple and bare appearance of the older building; still, he wrote, "It must be admitted that this old style has its beauties." Artistic beauties? Simplicity of line, form, contour, spatial relationships? Not exactly.

These walls standing modestly under the long steep roof which they support, this façade almost exactly pyramidal in front, with its clocher above, slender, single like the God of the church and the faith of the believers who gather here to pray—all this ensemble has something religious and national about it, precious to us . . ., dear as our old memories. Brittany, they say, furnished us the models; almost all the churches of our parishes have been built on this plan. We would be tempted to say that they are not merely more provincial, more Breton, more Canadian, than others, but that they have even a more Catholic spirit. Without overmuch imagination, one could perhaps add that for this reason Protestantism, so often our imitator in architecture, has never imitated this sort. One could make no mistake on this point, in fact, and even without the cross which they carry so proudly on their pinnacles, the most uninitiated traveller would recognize them for churches of our persuasion.[14]

Thus, the major interest that the old churches of Quebec held for Father Lalande was not aesthetic, but religious and patriotic. It was an attitude typical of his time in Quebec. Little protest was raised at the destruction of the old buildings, for that was considered small loss artistically; nevertheless, parish historians like Father Lalande give us a very great deal of our information about the church architecture of New France. Histories of Quebec parishes began to appear in volume from around 1860 onwards, and it is to them that the student

[13]Published at Montreal, 1890.

[14]P. 257 f. Built in 1801, the church of Boucherville, which is still extant, is one of the landmarks in the evolution of the Quebec tradition of church architecture. For it the curé, Pierre Conefroy, devised a type of plan used in dozens of Canadian parish churches subsequently. The elements of the Conefroy plan were derived intuitively from the Quebec tradition of the seventeenth and eighteenth centuries.

of church architecture must turn, after having considered the evidence offered by extant monuments and documents.[15] Their authors—particularly the early ones—were not interested in the architecture of old churches as such, and hardly wrote with art historians in mind; to search out facts amid a medley of anecdote, eulogy, and reminiscence is often an exasperating task. But in these books is preserved much primary and vital source-material that would otherwise be lost irreparably today.

The parish historians were basically antiquarians, and so the study of church architecture in the Province of Quebec begins with the antiquarian point of view. And this approach is still the one most common in writings which concern the art and culture of French Canada. However, to the antiquarian two sorts of emphases are possible, and one or the other nearly always dominates. Either he is basically an archivist, with an eye to the assembling and tabulating of facts, or he is a *curieux,* looking for the quaint and the romantic.

Practically all writings in English which have had to do with the culture of Quebec have fallen into the second category, from earliest times to the present. There have been excellent studies of French-Canadian history by English writers, but works written in English before 1920, with few exceptions, are not too useful for serious study by the art historian.[16]

After 1920, however, a series of valuable studies in English were made by what might be called the "McGill school." It centred around Ramsay Traquair, for many years Professor of Architecture at McGill University in Montreal. In collaboration with several McGill men, notably E. R. Adair and Gordon Neilson, and Marius Barbeau of the National Museum in Ottawa, Professor Traquair wrote a considerable number of very valuable single studies of old buildings and churches in Quebec.[17] He was also instrumental in obtaining for McGill a set of old photographs representing many now-vanished monuments, mostly in the Montreal area. In addition to these photographs, there appeared in his articles many measured drawings made by himself or by his students in the McGill School of Architecture under his supervision; they, too, constitute a valuable record. In his last book, *The Old Architecture of Quebec,*[18] Professor Traquair proposed to assemble these separate articles into a coherent stylistic account of the

---

[15]For a list of parish histories to 1938 the standard reference is Antoine Roy, *Bibliographie des monographies et histoires de paroisses,* Quebec, 1938. They are most conveniently accessible in the Collection Gagnon of the Bibliothèque de la Ville de Montréal, the Musée de la Province de Québec in Quebec, and the library of Université Laval, Quebec.

[16]Alfred Hawkins, *Picture of Quebec,* Quebec, 1834, is typical of such works; it has an immense amount of information, but only the scantiest references. Rather more reliable are several works published in English by *canadiens,* e.g., Désiré Girouard, *Lake St. Louis, Old and New,* Montreal, 1893; J. M. Lemoine, *Quebec Past and Present,* Quebec, 1876, and *Picturesque Quebec,* Montreal, 1882.

[17]These articles, which appeared in various periodicals over a considerable period of time, may be found assembled in *McGill University Publications,* Series XIII (Art and Architecture). This compilation will hereafter be referred to as *McG.U.P.*

[18]Toronto, 1947.

Quebec tradition of architecture and allied arts; the result was somewhat too diffuse to do him full justice, but his is a lasting and important contribution in the field.

In French, earlier works such as Lemoine's *Album du touriste*[19] and Leclaire's *Le Saint-Laurent historique*[20] displayed the viewpoint of casual *curieux*. But later French writers have consistently tended towards the archival approach. Its earliest exemplar was Benjamin Sulte, who throughout the last quarter of the nineteenth century busied himself in all phases of the past history of his native city, Trois-Rivières. Basically, Sulte was the antiquarian parish historian, but in quantity of production and depth of research he far surpassed all his contemporaries.[21] Sulte's great-uncle was the sculptor François Normand, and in addition to the true archivist's drive to search out names and sources of all sorts, Sulte had a particular interest in questions of artistic provenance. He it was, for example, who first discovered the name of Gilles Bolvin as the sculptor mainly responsible for the interior of the old church of Trois-Rivières. In Sulte, archivist and *curieux* blended together in such a way as to make him the prototype of the vast majority of later writers in French on the culture of the Province of Quebec.[22]

Joseph-Edmond Roy, a contemporary of Benjamin Sulte, busied himself in the same way with the history of the Quebec area, and more particularly of Lévis and the Lauzon coast, to which he was native. Edmond Roy was an official archivist for the Dominion Government, and the archivist's interest appears not only in the reports written in his official capacity, but also in his five-volume *Histoire de la seigneurie de Lauzon*.[23] Yet there was in him still a good deal of the antiquarian, as may be seen in early issues of the *Bulletin des recherches historiques* which was founded, with Joseph-Edmond's collaboration, by his brother Pierre-Georges Roy at Lévis in January 1895; on its masthead is still carried the motto "O notre histoire, écrin de perles ignorées, Je baise avec amour tes pages vénérées. . . ."

The *Bulletin,* however, rapidly changed complexion to become what it is today, the vehicle for much serious scholarship in the Province. Pierre-Georges Roy, its founder, was the first Provincial Archivist, and a scholar meticulous in sorting fact from fancy. He was primarily concerned with the history of the city of Quebec, as Sulte had been with Trois-Rivières, and his numerous publications are major source-material for the history of the Quebec area. These

[19]Quebec, 1873.

[20]Quebec, 1906.

[21]Benjamin Sulte was a particularly prolific writer. In addition to major works such as his *Histoire de la ville de Trois-Rivières,* Montreal, 1870, and *Chronique trifluvienne,* Montreal, 1879, he wrote an immense number of articles for out-of-the-way periodicals. These have been conveniently assembled in *Mélanges historiques, études éparses et inédites de Benjamin Sulte,* edited by Gérard Malchelosse and published at Montreal in twenty-one volumes, from 1918 to 1934.

[22]For an appreciation of Sulte by Gérard Malchelosse, see *Mélanges historiques,* XIX, 1932, pp. 82–83.

[23]Lévis, 1897–1904. Joseph-Edmond Roy died in 1913.

were largely incorporated in his two-volume *La Ville de Québec,* which appeared at Quebec in 1930. P.-G. Roy was also in charge of the Commission des Monuments Historiques de la Province de Québec, which published in 1925 *Les Vieilles Eglises de la Province de Québec,* in two languages, naturally of prime importance for this present study. In 1927 the Commission, under Roy's direction, also published *Vieux Manoirs, Vieilles Maisons,* on domestic architecture. And in 1931, following construction of the Musée de la Province de Québec, Roy succeeded in assembling for the first time under one roof a mass of important material—archival, archaeological, and artistic—formerly scattered through various government buildings.

Pierre-Georges Roy was succeeded as Provincial Archivist and director of the *Bulletin des recherches historiques* by his son, Antoine Roy, who now holds these offices. In his doctoral dissertation presented to the University of Paris, on *Les Lettres, les sciences, et les arts au Canada sous le régime français* (published at Paris in 1930), Antoine Roy carried on the family tradition of archival research. This work is a storehouse of facts culled from various archival deposits in Canada and France, and is prefaced by an extremely valuable bibliography of important works in the field up to 1930; it is essential to anyone interested in the culture of Quebec.

The cultural history of the Montreal area has been ably dealt with by two major figures—E.-Z. Massicotte, a contemporary of Pierre-Georges Roy, whose studies are mainly to be found in the *Bulletin des recherches historiques,* and Olivier Maurault. Mgr Maurault, rector of the Université de Montréal, began as a parish historian, publishing a history of Saint-Jacques (sometime cathedral church of Montreal) in 1923, and of Longue-Pointe in 1924. In 1929 two fundamental reference works by him appeared—*La Paroisse,* a history of the parish church of Montreal, and *Marges d'histoire: Montréal,* which deals as the name implies with varied aspects of the history of the city of Montreal, and with art in general. In 1930 Mgr Maurault published *Marges d'histoire: Saint-Sulpice,* a study of the achievements of the Sulpician Order in Canada, and particularly in the Montreal area.

The most active scholar in the field of *Québécois* culture today is M. Gérard Morisset, now director of the Musée de la Province de Québec. Morisset supported himself through the law school of Université Laval in Quebec by commercial art work. Upon graduation he discovered himself to be more interested in art than law, and found means to go to Paris for study, remaining there five years. In addition to the training in practical art which has made him government supervisor of art instruction for the Catholic Department of Education of the Province of Quebec, M. Morisset in Paris assembled material for his *Peintres et tableaux*[24] which won the Prix David in 1936, and the Prix de l'Académie des Beaux-Arts de France in 1938. In the process, M. Morisset began a system-

[24]Published in two volumes at Quebec, 1936 and 1937.

atic cataloguing of the artistic monuments of the Province, past and present, and information about the artists. This file came to form the major part of the Inventaire des Œuvres d'Art de la Province de Québec when M. Morisset became director of this project. With support of the provincial government, the Inventaire has been continually expanding, and M. Morisset has undertaken a programme of photography which, it is hoped, will come to constitute a permanent record of all objects of artistic significance now extant in the Province. M. Morisset has written a number of later books which make public a small fraction of the material assembled in the Inventaire, most important of which are his *Coup d'œil sur les arts en Nouvelle-France*,[25] and *L'Architecture en Nouvelle-France*.[26]

In all M. Morisset's books, the basic point of view is that of an educator. As he has himself written, the aim of his writings is to awaken the people of Quebec not only to an appreciation of their older heritage, but to the possibilities of new creation: "Notre architecture moderne devrait être parfaite; parfaite dans son dessin, parfaite dans ses matériaux, parfaite dans son éxécution. . . ."[27]

In this present study, I have attempted to combine all the above points of view; but I am well aware, of course, of the inevitable limitations of such an aim. And there are certain limitations, too, imposed on the work by the nature of the available material. It is not really feasible, I think, to attempt too specific aesthetic appreciations on the basis of such scanty monumental evidence. Nor is it possible, in view of the continual repairs and alterations of later years, to evaluate exactly the techniques of construction used by early builders. What evidence there is has been conveniently assembled by Antoine Roy,[28] Traquair,[29] and Morisset.[30]

The contribution of this present study lies, I hope, in the attempt to bring order and discipline into a chaotic mass of available source-material, and to derive from it a coherent picture of the stylistic evolution of the Quebec tradition of church architecture. To accomplish this with the minimum of hypothesis, my

---

[25]Quebec, 1941. Hereafter referred to as *C.O.A.*

[26]Quebec, 1949; hereafter referred to as *A.N.F.* Other works published by Morisset, aside from numerous articles in periodicals, include *François Ranvoyzé* (1942); *Philippe Liébert* (1943); *Evolution d'une pièce d'argenterie* (1943); *Les Eglises et le trésor de Varennes* (1943); *La Vie et l'œuvre du Frère Luc* (1944); *Le Cap Santé* (1944); *Paul Lambert dit Saint-Paul* (1945); a novel illustrated by himself, *Novembre 1775* (1948); *Québec et son évolution* (1952); *Les Eglises et le trésor de Lotbinière* (1953). All these were published at Quebec.

[27]*A.N.F.*, Part III, p. 107 f.

[28]*L.S.A.*, p. 151 f., and especially p. 160 f., "Principes et analyse de la construction: les matériaux, etc."

[29]*The Old Architecture of Quebec,* Toronto, 1947, chap. I, "Building in the Early Written Record."

[30]*A.N.F.*, pp. 18–24, "Matériaux et procédés." Of great value also are the descriptions of contemporaneous building techniques in Hugh Morrison, *Early American Architecture,* New York, 1952, chaps. I and II.

first task was to make as complete a *catalogue raisonné* as possible of all the church buildings erected in New France, in chronological order. Such a compilation has not been attempted before; I do not claim it is completely accurate, and, of course, it can never be final. But I believe this *catalogue raisonné* was essential, in order to subject the maze of fact and fancy represented by so much of the earlier writing to the discipline of art history; with it, I have been able to work out a theory of stylistic evolution which can be substantially supported by fact, not speculation.

The analysis of stylistic evolution in the churches of New France made on this basis represents an almost entirely new approach. I have seen in the seventeenth-century church architecture of New France two major and two minor categories. I have suggested that the style of the one major category grows from origins in the craft traditions of seventeenth-century France, and is thoroughly impregnated with late medieval forms. The other major category I believe to have derived its inspiration from the more advanced and proto-academic architectural trends current in Paris during the seventeenth century, and to have been introduced into New France by the missionary orders—Jesuits, Récollets, and Sulpicians. But from earliest times these two trends intermingled in the church architecture of New France, and the mature tradition as evolved in the last decades of the *ancien régime* represents a final synthesis, forming an indigenous and distinctly Canadian development.

# II

# THE HEROIC AGE, 1608-1665

THE FIRST FIFTY-SEVEN YEARS OF FRENCH SETTLEMENT IN CANADA have been most adequately characterized as the "Heroic Age," *les temps héroïques,* of New France. Champlain's foundation of Quebec in 1608 inaugurates the Heroic Age; it ends in the summer of 1665, with the arrival in the little city of all the panoply of Louis XIV's absolute power, in the persons of Viceroy de Tracy, Intendant Talon, the Carignan-Salières regiment, and hundreds of settlers from France. In that year it was made manifest that the destinies of New France were henceforth to be in the hands of the King of France and his powerful ministers. The great individuals who had laid the foundations of New France—gentlemen adventurers, intrepid merchants, and zealous missionaries—would still remain on the scene, but they would no longer dominate it.

Yet these men and women—Champlain, Maisonneuve, Dolbeau, Jeanne Mance, Marguerite Bourgeoys, Mère Marie de l'Incarnation, and the rest—left an indelible mark on New France. The efforts of Louis XIV and Colbert were soon seen to be ephemeral; it was the pattern set by the Heroic Age which in the end determined the fundamental orientations of New France.

In the material realm, the accomplishments of these founders of New France were not impressive. New France in 1665 was a poor, weak, and scantily populated colony. With few exceptions, the gentlemen adventurers had been interested in exploiting the colony, not in developing it. They saw in it an operating base for the fur trade, and as such an opportunity for immense fortunes; they used the colony as a means to an end, and kept always an eye on the markets of Europe, and the luxuries and comforts of life in France.

Had it not been for the need to protect the great river-highway of the St. Lawrence from the depredations of the Iroquois, New France might never have been settled at all. To defend the fur trade and its profits from these enemies, permanent garrisons had to be established along the river. At first, the expedient of garrisoning the banks with friendly, Christianized Indians was tried; it was only when this proved unfeasible that French colonists were brought over. At the same time, however, any extensive settlement, with a consequent growth

12

of agriculture, meant that fur-bearing animals and the Indians who supplied the traders would inevitably be driven farther and farther away—a result to be avoided at almost all costs. The quandary in which the fur traders found themselves explains their vacillating policies of colonization, and the fact that by 1665 the population was not more than 2500 people.[1] Such a highly unsatisfactory state of affairs, from the point of view of the nationalist- and mercantilist-minded Louis XIV and his ministers, was a fundamental cause of their direct intervention in the administration of the colony after 1660.

In spiritual affairs, the early founders of New France did much better. If the Récollets who came to Quebec in 1615, and the Jesuits who arrived ten years later, were at first and primarily concerned with their missions to the Indians, they nevertheless did not neglect the spiritual needs of those French settlers who came to the colony. They set a high, albeit somewhat narrow, spiritual tone in New France, the evidences of which are still with us in the Province of Quebec. Furthermore, in contrast to the traders and adventurers, they poured money and resources into the colony. In spiritually exalted seventeenth-century France, the Society of Jesus could draw on almost limitless resources for its missionary work. The Ursulines and the Hospitalières de Saint-Joseph likewise maintained themselves in the early colony at the expense of wealthy individuals and corporations in France. The Récollets, sworn to poverty and lacking the material wealth of the Jesuits, left New France in 1629 and did not return until 1670. This is significant of the fact that the colony throughout the Heroic Age was too poor to maintain out of its own resources adequate religious establishments.

There is, then, a fundamental dichotomy in early New France between the poverty of the country as a whole, and the comparative wealth of resources upon which certain elements in its society could draw. This characteristic of New France persists throughout its history. A parallel divergence can be seen in the stylistic character of its church architecture. An analysis of the church architecture of the Heroic Age in New France very well demonstrates this dichotomy in its embryonic form.

There is no evidence of importance in the form of monuments extant from the Heroic Age of New France. Our knowledge of the earliest church architecture of New France comes entirely from literary and documentary sources, and these do not enable us to visualize too clearly its specific details. But the general picture is clear enough. When the evidence is logically assembled,[2] I think there may be discerned even in this earliest period four categories of church architecture which may be traced throughout the subsequent history of New France. To distinguish these categories is, I believe, essential to an undistorted estimate of the church architecture of New France; the conception of it as entirely homo-

---

[1]Dominion Bureau of Statistics, *Chronological List of Canadian Censuses,* Ottawa, 1933.
[2]See the *catalogue raisonné* of the churches of this period.

geneous is one that in my opinion has given rise to many one-sided interpretations and misconceptions.

## THE MISSION CHAPELS

When Champlain came to Quebec for the first time, in 1608, he brought no clergy with him, and the *habitation* which he constructed had no chapel. But on his return in 1615, after a short stay in France, he was accompanied by several members of the Récollet branch of the Franciscan Order. These Récollets arrived in Quebec late in May, 1615, and immediately set about building a chapel, with the help of Champlain and the early settlers. Father Jean Dolbeau said the first Mass in this first church building of New France, on June 25, 1615.[3] It was the prototype of the first category of church architecture to be found in New France, the mission chapel.

Wherever a trading post or fort was established, wherever the Indians congregated, there would be found missionaries, and on many sites in New France the first building was a missionary chapel. Thus, when Champlain founded a strong post at Trois-Rivières in 1634, one of the first buildings was a chapel erected by the Jesuit Fathers,[4] and similarly, the mission chapel built by Maisonneuve in 1642 for his settlement of Ville-Marie was the first building erected on the Island of Montreal.[5]

On many sites later occupied by French settlers there were even earlier chapels, built in the virgin wilderness by missionaries to the Indians. Typical examples were the first chapel at Tadoussac, built by the Récollet Le Caron in 1617, and its successor built by the Jesuit de Quen in 1641;[6] the first chapel at Trois-Rivières, built by the Récollets in 1618;[7] and the first church at Cap-de-la-Madeleine.[8]

All these chapels, whether built for the earliest settlers or for the Indians, had

[3]P.-G. Roy, *La Ville de Québec,* Quebec, 1930, I, pp. 51–54. This important book will hereafter be referred to as *V.d.Q.*

[4]Benjamin Sulte, *Histoire de la ville de Trois-Rivières,* Montreal, 1870, p. 69.

[5]*Annuaire de Ville-Marie,* supplement to the 1864 edition, p. 315 f. The *Annuaire,* a vital source-book which contains, amongst much heterogeneous material, a series of parochial monographs covering the parishes of the Montreal district, will hereafter be referred to as *A.V.M.* It was published at Montreal in two volumes with numerous supplements, between 1863 and 1877.

[6]*V.E.,* p. 179.

[7]Sulte, *Histoire de la ville de Trois-Rivières,* p. 42 f.

[8]The Jesuits built a wooden church for their Indian mission at Cap-de-la-Madeleine in 1659; but French settlement of the region was so steady that only two years later the wooden church was replaced by a stone church erected with the help of the Jesuits, and served by them as a parish church for French settlers rather than as a mission for the Indians. The history of this parish is typical; whenever French settlers came into a neighbourhood, the missionaries moved their charges away, in order to avoid the contamination of civilized vices. Cf. Appendix, p. 107.

several features in common. They were extremely primitive, constructed of the
simplest materials in the shortest possible time. Of course, they have now
entirely vanished, most of them before the Heroic Age was over. But we may
form an idea of their construction from inferences in various writings, in lieu
of the kind of archaeological investigation which has made our knowledge of
the earliest architecture of the English colonies in America so much surer. The
basis of most of their construction was the type called by early writers *en pieux*
or *de pieux*—medium-sized trunks or branches or roughly squared timbers,
usually of spruce,[9] sharpened at one end or both, and driven side by side into the
ground to form walls; cracks between them were filled in with clay. The roof
was formed simply of pliable branches bent to form a sort of vault, the whole
being usually covered with some sort of bark. This kind of building is the
*cabane d'écorce* mentioned by early writers. The door of such a structure consisted of a sheet of bark or cloth; a table covered with a white sheet served for
an altar. A few candles burning in front of a crucifix suspended against the back
wall completed the interior furnishings[10] (Figure 1). A variant of this primitive

FIGURE 1. A *cabane d'écorce*, the type of chapel erected by the earliest
missionaries to the Indians.

[9]See the analysis of various timbers used by the early builders made by Antoine Roy in
*L.S.A.*, p. 160 f.
[10]Sulte, *Histoire de la ville de Trois-Rivières*, p. 43.

type of chapel is described in the *Jesuit Relations* of 1635 as serving the Fathers who came with Champlain to Trois-Rivières in 1634:

Notre maison [i.e., the chapel dedicated to l'Immaculée-Conception-de-Marie, built in 1634] en ce premier commencement, n'était que quelques bûches de bois jointes les unes auprès des autres, enduites par les ouverture d'un peu de terre, et couvertes d'herbes; nous avions en tout douze pieds en quarré pour la chapelle et pour notre demeure, attendant qu'un bâtiment de charpente qu'on dressait fut achevé.

This can hardly refer to log-cabin construction; it seems to be a kind of log-tent, a variant of construction *en pieux*.[11]

In essence, the construction *en pieux* of the early mission chapels of New France must have been similar to the "palisade" type of buildings found in the earliest architecture of the English colonies in America. Forman[12] has traced the origins of the "palisade" type of construction back to Anglo-Saxon times in England and the Palaeolithic age in Europe. Undoubtedly this primitive type of construction likewise survived into the seventeenth century in France, so that it was no invention indigenous to North America.[13] However, the use of pliable branches in construction is found universally in primitive societies, and the Indian "long-house" was one representative of it; it is probable therefore that the early builders of New France derived ideas from such aboriginal construction as well as from their own European heritage. But whatever the ultimate origins of construction *en pieux,* technically speaking it could hardly be called architecture at all. Mgr de Laval apparently shared this opinion; he refused to consecrate such buildings.[14]

Largely owing to Laval's initiative, construction *en pieux* became virtually obsolete in New France proper by the end of the seventeenth century. However, other French settlements in America perpetuated it well into the eighteenth century; there it generally went under the name of *poteaux* construction.[15]

[11]*Ibid.*, p. 69. Ramsay Traquair, discussing this question in *The Old Architecture of Quebec,* Toronto, 1947, p. 17, agrees with Shurtleff, *The Log Cabin Myth,* Cambridge, 1939, in rejecting the idea that log-cabin construction is involved here. However, there is a possibility that this construction was later found in New France; cf. chapter IV, the mission chapels at Nicolet and Forges-Saint-Maurice, p. 71 below.

[12]Henry C. Forman, *The Architecture of the Old South,* Cambridge, Mass., 1948, pp. 9–13, and Figure 1.

[13]Cf. T. T. Waterman, *The Dwellings of Colonial America,* Chapel Hill, 1950, pp.198–199. The author cites the old (second) Des Marest house in Bergen County, New Jersey, constructed by the Huguenot immigrant Daniel Des Marest in 1686 of *poteaux en terre (en pieux)* as evidence that this type of construction came directly from France and was not, therefore, a development peculiar to the French settlements in North America.

[14]In a letter from Duchesneau to Seignelay dated November 13, 1681, the writer speaks of churches "constructed of timber and plank . . .; the bishop . . . refuses to consecrate them, because, as he says, it is his duty and obligation not to consecrate any buildings except such as are solid and durable." The significant extract from this letter is found in W. B. Munro, *The Seigniorial System in Canada,* New York, 1907, p. 185, n. 3.

[15]Cf. Charles E. Peterson's studies of constructional techniques in French settlements of the old North-West Territory quoted by Rexford Newcomb, *The Architecture of the Old*

Newcomb finds that *poteaux* construction was common in the eighteenth-French settlements around Detroit and throughout the old North-West generally; he illustrates an eighteenth-century church built by French at Vincennes, Indiana, as reconstructed from contemporary descriptions, evidently a sizable elaboration of the type of mission chapels found in France a century before[16] (Figure 2).

FIGURE 2.  Church erected by French settlers at Vincennes, Indiana, in the eighteenth century. This type of construction was called *de pieux* in Canada. (From Rexford Newcomb, *The Architecture of the Old North-West Territory*)

## THE DEVOTIONAL OR EX VOTO CHAPELS

In 1636, Governor de Montmagny built a small chapel to honour the memory of Samuel de Champlain, the founder of Quebec, who had died the year before.[17] This building was the ancestor of a considerable number of *ex voto* chapels and devotional shrines erected sporadically throughout the later history of New France as an expression of piety on the part of individuals or small groups. Similar in conception to the "Chapelle de Champlain" was the devotional chapel

---

*North-West Territory*, Chicago, 1950, p. 21. Peterson distinguishes between *poteaux en terre* (posts in the ground) and *poteaux sur sole* (posts on sills), both found in the old North-West; he declares, however, that *poteaux-en-terre* construction was not found in Canada (*sic*).

[16]Newcomb, *The Architecture of the Old North-West Territory*, p. 26. The Vincennes church was 66 feet long, 22 feet wide, and 9 feet high; its closest approximation in New France was probably the 1640 wooden church at Trois-Rivières.

[17]Its exact location at Quebec has been the subject of considerable research, but is not yet decided. Cf. Ernest Myrand, "La Chapelle de Champlain," *B.R.H.*, IV, 1898, p. 290, and *V.d.Q.*, I, pp. 147–148.

built in 1658 at Sainte-Anne de Beaupré, known as the "Sailors' Shrine,"[18] and the chapel projected in 1657 at Montreal by Marguerite Bourgeoys, to honour Notre-Dame-de-Bonsecours.[19] Of these first devotional chapels we know little; presumably they were of primitive construction, rather similar to the mission chapels. The "Chapelle de Champlain" disappeared at the end of the Heroic Age; but the shrine at Sainte-Anne and that of Notre-Dame-de-Bonsecours both became the scene of miracles, and places of pilgrimage. New buildings, of considerably greater elaboration, were soon built at both sites.

### The Parish Churches

The mission chapels and these earliest devotional chapels represent minor categories of church architecture, more important in this earliest period than later. Two other categories of church architecture may be distinguished in embryonic form at this time, which are of much more lasting significance. The first of these major categories is that represented by the earliest parish churches.

Properly speaking, there was no such thing as a parish church in the Heroic Age. From 1608 to 1721 all French America was ecclesiastically considered as a mission. Until the appointment of a bishop for New France in 1658, the country's spiritual life was organized under the loosely defined control of the various missionary orders, and all churches in New France were mission chapels. But as the settlements grew in population, there arose a need for larger and more permanent buildings than mission chapels, suitable for holding regular services—parish churches in fact, if not in name. In many cases, as we shall see, outside orders based in France, especially the Jesuits, provided funds to assist the colonists to build these churches, and used them for their own services as well as those of the community, so that they did not function exclusively as parish churches. But in other instances the community erected a church out of its own resources, and used it exclusively for the community services, which would be conducted by a missionary curé assigned especially to that locality.

The main centres of population in the Heroic Age of New France were Quebec, Montreal (then called Ville-Marie), and Trois-Rivières. The parish churches of both Quebec and Montreal were built with the help of the outside orders. But around Quebec, the most thickly settled region of New France, there were several churches built by local communities. To the west of Quebec there was the "Chapelle Saint-Jean," built by Jean Bourdon, an important official and supervisor of buildings in early New France, for his family and used by the inhabitants of the district as a parish church;[20] to the east, on the Beaupré coast,

[18]Georges Bélanger in *Annales de la Bonne Sainte-Anne-de-Beaupré,* April, 1923. This article is summarized in *B.R.H.,* XXIX, 1923, p. 141, under the title "La 'Chapelle des Matelots' à Sainte-Anne de Beaupré." The first church replaced this chapel in 1660.

[19]*V.E.,* p. 25.

[20]Bourdon had a fief near Quebec in the district known as the Coteau Sainte-Geneviève. He was the leading engineer of the colony, surveyor, and *procureur général,* and presumably

a tiny church at Beauport,[21] and a larger one at Sainte-Anne de Beaupré,[22] and the first church of Château-Richer.[23] The only other building of this class was the parish church of Trois-Rivières, built about 1640, and replaced in 1664.

The parish church of Trois-Rivières is typical of the kind of church architecture produced by the colony's native resources in the Heroic Age. As we have seen, the Récollets built a mission chapel at Trois-Rivières in 1618, and when Champlain founded a strong post there in 1634 the Jesuits built another, "until such time as a proposed *bâtiment de charpente* should be completed," says the entry in the *Jesuit Relations* cited above. Not until 1640, however, do we hear from a Jesuit father that "We have a church for the savages at Trois-Rivières which, since it is not as old as that of Sillery, is not yet as flourishing."[24] This wooden building was taken over by the settlement at Trois-Rivières for its own services as the colony grew, and presumably altered and enlarged somewhat, but it still was not far removed from a mission chapel. Between 1645 and 1650 various projects were put forth for a more satisfactory parish church. Lack of resources, however, made them all abortive; not until 1661 were wardens (*marguilliers*) elected to handle business arrangements in connection with the new building, and not until 1663 were these officers actually able to purchase land for it. But the earlier project had gone far enough for a contract to be drawn up with a carpenter for work on the building. According to a census taken in 1665, there were some thirty-six persons calling themselves carpenters who lived in New France at that time.[25] One carpenter is listed as living in Trois-Rivières. He may well be that François Boivin who appears in a contract of June 24, 1649.[26]

This contract is a major piece of evidence for the local parish architecture of the Heroic Age, even if the church to which it refers was never built. In full its text reads (punctuation mine):

OBLIGATION DE FRANÇOIS BOIVIN DE BÂTIR UNE ÉGLISE
AUX TROIS-RIVIÈRES (24 JUIN 1649)

Fut present en sa personne François Boivin, maître charpentier, lequel s'est volontairement obligé à honorable homme Jean Bourdon, procureur et commis général de la Communauté de la Nouvelle france, d'écarrir et former le bois d'un comble d'une église aux trois-rivières, laquelle église aura quatre vingt dix pieds de long sur vingt

built the chapel himself. Cf. J.-E. Roy, "La Cartographie et l'arpentage sous le régime français," *B.R.H.*, I, 1895, pp. 17–18. The chapel was served by a priest who lived with the Bourdon family. *V.d.Q.*, I, pp. 203–204.

[21]Built in 1635. Cf. Appendix, p. 102.

[22]Built in 1660, replacing the "Chapelle des Matelots." Already in 1665 Mère Marie de l'Incarnation is describing in a letter "the church to Sainte-Anne in which Our Saviour does great miracles in favour of that holy mother of the Holy Virgin."

[23]"Notes historiques sur la paroisse de Château-Richer," *B.R.H.*, XXXIX, 1933, p. 716 f. Bishop Laval refused to consecrate this church until 1685, when it was rebuilt in stone.

[24]Benjamin Sulte, *Chronique trifluvienne*, Montreal, 1879, p. 6.

[25]*Statistics of Canada*, IV, *Censuses of Canada*, Ottawa, 1876, census of 1665.

[26]The text of this contract is published in *B.R.H.*, XXXI, 1925, p. 192.

sept pieds de large, avec des croisillons qui flanque le corps de l'église de seize pieds d'un cens, et dix neuf pieds de large de l'autre; le tout de dehors en dehors; et le dit comble sera forme en sept quartiers avec un culde-four paulme en sept pans avec les épaisseurs qui s'en suivent, sacvoir: les sablières auront de grosseur de sept pouces en un cens et huit en l'autre; les chevrons, et entraits, et jambettes, et liarnes, et corbles auront de grosseur quatre à cinq pouces pour les héritiers; et quatre noues renfoncés auront de grosseur suivant que le trait le requèrera. Et le dit entrepreneur doit observer tous les assemblages nécessaires suivant, et conforme en l'art de charpentier à dire à gens à ce connaissants, sous des bonnes visitations. Et le dit Bourdon lui promet faire fournir le harnois pour emmener le bois qui lui sera nécessaire pour la construction du dit comble, le tout moyennant la somme de mille six cent vingt livres. Et le dit Bourdon lui promet faire fournir six barriques de farine dans le tems du dit travail, au prix courant. Et, en outre, il a été promis par Monsieur le Gouverneur que le dit Boivin et un de ses hommes seront exempts de gardes pendant le dit travail.

Faict et arrêté au fort des Trois-Rivières en présence de Charles Sevestre, premier syndic, et le sieur Jacques Hertel, témoings, qui ont signé avec les parties à la minute.

> FRANÇOIS BOIVIN
> BOURDON
> CH. SEVESTRE
> HERTEL.

Judging from the terms of their contract, the syndics in charge of building the new parish church of Trois-Rivières had an ambitious programme. Since no mention of walls is made in this carpenter's contract, they were presumably to have been of stone. The proposed dimensions of the church were generous indeed for the time—larger, in fact, than the parish church then under construction with Jesuit help at Quebec. Ninety feet long by twenty-seven feet wide, the church was to have terminated in a round apse, with flanking chapels forming a transept. There is no mention of any kind of steeple or belfry. Apparently this was not unusual for a church of this type and time; in 1749 Peter Kalm noted that the church of Baie-Saint-Paul, which was then considered one of the oldest churches in the country, "has no steeple, but a bell fixed above the roof, in the open air."[27]

The contract is specifically concerned with roofing the proposed church. The round apse is to be covered in seven panels, a method common enough in later times that we can visualize its probable appearance; an example of it is to be seen in the church of Repentigny, begun in 1725 (Plate XXXIX). The bulk of the contract, however, has to do with the thicknesses of the various rafters, beams, joists, and so forth, that Boivin was to use. Inasmuch as no dimensions in height are given, it is considerably more difficult to reconstruct the way in which it was proposed to relate the roofs of apse, transept, and main body. On

[27]*P.K.T.*, p. 483.

the evidence of later examples, I have made a rough sketch of what I conceive to be the most probable scheme (Figure 3).

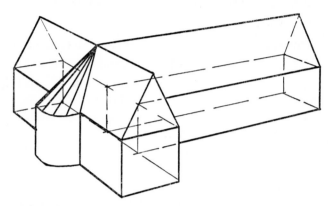

FIGURE 3. Hypothetical reconstruction of the church proposed for Trois-Rivières in the contract of 1649.

Significant, I think, is the omission of any reference to a plan to be followed. It is stated that "le dit entrepreneur doit observer tous les assemblages nécessaires suivant, et conforme en l'art de charpentier à dire à gens à ce connaissants, sous des bonnes visitations"; such a clause seems to mean simply that he will be checked for possible malfeasance. François Boivin's church will be designed by no architect; rather, its outlines will be determined by that "art de charpentier" in which Boivin, as a master craftsman, has been trained. It represents the transplantation to New France of a craft architecture based on traditional techniques and designs, and learned through apprenticeship, the origins of which go back to the Middle Ages and even earlier.

Such craft architecture appears in all the colonies of the New World in the seventeenth century. Perhaps the most familiar *Québécois* example of it is the *habitation* built by Champlain in 1608; a drawing of this structure, taken from the illustration in Champlain's *Voyages,* adorns practically every book on Canadian history. But because it is so familiar, and because the craft tradition in architecture persisted so much longer in Quebec than in the United States, there has arisen what I believe to be a fundamental misconception about the whole architectural tradition of Quebec—a prevalent assumption that the kind of simple craft building represented by the *habitation* was the only kind of architecture known in New France. It is undoubtedly true that in the Heroic Age, and for two centuries afterwards, the architecture of traditional craftsmanship was a major element in the architectural history of New France and the Province of Quebec. But even in this earliest period, I believe there is considerable evidence that it was not the whole story, by any means. There remains to be considered in our analysis that category of church architecture represented by the stone churches erected in the early colony by the religious orders with outside resources.

### CHURCH BUILDING OF THE RELIGIOUS ORDERS

Of twenty-eight examples of church architecture in New France between 1615 and 1665, nine, or about a third, were built in stone. This is a high percentage, in view of the poverty-stricken condition of the early colony. But it is explained by the fact that every one of these stone churches was erected by a religious order with outside resources.

The first stone church of New France was that attached to the Récollet residence of Notre-Dame-des-Anges in Quebec, the cornerstone of which was laid June 3, 1620. The arms which this stone bore—those of France, and of the Prince de Condé, viceroy of New France—suggest the outside patronage which was responsible for the church's erection.[28] Apparently it was never used as a parish church. The tiny population of Quebec continued to worship in the mission chapel built in 1615 until the year 1629, when both churches were ruined by the English, who captured Quebec and temporarily wiped out the colony.

The Society of Jesus was responsible for five, or more than half, of the early stone churches. The Jesuits' first church in New France was a chapel attached to their residence in Quebec; it was begun in August, 1625, and completed in April, 1626. Like the Récollets', it was also dedicated to Notre-Dame-des-Anges, and it too was ruined in 1629.[29] Following the restoration of Quebec to France, in 1632, the Récollets did not return; the Jesuits thereupon repaired the Récollet residence and church of Notre-Dame-des-Anges, using the residence until 1648,[30] and the church until 1666.[31]

While using these buildings at Quebec, the Jesuits also built a residence for themselves at Sillery, with a church dedicated to Saint-Joseph, begun about 1638;[32] a stone church at Tadoussac, in 1661;[33] one at Cap-de-la-Madeleine, also in 1661;[34] and of most importance, the third parish church of Quebec, Notre-Dame-de-la-Paix, of which we shall speak shortly.

[28]*V.E.*, pp. 17–18.          [29]*V.d.Q.*, I, pp. 85–86, 141–142.          [30]*Ibid.*, pp. 231–232.

[31]From a letter written by the Jesuit Father Thierry Beschefer, dated October 4, 1666, we learn that in that year the Jesuits were building a new church for themselves. He continues: "The little chapel which we are using at present is very well ornamented with fine decorations, large silver chandeliers, lamps, and all the rest. . . ." Quoted in *B.R.H.*, XXXV, 1929, p. 335.

[32]The *Liber Baptisatorium de Sillery*, in the Archives de l'Evêché de Québec, sets the date for the residence as 1637. The church is the one referred to in the passage cited above, note 24.

[33]Replacing the chapel of 1641. Destroyed by fire in 1664; another stone church was not built until 1747. *V.E.*, p. 179 f.

[34]Although only 30 feet long and 18 feet wide, it served as a parish church until 1714. *V.E.*, p. 57.

The remaining stone churches of the Heroic Age were erected under the auspices of nuns drawing their resources from France. The foundations of the Hôtel-Dieu and its chapel in Quebec were laid August 12, 1638, although the building was not completed until the fall of 1644;[35] served by the Sœurs Hermites de Saint-Augustin, a nursing order, the funds for its erection were provided by the Duchesse d'Aiguillon.[36] In the spring of 1641, the first stone of the Ursuline convent was laid in Quebec, and the building with its chapel completed late in 1642. It was gutted by fire in 1650; repaired, it existed until 1686 when a second fire destroyed it.[37] Our rather extensive knowledge of the convent, which unfortunately does not include very much about the chapel, is derived from the letters of Mère Marie de l'Incarnation, mother superior of the order, to her relatives and patrons in France who provided its financial backing.[38]

Funds for the erection of the Hôtel-Dieu in Montreal were provided by Mme de Bullion, a wealthy Parisian widow whom Jeanne Mance met in 1640.[39] With her help, the Hospitalières de Saint-Joseph were able in 1644 to build a little *oratoire* in stone about nine or ten feet square, beside their hospital.[40] This little chapel and the wooden "Chapelle du Fort" erected by Maisonneuve in 1643[41] served conjointly for parish services until 1656.

From 1654 on, Maisonneuve had projected a new parish church, but he could not raise the funds from the native resources of the settlement. He would have met with no greater success than the Trois-Rivières community had it not been for the help of the Hospitalières. The fact that this third parish church of Montreal, the foundations for which were finally laid on August 28, 1656, was located beside the Hôtel-Dieu, and was used by both the community and the hospital, suggests that in the end some of Mme de Bullion's bequest of 60,000 *livres* had to go into its construction.

This whole episode points up again the disparity between the resources of the religious orders in the colony and those of the colony itself. Without outside aid, the communities of Trois-Rivières and Montreal could not build the kind of parish churches they needed. But with the financial aid received from the Hôtel-Dieu, it was possible for Montreal to have a fine church, nearly fifty feet long. This church was of wood, but it was not of the same class as those wooden

---

[35]*V.d.Q.*, I, pp. 159–160.
[36]Cf. "Les Congrégations de femmes au Canada," *B.R.H.*, L, 1944, p. 33.
[37]*V.d.Q.*, I, pp. 211–212, 465–466.
[38]Cf. the extract from Benjamin Sulte, *Lettres historiques de la Vénérable Mère Marie de l'Incarnation*, quoted in Ramsay Traquair, *The Old Architecture of Quebec*, p. 10. The collected letters were first published in Paris, 1681.
[39]E.-Z. Massicotte, "Jeanne Mance," *Canadian Antiquarian*, 3rd series, IX, 1912, p. 1 f.
[40]*A.V.M.*, I, p. 59 f., "Notice historique sur l'Hôtel-Dieu de Ville-Marie."
[41]The first parish church of Montreal was a primitive *cabane d'écorce* erected by Maisonneuve the year he founded the settlement, 1642. The next year, he built a somewhat larger chapel, known throughout its history as the "Chapelle du Fort." Cf. *A.V.M.*, supplement to the 1864 edition, p. 315 f.

churches built by communities without outside assistance; rather, it belonged to the category of the more elaborate churches in stone built by the religious orders, and as a mark of elaboration it had a clocher "de forme regulier et élégant,"[42] with two bells.

How splendid these churches built by the religious orders were, in comparison to the parish churches built from native resources, is suggested by the third parish church of Quebec, which was built mainly at Jesuit expense. The church of 1615 dedicated to l'Immaculée-Conception de la Sainte-Vierge, and the 1633 building dedicated to Notre-Dame-de-Recouvrance, were really nothing better than mission chapels.[43] When the latter was destroyed by fire in 1640, the community lacked resources to build a suitable church, and was reduced to using a room in the house of the Compagnie des Cent-Associés.[44] A church for Quebec was badly needed, but no simple structure such as that of the parish churches on the Beaupré coast, or of Trois-Rivières (i.e., patched-up Jesuit chapel of 1640), could do. Like Montreal and Trois-Rivières, however, the community was too poor to do more than consider building until an outside

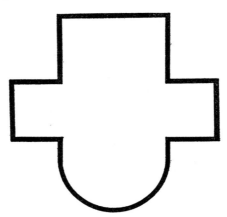

FIGURE 4. Ground-plan of the church of Notre-Dame-de-la-Paix, from the *Vrai Plan de Québec* made in 1660.

order, in this case the Jesuits, came to its assistance. With their support, work on the new church was finally begun in 1647, on land donated for the purpose two years before. The church was dedicated to Notre-Dame-de-la-Paix in commemoration of a peace concluded with the Iroquois in 1645. With Jesuit help, and undoubtedly under Jesuit supervision, a fine stone church was completed

[42]*Ibid.*, p. 343 f. The English word "belfry" does not correspond in meaning to "clocher." "Clocher" includes not only the actual belfry, but a drum, usually square or nearly so, upon which the belfry rests, and the spire (*flèche*) above it. "Steeple" is closest in meaning to "clocher," but I have preferred to keep the French term throughout.

[43]*V.d.Q.*, I, pp. 53–54, 117–118.

[44]This room was somewhat grandiloquently styled "L'église de la Conception de la Bienheureuse Marie à Québec." *V.E.*, p. 1.

in 1650, absolutely incomparable with its predecessors. Its construction was an accomplishment far beyond the community's meagre resources, but well within the means of the Jesuits. In 1664, the new Bishop of Quebec, in a letter to the Holy See, expressed his pleasure and surprise at finding such a building in New France: "There is a basilica here . . .," he wrote; "it is large and magnificent."[45]

Of all the church buildings erected by the religious orders with outside resources, Notre-Dame-de-la-Paix, the third parish church of Quebec, is the only one that we can visualize at all certainly. It stood in its original state for about thirty-five years—from its completion in 1650 to its rebuilding between 1684 and 1689—but we can form an idea of its original appearance from two contemporary sources. A rough floor plan of the church appears on the *Vrai Plan de Québec* of 1660 (Figure 4). We also have the text of a contract[46] made for its construction in 1646, which was renewed in 1647 and again in 1648:

MARCHEZ FAICTS EN 1646 ET 47 JUSQUE EN 1648 AU MOIS DE SEPTEMBRE POUR LA CONSTRUCTION DE L'ÉGLISE ET DU FORT A QUÉBEC.

### Pour l'église. Pour la Massonnerye

Par Denis Bochard Jacob Desbordes et Jean Garnier marchez faict du corps de l'église contenant quatre vingt pieds de long avec ung point rond au bout devers l'est, le tout suivant et conforme au dessin p$^r$ le prix et somme de 4200 lb et deux barriques de vin faict le 18 avril 1648. . . .

Item pour le charoy qu'il a fallu faire ceste année pour le sable, pierre, chaux et bois du comble et aporter les estempars la somme de 1122 lb. . . .

### Pour le comble de l'église

Marchez faict avec M$^e$ Nicolas Pelletier charpentier, prix 1500 lb et 30 lb pour le vin le marché faict et passé le 24 de novembre 1647.

Il reste du charoy qu'il conviendra faire pour l'église et la place pour la couvrir et faire le planchez de bas, le lambris, la menuiserye, la ferrure et le frontispice, mesme la prolonger de deux toises.

. . . faict à Quesbecq le 20 de septembre 1648. . . .

Collation faicte à l'original pour moi secrétaire et notaire royal estably en la Nouvelle-France le saizième jour d'octobre mil six cent quarante huist.

BERMEN

The contract is by far the more important source of the two. Some of the terms are open to misinterpretation, but the general picture of the church which these specifications present is clear. It was eighty feet long, with a round apse at the east end. Its walls were of stone, entirely clapboarded on the outside—a method of insulating a building against the cold known in several provinces of France and often used in Canada.[47] The phrase "prolonger de deux toises" is

---

[45] *V.d.Q.*, I, pp. 179–180.

[46] *B.R.H.*, VII, 1901, p. 269 f; quoted in part. This document is in the archives of the Ursulines in Quebec.

[47] *L.S.A.*, pp. 161–162. The practice of covering the outer stone walls of buildings with boards seems to have come into New France with the earliest settlers. Its primary use was for insulation, both here and in the English colonies in America (Forman, *The Architecture*

somewhat obscure; it may refer simply to the practice of splaying out the eaves, later so common in French Canada.

But clearly Notre-Dame-de-la-Paix was not simply the product of craft traditions. It had many elaborate features for the time—a wooden floor,[48] possibly a wood-panelled vault and panelled walls,[49] and, as we know from a letter written by Laval in 1680,[50] a clocher of wood built over the crossing. In form, this clocher probably resembled the little dome-like structures so commonly found in sixteenth- and seventeenth-century French architecture of the more "classical" trend,[51] and in both form and location, this earliest Quebec clocher undoubtedly depended upon Jesuit architectural concepts.[52]

---

*of the Old South*, p. 17). But in New France, as Traquair has pointed out (*The Old Architecture of Quebec*, p. 12), clapboarding also served the vital purpose of keeping the wall dry and hence safe from the ravages of hard Quebec frosts. This use seems to have superseded the original one as the main *raison d'être* of clapboarding in Canada; the cracking of stone walls due to frost early became the perennial problem of the Quebec builder. Gérard Morisset, *A.N.F.*, pp. 61–62, emphasizes this point in connection with niches on façades, many of which had to be walled up during the nineteenth century because water ran into them, froze, and cracked the wall. The earliest mention of clapboards in Canada comes in connection with the Jesuit residence at Sillery, begun in 1637; this building appears to have been entirely covered by clapboards, not only the walls, but the gables and even the chimneys (W. Carless, appendix to P.-G. Roy, *Vieux Manoirs, Vieilles Maisons*, Quebec, 1927, pp. 324–326, 335). Mère Marie de l'Incarnation, writing in 1644, says: "The coverings of the houses are in two layers of planks or of shingles laid on planks" (quoted by Traquair, p. 10). Then there is the reference to "le lambris" in this contract for Notre-Dame in 1646–1648. In 1663 Pierre Boucher says of New France, "all the houses are covered . . . with boards" (Traquair, p. 12). In 1680 the chapel in the "Fort des Sauvages" designed by Vachon de Belmont at the foot of the Côte des Neiges in Montreal is described as "clapboarded with shingled planks" (Olivier Maurault, *Marges d'histoire: Saint-Sulpice*, Montreal, 1930, p. 23 f.). And so forth. Cf. chap. v, n. 31.

[48]This was apparently not the usual thing in early churches. Charlevoix in 1720 singles out the Jesuit church of 1666 in Quebec, which was as close in appearance as in date to Notre-Dame-de-la-Paix, for special comment on this score: "It has no stone pavement, in place of which it is floored with strong planks, which makes this church supportable in winter, whilst you are pierced with cold in the others." Charlevoix seems to imply this was a very elaborate and desirable feature. Cf. Alfred Hawkins, *Picture of Quebec*, Quebec, 1834, pp. 192–193.

[49]"Menuiserye" presumably refers to such treatment; there are no other references to such panelling in this earliest period. It later became the rule.

[50]"The clocher [of Notre-Dame-de-la-Paix], being only of wood, has been totally ruined by the snows and severe climate of this country. . . . For eighteen months now, we have rung no bells, for fear that the clocher would collapse upon the building of which it forms part. . . ." Written to Louis XIV, preserved in the archives of the Seminary of Quebec. See Auguste Gosselin, *Henri de Bernières*, Quebec, 1902, p. 159.

[51]Louis Hautecœur, *Histoire de l'architecture classique en France*, II, pt. II, Paris, 1948, p. 744: "In many classical churches the clocher is reduced to a little campanile in wood, situated at the extremity of the roof or behind the gable."

[52]Father Beschefer's letter of 1666 (cf. n. 31) refers to a clocher on the Jesuit residence in Quebec, built in 1648, which also served as a college. As he describes it, the residence was "all in stone, covered in tile, with a fine cupola for bells." The only other mention of a clocher in this period concerns the parish church of Montreal built in 1656 with the help of the Hospitalières d'Hôtel-Dieu; of its form we know nothing. On Jesuit influence in New France during the seventeenth century, see further chapter III.

Most significant of all, I think, especially in comparison to the contemporaneous plan for the Trois-Rivières church, is the reference to a plan ("dessin") in the Notre-Dame-de-la-Paix contract. The exact specifications which bulk so large in the Trois-Rivières contract are absent; presumably the master plan took care of them. Someone other than the workmen named in the contract was responsible for the design of the church of Notre-Dame-de-la-Paix. Who this might be we do not know for sure; a good guess would be one of the Jesuit Fathers— possibly Father Vimont, who consecrated the building. The important thing is that there *was* a plan for this and, presumably, for other stone churches of the period.

With the limited means to hand, such a plan need not have been elaborate— indeed, it could not have been. But for succeeding epochs in New France, these early stone churches with a definite designer set an important precedent. In later times of greater prosperity, an attempt could be made, following this precedent, to erect in New France churches whose plans resembled so far as could be the great seventeenth-century churches of up-to-date style in Old France, rather than the small, provincial, *retardataire* examples of the mother country.

Of the four categories discernible among the early examples of church building in New France the two of most importance were thus parish churches, representing a craft tradition, and churches built by the orders, based on a more "academic" approach. In the second half of the seventeenth century, we have considerably more evidence for specific buildings, and can attempt a much more concrete reconstruction of these two types than is possible in an analysis of the earliest church architecture of New France.

# III

# THE AGE OF LAVAL,
# 1665-1700

AT THE BEGINNING OF THE YEAR 1665, NEW FRANCE WAS IN A precarious state. There were only some two thousand people in the colony;[1] its settlements were straggling and its twelve churches mostly small and crude.[2] Acts of God and man alike threatened it with annihilation.[3] Yet before the year was out, all this had changed. In 1665 almost as many persons came to the colony as during its entire previous history—a new Governor, an Intendant, a complete regiment of 1200 infantry, and numerous settlers.[4] There followed an attack on the Iroquois which made the colony secure from them for two decades, an invigorating reorganization of the colony's resources by Intendant Talon, flourishing new settlements, and an outburst of church building all over the country.[5] Despite occasional pessimism,[6] the future of the colony, at least its physical existence, was assured. It was truly the beginning of a new age.

This rejuvenation of New France was initiated by Colbert, Louis XIV's great

[1]*Statistics of Canada*, IV, *Censuses of Canada*, Ottawa, 1876.

[2]Viz.: Five in Quebec: the parish church of Notre-Dame-de-la-Paix, the "Chapelle Saint-Jean," and chapels connected with the establishments of the Jesuits, Ursulines, and the Hôtel-Dieu; one each at Tadoussac, Trois-Rivières, Château-Richer, Sillery (the Jesuit foundation), Sainte-Anne de Beaupré, Montreal, and Cap-de-la-Madeleine.

[3]During the 1650's, Iroquois raids came near wiping out the whole colony; following Dollard's exploit at the Longue-Sault, this danger abated somewhat, but the rigours of the climate and the terrible series of earthquakes in 1663 continued to take a heavy toll of lives and energy.

[4]Between 1660 and 1680 some 2550 immigrants entered New France—more than twice the number that had arrived during the preceding half-century. See the figures compiled by S.-A. Lortie, *Bulletin du parler français*, 1903–4, p. 18. Of this number, about 2000 arrived during the period of mass immigration from 1665 to 1672.

[5]Within ten years, new churches and chapels appeared at Chambly, Gentilly, Sainte-Foy, Sainte-Famille (Ile d'Orléans), Boucherville, Montreal (Bonsecours), Charlesbourg, Quebec (Récollet chapel, Seminary chapel), Beauport, Ancienne-Lorette, Pointe-aux-Trembles (Montreal), Ange-Gardien, Contrecœur, Baie-Saint-Paul, Nicolet, Lauzon (Saint-Joseph de la Pointe de Lévy), Lanoraie, Lachine, Saint-Pierre (Ile d'Orléans); and churches were rebuilt on a new and larger scale at Sainte Anne de Beaupré, Montreal (Notre-Dame), Quebec (Jesuits, Ursulines). See further the chronological list in the *catalogue raisonné*. (Ile d'Orléans will henceforth be abbreviated to "I.O.," following general usage.)

[6]E.g., M. de Brisacier, superior of the Foreign Missions in Paris, wrote in 1687 that "New France has been on the verge of being abandoned this year. . . ." Quoted in H. A. Scott, *Bishop Laval*, Makers of Canada series, Anniversary ed., Toronto and London, 1926, I, p. 311.

minister, as part of his world-wide policy of mercantilist expansion. But its permanent success was the work of another man, with very different ends in view—François de Laval-Montmorency, first Bishop of New France. Laval's influence on the future culture of New France was so pervasive that it will be worth while to review his accomplishments in some detail.

Laval was born at Montigny-sur-Avre (Eure-et-Loir) in 1622 or 1623.[7] In 1658 he was given charge of the spiritual destinies of New France as apostolic vicar, under the title Bishop of Petræa, and arrived in Quebec in June, 1659. After three years' study of the colony, he returned to France in 1662 and placed suggestions for various reforms before the King. In 1663 the old Compagnie des Cent-Associés was dissolved; all its rights were resigned to the King, and a Conseil Souverain was established to govern the country—an act which set Canada on almost the same footing as many provinces in France, ensured direct intervention of the Crown in the colony's affairs, and created the framework for the vigorous programme of colonization which began in 1665. That Laval was responsible for this momentous act there is little doubt; his first biographer, Bertrand de La Tour, stated it flatly,[8] and Canada's classic historian Parkman agreed.[9] And the Bishop took a deciding hand in the new immigration programme; it was at his insistence that settlers from Perche and Normandy were encouraged, rather than from the La Rochelle area.[10]

New France's religious life was, of course, the Bishop's primary interest, and from 1663 on he began a complete reorganization of it.[11] In 1663 he published a mandate which made the Seminary of Quebec a focus for parochial administration; successive moves tightened his personal control over all aspects of religion in the colony.[12] In 1664 the Bishop's church, Notre-Dame de Québec, was given the rank of a parish church by canon law, the only one with this rank in

[7]The date cannot be determined exactly. Among other biographies of Laval, see especially Auguste Gosselin, *Vie de Mgr de Laval*, Quebec, 1890, 2 vols., and abridged edition, Quebec, 1901.

[8]"The Conseil Souverain of Canada was the work of its first bishop." *Mémoire sur la vie de M. de Laval, premier évêque de Québec*, Cologne, 1751.

[9]Francis Parkman, *The Old Régime in Canada*, London, 1904 (Parkman's *Works*, IV).

[10]Scott, *Bishop Laval*, p. 193. In 1665, following Laval's return to Quebec, Colbert wrote to him: "During your stay here you mentioned to me that the people coming from around La Rochelle were not laborious. The king, after your advice, has taken the resolution to levy three hundred men in Normandy and the neighbouring provinces. . . . I hope that contingent shall be a benefit to the colony."

[11]Cf. Claude de Bonnault, "La Vie religieuse dans les paroisses rurales canadiennes au dix-huitième siècle," *B.R.H.*, XL, 1934, p. 645 f.

[12]"I desire it to be a perpetual school of virtue and a body of reserve from which I may draw pious and able subjects and send them, in all emergencies, into parishes or any other places of this country, in case of need: . . . retaining forever . . . the right of revoking from office all the ecclesiastics sent . . . whenever and as many times as it shall be deemed necessary; none of them being by special title particularly bound to any parish: but, on the contrary, my will being that they be rightfully removeable, revocable, liable to dismissal, according to the will of the bishop, or of the aforesaid seminary. . . ." Scott, *Bishop Laval*, p. 148.

the colony.[13] And on a second visit to France in 1671, he secured the erection of Quebec into a bishopric, something he had desired since 1662. By Clement X's bull dated October 1, 1674, François de Laval became Bishop of the whole of North America except New England. The parish of Quebec was suppressed, and the care of souls confided directly to the bishop, who was to administer affairs either himself, or through priests under his direction, or in any other way he saw fit.[14] Even before these developments, Laval had been influential enough to defy royal governors like d'Avaugour and de Mézy; he now was unquestionably the most powerful single figure in the colony. His authoritarian ideas of centralized government triumphed in both secular and ecclesiastical fields, largely due to his own efforts. No aspect of the life of New France could be considered beyond his paternal oversight. The period of church architecture in Quebec from 1665 to 1700 may therefore be designated aptly as the Age of Laval.

Laval's influence was by no means limited to the seventeenth century, however. The authoritarian tradition which he established continued strong in the colony up to the end of the *ancien régime*. The Jesuits, who had been Laval's early teachers in their French colleges, gained by his constant firm support an early predominance in the colony which they never lost; by 1760 the Society of Jesus was by far the largest single landowner in New France.[15] And the traditions of church architecture which Laval established continued to be felt well into the nineteenth century in Quebec, and may perhaps be detected even at the present time.

For purposes of study, church architecture in the Age of Laval may be most conveniently considered as falling into four categories. In order of increasing elaborateness, these are mission and devotional chapels; parish churches; a group of buildings erected by the architect Claude Baillif under the patronage of Laval's immediate successor Mgr de Saint-Vallier; and the churches erected by and for religious orders. Very little of any of them has survived; what extant evidence we have may be briefly mentioned at this point.

The earliest building which has survived from the Age of Laval is the Récollet chapel of Notre-Dame-des-Anges, built in 1671,[16] and now encased in the buildings of the Hôpital-Général. By 1692, however, the Récollets had already taken away everything movable from the interior; its present appearance is substantially the work of Pierre Emond between 1770 and 1780. The apse of Ange-Gardien, built in 1675, was extant until 1930, but its original interior was ruined by Wolfe's army in 1759 and restored at least twice afterwards.[17] The

[13]P.-G. Roy, *Les Petites Choses de notre histoire*, 5e série, Lévis, 1925, pp. 107–108.

[14]A. Gosselin, *Vie de Mgr de Laval*, Quebec, 1901, pp. 395–396.

[15]Cf. W. B. Munro, *The Seigniorial System in Canada*, New York, 1907, p. 180.

[16]I am speaking here about church architecture only. For bibliography and other factual data on the monuments mentioned in this section, see the *catalogue raisonné*.

[17]In the present church of Ange-Gardien there still exists in mutilated form a retable *à la récollette* made by Jacques Leblond *dit* Latour *c.* 1700. This work escaped destruction

chapel of Notre-Dame-de-Bonsecours in Montreal, built in 1675, was destroyed by fire in 1754. Although it is claimed that the rebuilding followed the old lines exactly, it was on a slightly larger scale, and drawings of the chapel as it was in the nineteenth century show all the characteristics of late eighteenth-century work; certainly as "refurbished" by Edouard Meloche in the 1880's, it now bears only the slightest resemblance to the original. Of the old church of Sainte-Anne de Beaupré as reconstructed after 1689, likewise only photographs and drawings remain; it was demolished in 1878. The clocher from this church, however, was transferred to the Commemorative Chapel at Sainte-Anne and is still extant.[18] A clocher built in 1709 for the old church of Saint-Laurent, I.O., also survives, as part of a summer chapel at Mont-Tremblant; it is of the same type. From the 1684–1689 rebuilding of the Cathedral in Quebec, little has been left after alterations in 1744, siege in 1759, restorations in 1845, and fire in 1922. Notre-Dame-des-Victoires, in Quebec's Lower Town, built in 1688, has fared no better; as we see it today, it substantially dates from the first half of the nineteenth century. The apse of Neuville, built in 1696, is perhaps the best preserved of any building from the Age of Laval, excluding domestic architecture; its interior decoration, however, all dates after 1760. Therefore, just as in the Heroic Age, so in the Age of Laval we must reconstruct its church architecture mainly from documentary and literary sources.[19]

## MISSION AND DEVOTIONAL CHAPELS

Two general sorts of mission chapels may be distinguished in the Age of Laval: those erected by or for the large number of new French settlements founded during this period of rapid growth, and those built for Indian converts. Curiously enough, Indian mission chapels were usually somewhat more elaborate than those built by the French. They were largely built by Jesuit missionaries; evidently having outside resources to draw upon made the difference, as it had in the Heroic Age.

The bulk of our information about the chapels in French settlements is contained in the *Plan général de l'état présent des missions du Canada fait en l'année 1683*.[20] This source, and other incidental references, make it clear that in the majority of them the poor and primitive construction of the mission chapels of the Heroic Age lived on. Typical was the first chapel at Charlesbourg, built about 1670. It was covered with thatch, for a notice of 1674 tells of a *habitant*

---

in 1759, but was broken up in 1801 or 1802 by the curé, who made three retables out of it; so divided, the old retable was saved from the fire of 1931. (Note supplied by Gérard Morisset.)

[18]See further the discussion of this church, and Figure 6.

[19]These are outlined in chapter I.

[20]*P.G.M.*, p. 115 f. See pp. 5, 117–118.

who made up his church dues by providing straw for the roof of the chapel.[21] The *Plan général* of 1683 describes it as built "only *de pieux*," and ruinous.[22] Yet this primitive building served for divine worship at Charlesbourg until 1695. The *Plan général* further suggests the miserable condition of many of these churches by inference—for example, the chapel at Sorel "which the *habitants* have promised to repair"; the chapel at Grondines "which the *habitants* have promised to finish"; at Saint-Ours "a little chapel *de pieux* . . . thirty feet long by twenty feet wide"; at Contrecœur "a wooden chapel" of the same tiny dimensions; at Sainte-Anne de La Pérade a "wooden chapel" even smaller, twenty by fifteen; at Pointe-aux-Trembles, Montreal, "a chapel thirty-six feet long by twenty-four feet wide."[23] The records preserved in the latter church are most enlightening; projected in 1674, the diminutive chapel took four years to complete.[24] And we may be sure that mission chapels like those of Beaumont,[25] Cap Santé,[26] Rimouski,[27] or L'Islet[28] were of the same sort; they were served by Récollets, who were customarily assigned to the poorest stations.

Around 1680, however, the architecture of mission chapels in the settlements began to improve rapidly. One by one the older chapels *de pieux* were replaced by more substantial structures of squared timbers (what the *Plan général* calls *bois équarris*), a process which undoubtedly reflected the growing prosperity of New France. Typical of these was the chapel provided for garrison, settlers, and transient Indians at Fort Rémi (Lachine); it was built by Pierre Gaudin *dit* Chatillon, a local carpenter, in 1676,[29] and we may envisage it from a reconstruction after Gédeon de Catalogne's plan of the fort in 1689—a simple

---

[21]C. de Bonnault, "La Vie religieuse dans les paroisses rurales canadiennes au dix-huitième siècle," *B.R.H.*, XL, 1934, p. 645.

[22]*P.G.M.*, p. 118.

[23]*Ibid.*, p. 122 f.

[24]*A.V.M.*, I, p. 209 f. It is not certain whether this church was built of stone or wood. The *Plan général* does not indicate the material, an omission that would suggest wood. E. R. Adair, in his article "The Church of L'Enfant-Jésus, Pointe-aux-Trembles," *B.R.H.*, XLII, 1936, p. 411 f., assumes that it was wood. On the other hand, it may have been partly of stone. Two factors suggest this: the length of time in building, and the known builders, a pair: François Beau and Laurent Archambault: mason and carpenter, perhaps?

[25]The first parish register here was signed by Father Guillaume Beaudoin, Récollet, in 1693; the chapel was built in 1694. Cf. J.-E. Roy, "Saint-Etienne de Beaumont," in *B.R.H.*, XIX, 1913, p. 210 f.

[26]*Ibid.*, p. 217. The same Récollet father signed the first parish register here in 1693. The chapel was built *c.* 1700.

[27]Built about 1700. Cf. P. Hugolin, "Les Registres paroissiaux de Rimouski," *B.R.H.*, XVIII, 1912, pp. 129–130.

[28]The first chapel, built *c.* 1700, measured only 25 feet long by 20 feet wide, and contained eleven pews. It was replaced by a church begun in 1721. Cf. P.-G. Roy, *L'Annonciation de Notre-Dame de Bonsecours de l'Islet*, Lévis, 1901, p. 6 f.

[29]Désiré Girouard, *Lake St. Louis, Old and New*, Montreal, 1893, p. 45 f. Pierre Gaudin *dit* Chatillon was an Acadian, born in 1632. He was married in 1654 at Montreal; died at Quebec in 1700. Cf. Cyprien Tanguay, *Dictionnaire généalogique des familles canadiennes*, I, Quebec, 1871, p. 256. This work will hereafter be referred to as *D.G.F.C.*, and the first volume is meant, unless otherwise indicated.

frame building, rectangular,[30] with a tiny belfry (Plate IV). Such, too, must have been the appearance of the second church of Saint-Thomas de Montmagny, begun in 1685 to replace a chapel *de pieux* built only six years before;[31] by no means pretentious, it still denoted progress, so that Mgr de Saint-Vallier could express considerable satisfaction with it: ". . . the church which is only in wood," he wrote, "is handsome enough, but just as poor [in furnishings] as the others, despite its being in the most populous territory of the mission."[32] Probably of the same type were the chapels at Champlain (described by the *Plan général* as fifty-five feet long and twenty-five feet wide), and Batiscan (forty-five by twenty-two), and in the Sulpician-fostered settlements around Montreal, such as Saint-Louis au bout de l'Isle,[33] Saint-Sulpice,[34] and Vaudreuil.[35]

The Jesuits, too, could afford such buildings in the French settlements on their seigniories. At Laprairie, which they began to colonize in 1667, they built a wooden fort and chapel near the Sault-Saint-Louis around 1668, replaced it by a second and presumably more substantial church of wood in 1687, and finally constructed a stone church in 1704.[36] This history is typical of the development of French mission chapels in the Age of Laval; by 1700 the squared timber construction which came in around 1680 was everywhere beginning to give place in its turn to stone.[37]

The architecture of mission chapels for the Indians showed the same progress. At Sault-au-Récollet, for example, the original chapel was *de pieux*; it was destroyed in a storm, and in 1684 replaced by a building of squared timbers, described in the *Jesuit Relations*: "When the logs were hewn, carting was out of the question; but the Indians carried pieces sixty feet long and proportionately thick, and thus assembled all the timbers where the building was to be erected. . . . When spring arrived, we began to build the chapel, [the parts of] which had been shaped during the winter. . . . The posts and beams are very clumsy and heavy—for it may be imagined that timbers for a building sixty feet long and

[30]Girouard (*Lake St. Louis*, p. 45) says this chapel was 36 feet square, which would be hard to believe. Perhaps one dimension was 36 feet, as in the Sault-au-Récollet chapel.

[31]F.-E.-J. Casault, *Notes historiques sur la paroisse de Saint-Thomas de Montmagny*, Quebec, 1906, pp. 17–18 and 82–83.

[32]Quoted in *ibid.*, p. 25.

[33]Built by the Sulpician missionary d'Urfé about 1686, it was wiped out during the Iroquois wars beginning in 1688. Until 1713 no church existed on the site. In 1714 a church was built and dedicated to Sainte-Anne. Girouard, *Lake St. Louis*, p. 145 f.

[34]Built in 1706. Cf. A. Leclaire, *Le Saint-Laurent historique*, Quebec, 1906, p. 145 f.

[35]Built about the same time as Saint-Sulpice. Cf. E. R. Adair, "The Church of Saint-Michel de Vaudreuil," in *B.R.H.*, XLIX, 1943, pp. 38–40, 75–89.

[36]Laprairie was granted to the Jesuits as a seigniory in 1647. See further Appendix, pp. 109, 122, 131.

[37]Not that there was a regular sequence of the three building types on every site, of course. For one example, at Chambly a chapel in the fort built *de pieux* in 1665 stood until 1710, when it was rebuilt in stone. Cf. F.-A. Baillargé, "Le Fort de Chambly," *B.R.H.*, XV, 1909, p. 32.

twenty-five feet wide are not light."[38] People still living remember this process of construction, of course, from the barn-raisings which remained common until the early twentieth century, when balloon- and metal-frame construction finally displaced it everywhere.

The architecture of Indian chapels benefited not only from the outside resources upon which their builders could often draw, but also from concentration of the missions near the greater centres of French population, where materials and technical skill were more readily available. The reason for this concentration was twofold. Iroquois aggression, which wiped out the Huronia mission field, also rendered outlying missions unsafe, so that many of them, such as Tadoussac and Gentilly, were abandoned.[39] (Outlying French settlements, too, were threatened; only towards 1700 did New France begin to expand any great distance from the settled riverside strip between Quebec and Montreal.[40]) And Laval's policy of building up French parishes made him averse to great expenditures on the Indians. Therefore there was a general tendency to concentrate Indian missions in a few defensible places, and encourage converts to settle there. Greater resources were thus made available for each mission. So at Bécancour, where a group of Christianized Algonquins persecuted by the Iroquois had already been settled by its seignior,[41] the Jesuits took charge, encouraged further settlement, and provided a substantial church.[42] Around Montreal, the Sulpicians built solid chapels for several Indian missions. Their earliest was the "Fort des Sauvages" at the foot of the Côte des Neiges, built in 1680; in 1696 this mission was consolidated with the one at Sault-au-Récollet, and the Jesuit-built chapel there was replaced by an even finer structure.[43] Another Sulpician Indian mission was on the Ile-aux-Tourtes, where a chapel was built in 1699.[44] And at Ancienne-Lorette, the Jesuits provided a chapel so elaborate, by comparison with other mission chapels, that we shall properly consider it under the category of Jesuit churches.

The centralization achieved by Bishop Laval in the later seventeenth century in New France is reflected in the fact that only two commemorative or *ex voto*

[38]Cf. R. G. Thwaites (ed.), *The Jesuit Relations*, LXIII, Cleveland, 1900, p. 233.

[39]At Tadoussac, the Jesuit mission for the Indians was abandoned when the stone church built in 1661 was destroyed by fire in 1664. *V.E.*, p. 179. The Indian mission at Gentilly, in connection with which a chapel had been built at Fort La Présentation in 1668, was abandoned in 1686. Girouard, *Lake St. Louis*, p. 61 f.

[40]E.g., towards 1700 the Jesuits founded Chicoutimi and built a chapel there, beginning to open up the Lake St. John country. Cf. "Chicoutimi, la reine du Nord," *B.R.H.*, XIX, 1913, p. 351.

[41]Sieur de Bécancour, Baron de Portneuf; settlement dates from about 1650. Cf. Leclaire, *Le Saint-Laurent historique*, pp. 48–49.

[42]"Notes sur les premiers temps de la colonisation à Bécancour," *B.R.H.*, VIII, 1902, p. 42.

[43]C.-P. Beaubien, *Le Sault-au-Récollet*, Montreal, 1898, pp. 143–144, 149.

[44]Olivier Maurault, *Marges d'histoire: Saint-Sulpice*, Montreal, 1930, p. 205 f. This work will hereafter be referred to as *M.H.: S.-S.*

chapels of importance appear to have been built in his régime, and, significantly enough, both in Montreal. One dates from the beginning of the Age of Laval, the other from the end of it. The first, and by far the most important, was the chapel of Notre-Dame-de-Bonsecours in Montreal. Projected by Marguerite Bourgeoys in 1657, the first wooden chapel was built by her in 1670. Following the acquisition of a miraculous statue of the Virgin, it became a place of pilgrimage, and Mère Bourgeoys was soon able to build a stone chapel, in 1675.[45] This chapel was destroyed by fire in 1754, and not rebuilt until 1771. Its successor occupied the same site, but it was a little larger, and probably had nothing more than a general relationship to the seventeenth-century building.[46]

The other devotional chapel of importance in Laval's time was erected just outside Montreal in 1697 by Pierre Le Ber. One François Charon was the mason. Like Bonsecours, the "Chapelle Sainte-Anne" did not survive the Cession; abandoned after the conquest, it soon fell into ruins and disappeared.[47]

The ground-plans of both these chapels appear on the "Plan de la Ville de Montréal" made by Chaussegros de Léry in 1729 (Figure 5). That of the

FIGURE 5. Ground-plan of the chapels of Sainte-Anne (left) and Bonsecours in Montreal, enlarged from the "Plan de la Ville de Montréal" drawn by Chaussegros de Léry.

Chapelle Sainte-Anne" is a Latin cross with round apse, the regular plan for a parish church of the Age of Laval, as we shall see. The plan of Bonsecours was the same, except that it lacked one lateral chapel. This kind of asymmetry is

[45]*A.V.M.*, I, p. 22 and n. 1. Olivier Maurault, *Marges d'histoire: Montréal,* Montreal, 1929, p. 189 f. This latter work will hereafter be referred to as *M.H.: M.*

[46]O. Lapalice, "Les Pierres angulaires de la chapelle de Notre-Dame-de-Bonsecours, à Montréal," *B.R.H.*, XXXVI, 1930, p. 499. The 1771 chapel is well known from numerous nineteenth-century drawings, engravings, and photographs. It is still extant, but from 1885 on, it underwent a series of alterations which changed its appearance unrecognizably. Cf. *V.E.*, p. 25 f.

[47]Le Ber, a painter, was in Montreal from 1669, and died there in 1707. *A.V.M.*, I, pp. 350–351; cf. Appendix, p. 127. *D.G.F.C.*, p. 118, lists a François Charon, born in 1678, married in 1701, the son of Pierre Charon of Montreal (1640–1700). See also E.-Z. Massicotte, "La Première Chapelle de Sainte-Anne à Montréal," *B.R.H.*, XLVIII, 1942, p. 51.

not an isolated case in the architecture of New France; it may be that it represents a survival of late medieval architectural ideas from Europe.[48] Whatever the explanation, it seems most probable that these two commemorative chapels resembled quite closely the conventional type of parish church set by Laval, and would suggest that Laval's example inspired a fairly uniform architectural form in the colony, even outside his own immediate area of jurisdiction.

## PARISH CHURCHES

*Laval's influence on parish church building.* Next to thorough reorganization of the ecclesiastical set-up, the pressing need of the Church in New France, swollen by later seventeenth-century immigration, was for more, larger, and better parish churches. In his mandate of 1663 establishing the Seminary of Quebec, Laval made specific provision for new church building: "As it is necessary to build several churches for . . . divine service . . ., I order, though without prejudice to the obligation that the faithful have in each parish to contribute to the building of churches, that when the annual expenses have been covered, all the rest [of the Seminary funds] shall be spent on the construction of churches, or in . . . other good works for the benefit of the Church, according to the orders of the bishop."[49] In addition to these resources, Laval, who was always on most cordial terms with Louis XIV,[50] solicited and obtained fairly regular and quite substantial grants from the King, specifically earmarked for parish church building.[51]

These two methods of raising funds for church building were obviously under Laval's direct control. There were two other means available for financing parish church building—tithes, and grants from local seigniors. Over them Laval's authority was almost as great, although more indirect. Before con-

[48]In conversation with me, M. Gérard Morisset has advanced the theory, suggested to him by Louis Hautecœur in Paris, that the architecture of New France was in some way influenced by the "deliberate asymmetry" of late medieval architecture in Europe. He would thus explain such anomalies as the single chapel on Bonsecours, the single tower built for the 1684 cathedral of Quebec, etc. In general, I would agree with this theory; it accords with the strong element of craft traditions in the architecture of New France. On the other hand, there is a strong, I think perhaps stronger, element of symmetry in this period, embodied in the regular Latin-cross plans of Laval's parish churches, and other examples which we shall shortly consider. It is to be noted that in seventeenth-century American architecture also there is to be found a mixture of medieval picturesqueness and Renaissance symmetry. I shall discuss this point further in chapter v.

[49]Scott, *Bishop Laval*, p. 150.

[50]Laval's ideas on government and society so well paralleled those of Louis XIV that there was the closest co-operation between them. In 1664 the King wrote: "M. the Bishop of Petræa, I have received all your letters, and seen all that you say about the events of Canada . . . this dispatch is to testify my satisfaction for your devotedness to the welfare of the country. I hope that you will continue and exhort you to do so. Remain sure of my protection, proofs of which you shall receive on every occasion." *Ibid.*, p. 193.

[51]E.g., 6000 *livres* in 1666 (*ibid.*, p. 194), and 4000 *livres* in 1675 (J.-E. Roy, *Histoire de la seigneurie de Lauzon*, I, Lévis, 1897, p. 272). This grant is specifically directed to "le curé de Québec et les prêtres du séminaire de Québec pour le bâtiment des églises."

struction could begin on any parish church, whether financed by local tithes or otherwise, the Bishop's permission had to be obtained, and he could withhold it if he considered the project unsatisfactory. He had a further indirect control by virtue of his relationship with the Intendant, as provided in the legislation of 1663: the Intendant had the last word in all financial matters pertaining to church building, including the assignment of individual contributions,[52] and he almost invariably followed the Bishop's recommendations.[53] Laval's control over churches privately financed by seigniors was in theory more tenuous, but in practice hardly less absolute. An act of 1679 stipulated that if a seignior were able to build a church out of his own funds, he had the right of veto over the appointment of its curés; presumably he was free to dictate its type of construction also.[54] But most seventeenth-century seigniors were no wealthier than their tenants, and able to afford only the humblest structures, so that if the Bishop found them not to his liking, he could and did refuse to consecrate them, on grounds of impermanence.[55] Thus, to all intents and purposes the Bishop of Quebec could effectively dictate all the church building of New France in the seventeenth century.

*Locally financed parish churches.* Tithes and requisitions on parish members provided a traditional source of Church revenue for all local purposes. In 1663

---

[52]Cf. Gustave Lanctot, *L'Administration de la Nouvelle-France*, Paris, 1929, p. 76 f.: "In the realm of religion, which he shared with the Governor, the Intendant had a very wide jurisdiction. He had a general obligation to advance the Faith, and to see to the execution of ordinances pertaining to religion and clerical affairs. He was pledged to give the curés all the support of his authority. . . . With the Governor and the Bishop, he assigned curial charges. . . . Finally, he alone had charge of parochial affairs, i.e., everything concerning the construction of churches, presbyteries, the estimating of necessary repairs. It was from him that permission had to be obtained to convoke an assembly of parishioners, and it was he who authorized the execution of its decisions, and who, if necessary, ordered those assessed to pay their contributions to the project."

[53]As one instance among many, we may cite the following, quoted from Lemoine's *Album du touriste* by A. Béchard, *Histoire de la paroisse de Saint-Augustin, Portneuf*, Quebec, 1885, p. 19: "About 1690, a little wooden chapel was constructed at the edge of the river, in the Anse-à-Maheut. . . . Since the tide made this site difficult of access, the ecclesiastical authorities chose another more convenient, and ordered the chapel and cemetery moved there. The inhabitants of the neighbourhood opposed this order, but the Intendant supported the Bishop, and obliged the people to execute his ordinance."

[54]Amédée Gosselin, "Le Patronage des églises de la Nouvelle-France," *Rapport de l'Archiviste . . . de Québec . . . pour 1922–23*, p. 118.

[55]Duchesneau, writing to Seignelay on November 13, 1681, describes such incidents: "Every one here [in New France] is puffed up with the greatest vanity; there is not one but pretends to be a patron, and wants a curé on his land, yet all are heavily in debt and in the most extreme poverty. Exclusive of that at Quebec, there are, throughout the entire colony, only seven stone parochial churches. These are in the seigniories of the Bishop, of the Jesuits, of the Seminary of St. Sulpice, and in two private seigniories. The rest are constructed of timber and plank at the expense of the proprietors of the fiefs, and of the settlers; the bishop, however, refuses to consecrate them, because, as he says, it is his duty and obligation not to consecrate any buildings except such as are solid and durable." *Correspondance générale*, vol. 275, quoted in W. B. Munro, *The Seigniorial System in Canada*, p. 185, n. 3.

Laval set the tithes at one-thirteenth of the grain crop, assuming that after the curés had been provided for, enough would remain for church construction; unfortunately for his plan, there was a general outcry against this amount, and in 1667 the figure had to be reduced to one twenty-sixth, where it remained down into the twentieth century. The resulting revenue barely met the clergy's meagre stipends, and parishes which had to depend upon what was left over for building their churches fared poorly indeed. Mgr Saint-Vallier's report on the Canadian Church in 1686 made a great point of their distressing condition:

[In the Beaupré coast region] there are only three or four churches which have been built in stone, by the efforts and with the help of the Gentlemen of the Seminary of Quebec: the rest are merely of wood, and all need to be repaired, or rebuilt, or completed, or decorated on the interior. . . . I visited on my way [to Montreal] all the churches . . . on both sides of the river; that of the little town of Trois-Rivières . . . was the only one that gave me any satisfaction; all the rest are either so near ruin, or so lacking in the most elementary necessities, that the poverty in which I saw them touched me deeply; and I have no doubt that if pious persons in France had seen as I did these shrines covered in thatch, quite bare, without sacred vessels and without ornaments, they would be so sensibly affected as to direct their charity to these places, so that the divine mysteries might be celebrated in them with decency.[56]

It is a dismal enough picture, even allowing for some exaggeration in the interests of exciting sympathy in influential quarters. Indeed, we have considered these churches architecturally under the category of mission chapels, which, strictly speaking, they were.

*Parish churches in lay seigniories.* Most churches built by lay seigniors, it seems, were equally poor affairs. Typical was the chapel built at Lanoraie in 1675 by Sieur Dautray, following concession of the seigniory to him in 1672; since it was served by a priest from Sorel, Laval must have adjudged it too insubstantial to consecrate.[57] Sometimes the seigniorial church was nothing but a chapel in the manor house, where priest and seignior lived together.[58] And it often happened that seigniors would even refuse offers of financial aid from the Bishop to provide more suitable places of worship, for fear of losing their rights of patronage. So stubborn were some of them that in 1699 Mgr de Saint-Vallier

[56]Têtu and Gagnon, *Mandements des évêques de Québec*, I, p. 191 f.
[57]It was destroyed when the Iroquois wiped out the Lanoraie settlement in 1689. Cf. "Notes historiques sur Lanoraie," *B.R.H.*, XXVI, 1920, p. 337 f.
[58]A hint of the probable appearance of such structures is given by the Ferme Saint-Gabriel, and the old presbytery of Batiscan. The former was built in 1698 as a house for the Sœurs de la Congrégation Notre-Dame; with wings added in 1726 and 1728, it is known from an old painting of it in the McCord Museum, Montreal, and from a photograph by Edgar Gariépy. Cf. *V.E.*, pp. 103–104; Gérard Morisset, *A.N.F.*, Figure 37. The old presbytery of Batiscan, built about 1680, repaired in 1734, 1836, and 1865, still preserves a fair approximation of its original appearance. Cf. Ramsay Traquair, *The Old Architecture of Quebec*, Toronto, 1947, pp. 45–46.

had to obtain a royal mandate authorizing erection of stone churches in seigniories needing them, regardless of a seignior's opposition.[59]

However, if a lay seignior had initiative or private means, he could always provide a parish church considerably superior to those built with the colonists' own resources. The energetic Pierre Boucher wrote a book in 1663 to attract colonists to New France, entitled *Histoire véritable et naturelle des mœurs et productions du pays de la Nouvelle-France,* which contains, among other things, a great deal of information about early materials and building techniques; the parish church he built at Boucherville in 1670,[60] fifty feet long and twenty-five feet wide, presumably made his seigniory that much more attractive to settlers. Pierre Le Gardeur, who became seignior of Repentigny in 1676, was equally conscientious; in 1679 he built a church which stood until 1725.[61] Both these churches were solidly built of wood.[62]

At Neuville the seignior was even more ambitious. His church, built in 1679, was *en colombage.* This construction was a sort of intermediate step between stone and wood, much favoured by those who wished to have the durability of stone without its cost; Laval recognized its solidity by consecrating the church of Neuville on December 3, 1684.[63] Like construction *en pieux, en colombage* seems to have been another survival of medieval European building traditions. It also has parallels in the seventeenth-century architecture of the American colonies (where it was called "puncheoned" construction[64]); an eye witness described its appearance in New France[65] as follows: ". . . the walls are formed of timbers, erected perpendicularly about two feet from each other. . . . Between these pieces of timber, they have made the walls of the church of black slate [rubble fill]."

And in Sieur Le Moyne's manorial establishment at Longueuil there was a seigniorial church of genuine stone construction. In a seventeenth-century document we read that "he has had a fort constructed . . . flanked by four good towers . . . all in stone and masonry, with a guard house, several fine residences, and a very fine church, all distinguished with the marks of nobility."[66] Since

[59]See the discussion by Antoine Roy, *L.S.A.,* p. 151 f.

[60]The date was established by Huguet-Latour, *A.V.M.,* I, p. 275 f., and followed by L. Lalande, *Une Vieille Seigneurie—Boucherville,* Montreal, 1890.

[61]*V.E.,* pp. 97–98.          [62]*P.G.M.,* p. 125 f.

[63]*Ibid.,* p. 121. Evidently it was one of the two stone churches referred to in Duchesneau's letter of 1681 (cf. n. 55). For its consecration see P.-G. Roy, "Saint-François-de-Sales de la Pointe-aux-Trembles, Québec," *B.R.H.,* III, 1897, p. 129 f.

[64]Cf. Henry C. Forman, *The Architecture of the Old South,* Cambridge, Mass., 1948, pp. 16–17, Figure 2, *et al.*

[65]In the church of Baie-Saint-Paul, probably built *c.* 1675. According to Tanguay, *D.G.F.C.,* p. 601, the parish records commence in 1681. Cf. "Notes historiques sur la Baie-Saint-Paul," *L'Abeille,* Quebec, Nov.–Dec., 1859. For the description quoted see *P.K.T.,* p. 483.

[66]Quoted in *B.R.H.,* VI, 1900, p. 76.

Duchesneau mentions it in 1681 as one of two stone churches standing in lay seigniories, the church must have been built about that year; in 1724 its functions were taken over by a church provided by the parishioners.[67] Among lay seigniorial churches, however, such magnificence was a distinct exception; it was in the ecclesiastical seigniories, particularly those of Bishop Laval, that the real development of seventeenth-century church architecture in New France took place.

*Parish churches in Laval's seigniories.* Most important of the ecclesiastical seigniories of later seventeenth-century New France were those of the Bishop of Quebec, located on the Beaupré coast and the Ile d'Orléans.[68] As early as 1667, Laval was able to point with pride to the fact that they contained more than a quarter of the colony's total population.[69] Here were built, under the Bishop's personal supervision and aided with grants from the Seminary funds and royal moneys, the largest and best of the parish churches of the Age of Laval, those that had the most lasting significance for the tradition of church architecture in French Canada.

Most of them were of stone. A few, however, resembled the simple structures discussed earlier. Laval used the construction *en colombage* on several occasions for his churches, notably in two early churches on the Ile d'Orleans—Saint-Pierre and Saint-Jean. At least one of his churches was of wood—the small church of Saint-François, I.O.[70] But in general Laval preferred to build in stone if at all possible, and it is his stone parish churches which entitle him to be considered founder of the Quebec tradition of parish church architecture.[71] There were six of them—Sainte-Famille, I.O. (begun 1669), Beauport (1672),

[67]A. Jodoin and J.-L. Vincent, *History of Longueuil*, Montreal, 1889.

[68]The Ile d'Orléans was first settled by Christianized Indians driven from Huronia by the Iroquois about 1651. In 1668, with the tremendous growth in French population, the Indians under the care of the Jesuits were removed to Sainte-Foy.

[69]Munro, *Seigniorial System in Canada*, pp. 185–186.

[70]Saint-Pierre, built about 1676, is described in the *Plan général* as 50 feet long and 22 feet wide; Saint-Jean, begun shortly before 1683, was 45 feet long and 20 feet wide, and in 1683 was not yet finished; built in 1683, Saint-François was 30 feet long and 20 feet wide. Cf. Traquair and Barbeau, *McG.U.P.*, nos. 22, 23, 14.

[71]Throughout the seventeenth century, the term "stone" refers only to the walls, as far as we can judge, the roofs and interiors being universally of wood. In case of fire, these wooden interiors were gutted and the stone walls often used *in situ* for rebuilding, as was for example the case in the fire which burned out the Ursuline convent in December, 1650. Mère Marie de l'Incarnation describes this fire in a letter: "In short, everything was enveloped in flames in less than one hour, and all we possessed in the way of clothes, supplies, furniture, and such things, was consumed." But the building was rebuilt shortly thereafter on the old walls. Cf. *V.d.Q.*, I, pp. 211–212. Such events account for the great confusion existing in the records between "rebuildings" and "new buildings," and also attest to the thickness of the walls. This thickness came either from the use of fieldstone, or construction *en colombage.* Cut-stone work was usually restricted to the quoins, door- and window-frames. Cf. *L.S.A.*, p. 164 f. Not until very late in the seventeenth century are there records of buildings made of cut stone throughout, and writers always make a point of specially mentioning it.

Saint-Joseph de la Pointe de Lévy (1675), Ange-Gardien (1675), Sainte-Anne de Beaupré (1676, rebuilt 1689–1695), and Château-Richer (c. 1680).

When Laval arrived in New France, he found one fine stone parish church already standing in his territory—Quebec's Notre-Dame-de-la-Paix, built with Jesuit help in 1647. It was, in fact, the largest church in the colony, measuring eighty feet in length and about thirty-eight feet in width.[72] So impressed was the Bishop with it that in 1664 he expressed his pleasure in a letter to the Holy See: "There is a basilica here," he wrote, "built in stone; it is large and magnificent."[73] But what is more important, he may well have decided to make Notre-Dame his architectural model for all the parish churches in his seigniories. To do so would have been entirely consistent with all we know of Laval's character; it would result in a uniformity most congenially symbolizing the control of the Bishop over New France's spiritual life, and encourage a high standard of construction as well.

The dimensions of Laval's parish churches certainly suggest that Notre-Dame-de-la-Paix was their model. His first one, Sainte-Famille, was almost exactly the same size—eighty feet long and thirty-six feet wide.[74] None of the others were so large (when the Plan général was compiled in 1683, Sainte-Famille parish's population of 384 was one of the largest in the whole colony), but there is an even more revealing similarity in the fact that all of them shared with Notre-Dame and Sainte-Famille a curious proportion of length to width, roughly two to one. Beauport, Ange-Gardien, and Château-Richer were all sixty feet long and about thirty feet wide.[75] Saint-Joseph de la Pointe de Lévy and Sainte-Anne de Beaupré were also thirty feet wide, but varied in length from the others, Saint-Joseph being forty-five feet and Sainte-Anne eighty (the same length as Sainte-Famille and Notre-Dame); however, these deviations are easily explicable, since Saint-Joseph was located in the sparsely populated seigniory of Lauzon, and Sainte-Anne already needed a longer nave to accommodate pilgrims.[76] Now this two-to-one proportion is reasonable in a church intended partly for the use of a religious order (as the 1647 church of Notre-Dame, built with Jesuit help,

---

[72]"Marchez faicts en 1646 et 47 jusque en 1648 au mois de septembre pour la construction de l'église et du fort à Québec," B.R.H., VII, 1901, p. 269 (see. chap. II, p. 25). See also V.E., pp. 1–2. Notre-Dame remained the largest until the erection of the Jesuit church in Quebec, in 1666, which was 100 feet long.

[73]Quoted in V.d.Q., I, pp. 179–180.

[74]Traquair and Barbeau, McG.U.P., no. 13; V.E., p. 171 f.

[75]All dimensions cited from the Plan général; P.G.M., pp. 116–118.

[76]Lauzon was in fact so sparsely populated that Laval had to solicit a royal grant to help build the church. As for Sainte-Anne, a letter written by Mère Marie de l'Incarnation, dated 1665, testifies to its early popularity: "Seven leagues from Quebec there is a place called Le Petit Cap, where there is a church dedicated to Ste Anne, in which Our Saviour does great miracles. . . . There one may see paralytics walking, the blind recovering their sight, and the sick being cured of whatever afflicts them." Cf. "La 'Chapelle des Matelots' à Sainte-Anne de Beaupré," B.R.H., XXIX, 1923, p. 141.

was), because, with lateral chapels particularly, it provides a relatively greater space at the east end for the services of regular clergy; its appearance in Laval's parish churches would be difficult indeed to explain without the assumption that Notre-Dame was their prototype.

If it is correct, then, to think that all Laval's churches were based on a common model, they clearly made up a group embodying the first consistent architectural tradition in New France, and must have been a compelling influence on subsequent generations. To understand later developments, it would be essential to form an idea of their appearance. Can we reconstruct it? As we have noted, actual remains from the period are practically nil. Nevertheless, there is circumstantial evidence enough for a reconstruction which, if not absolutely sure, is very nearly so.

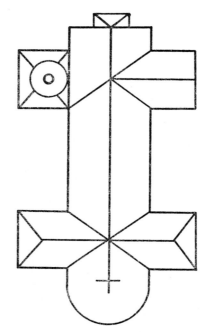

FIGURE 6. Ground-plan of the Cathedral of Quebec from a map made in 1714, showing the additions of 1684–1687.

We have evidence from several sources about Notre-Dame-de-la-Paix. There is the contract of 1648, discussed in chapter II, and ground-plans appearing on maps dated 1660 and 1714 (Figures 4, 6; the map of 1714 represents the church as it was after the twenty-foot lengthening of the façade in the years 1684–1687). These agree in showing a Latin-cross plan, twice as long as its width, terminated by a round apse. Roof construction also seems to be indicated on one map—the ridge-pole of the nave roof is crossed at right angles by a ridge-pole common to the twin lateral chapels.

From other sources we also happen to know that the first clocher of Notre-Dame-de-la-Paix was built in wood over the intersection of the two ridge-poles. Such a location is at first hard to square with an assumption that Notre-Dame was a prototype for the Quebec parish church tradition, because in this tradition clochers are almost invariably located over the façade. But there is a simple explanation: the clocher so located was the one feature of Notre-Dame that Laval heartily disliked, so much that in 1680 he wrote to the King himself about it: "The clocher, being only of wood, has been totally ruined by the snows and severe climate of this country; it cannot be repaired, which is why we find it necessary to build one in stone. For eighteen months now, we have rung no bells, for fear that the clocher would collapse upon the building of which it forms part."[77] Laval would hardly have repeated such an undesirable feature in his parish churches; but to build a stone tower beside the façade such as he eventually provided for the cathedral, or to reinforce the crossing with stone piers, was too expensive for parishes. The best solution was to follow a tradition long established in northerly parts of Europe, and incorporate a base for the clocher into the stonework of the façade. And this, we may reasonably believe, was the scheme followed in all Laval's parish churches.

There emerges, then, a good idea of the general outline of Notre-Dame-de-la-Paix, and hence, with the assumption of a clocher over the façade, of the general type of Laval's parish churches. And I think evidence exists which permits us to go further, and reconstruct something of the actual appearance of these churches.

No example of a parish church interior from this age survives, as we have noted earlier. However, as late as 1930 the church of Ange-Gardien preserved an apse built in 1675, and the apse of the seigniorial church of Neuville, begun in 1696, is still extant (Plates II, III).[78] Both show a semi-circular apse, roofed with a false vault in wood; windows are spaced around the curving wall, which is articulated by carved wooden pilasters and cornice. But in both cases the actual work is much later, typical of Quebec church interiors of the eighteenth and early nineteenth centuries; we cannot assume that Laval's churches were as pretentious. On the other hand, we know of a chapel at Armenonville in France with an extant interior dating from the 1660's which for reasons discussed in chapter v must be considered very similar to one of Laval's churches (Plates XLVI, XLVII); it shows only a crude prototype of the wall articulation and wooden ceiling vault of the later Quebec tradition. Laval's parish churches

[77]See Auguste Gosselin, "L'Eglise paroissiale de M. de Bernières," in *Henri de Bernières,* Quebec, 1902, p. 159. The letter is in the archives of the Seminary of Quebec.

[78]René-E. Casgrain, *Histoire de la paroisse de l'Ange-Gardien,* Quebec, 1902, *passim.* The interior decoration of Neuville dates mostly from the years 1777–1794; cf. P.-G. Roy, "Saint-François-de-Sales de la Pointe-aux-Trembles, Québec," *B.R.H.,* III, 1897, p. 129 f.

were probably somewhat more elaborate than this; I think, therefore, that if we imagine their interiors as looking rather like Armenonville, but more elaborately developed in the direction of the work of Ange-Gardien and Neuville, we shall have about as accurate a picture of them as extant evidence can provide.

For the external appearance of Laval's churches our evidence is much better. We have good photographs of two churches, now demolished, which were built a few years after Laval's resignation as Bishop but still reflected the tradition he established. The first of these is the old church of Saint-Laurent, I.O., demolished in 1864 (Plates VI, XLIX). Most of this church dated from 1695, and shows the Latin-cross plan and relation of nave to transept characteristic of Laval's parish churches; its façade followed the same tradition, although it was built in 1708 by Jean Maillou, who later in the eighteenth century developed a somewhat different type of plan for country churches.[79]

Our photographs of Saint-Laurent show the west end particularly well.[80] The gable is high and steeply sloped, constructed of rough fieldstone masonry which has been whitewashed or plastered over, probably at some later time.[81] A round-headed door and an oculus above it—known in Quebec as an *œil de bouc*—both framed in cut stone, are the only openings. The clocher is located where we have been led to expect it, just behind the point of the gable. This clocher is of particular interest, not only for its early date (according to the *Livre de Comptes* of Saint-Laurent, it was constructed in 1709 by Joseph Chabot, master carpenter of Quebec), but because it is still in existence, incorporated in the near-replica of Saint-Laurent which serves as a summer chapel at Mont-Tremblant[82] (Plate IX). It consists of a squarish drum set into the roof, supporting a hexagonal base upon which are set two little superimposed lanterns, the uppermost capped with a small *flèche*.

But we need not rely solely on Saint-Laurent to form an idea of the exteriors of Laval's parish churches. Another, and in some ways more important, reflection of that tradition has been preserved in photographs of the third church of Sainte-Anne de Beaupré, demolished in 1878, and in its clocher which still stands on the Commemorative Chapel there (Plates VII, VIII). Recent investigations by Gérard Morisset have revealed that this church was built in the years

[79]Maillou was born in Quebec in 1668, and died there in 1753 (*D.G.F.C.*, p. 405). The plan he developed is discussed in chapter IV, p. 80 f.; the church of Saint-Laurent already embodied its characteristic proportions (it was 55 feet long and 22 feet wide), but otherwise seems to have followed the precedent of Laval's churches.

[80]"West end" here, and commonly in Quebec churches, is synonymous with "front façade," their orientation generally following traditional liturgical usage. Exceptions are fairly widespread, however: e.g., Notre-Dame-des-Victoires in Quebec faced north; La Paroisse in Montreal faced south; the Jesuit church of Montreal east, etc.

[81]On the introduction of whitewashing and plastering in the church architecture of Quebec, cf. chap. v, n. 31.

[82]See Appendix, p. 127.

1689–1695 as a replacement of Laval's parish church of 1676,[83] and that it was not completely rebuilt in 1787 as formerly believed,[84] but survived substantially intact until its demolition in 1878. Except for some difference in proportions, and the fact that the *flèche* of its clocher is more domical in form, the third church of Sainte-Anne de Beaupré appears to be practically identical with the first church of Saint-Laurent, I.O. This coincidence, plus the correspondence of both churches to what we have deduced about Laval's parish churches from documentary evidence, leaves little room for doubt they represent the tradition Laval established, the core of all later developments in Quebec church architecture.

A traveller visiting the parishes of New France at the turn of the eighteenth century would, then, find a considerable contrast in church buildings. In a few of the newer parishes he might still meet with primitive chapels *de pieux*; in some of the others unpretentious structures of squared timbers or somewhat more elaborate ones *en colombage*. Often he would find a new church in stone standing beside the older one, or hear of preparations to that end underway. But particularly in the region around the capital of Quebec, he would find parish after parish with a fine substantial stone church, and he would be surprised to find that these had already been standing for a good many years. He would notice that they all looked the same; each had heavy walls of fieldstone set in mortar, with cut fieldstone framing a round-headed door and oculus in front, and a few round-headed windows along the sides. Our traveller might remark on the steep slope of the roofs, and wonder if it were to take care of heavy winter snowfalls; he might also wonder why these churches were so short in comparison to their width, and be told that Bishop Laval had modelled them upon the Cathedral in Quebec. Or he might comment upon the prominence of the wooden clochers which stood above the gables of these buildings and learn that they were really units separate from the stonework of the façade, which could be assembled or taken down without disturbing the fabric of the structure,

[83]To my knowledge, M. Morisset has not yet published this information. He gave it to me personally in 1950 in his capacity as director of the Inventaire des Œuvres d'Art de la Province de Québec. Within thirty years there were four buildings on the site of Sainte-Anne de Beaupré, viz.: the "Chapelle des Matelots" of 1658, the first church of 1660, the second church of 1676, and the third church (a complete rebuilding of the second) commenced in 1689. See also "La 'Chapelle des Matelots' à Sainte-Anne de Beaupré," *B.R.H.*, XXIX, 1923, p. 141; *V.E.*, p. 311 f.

*Le Courrier du Canada* for August 1, 1870, has a long article on Sainte-Anne signed by "A Pilgrim," which is copied in H. Lemoine's *Album du touriste*, Quebec, 1873 (and may have been written by him originally); it mentions a "restoration" of the second church in 1694, without giving the name of any architect or saying what precisely was done. Evidently this is a garbled reminiscence of the programme of 1689–1695, of which M. Morisset has found accurate record in the *Livre de Comptes* of Sainte-Anne de Beaupré.

[84]E.g., cf. David Gosselin, *Manuel du pèlerin à la bonne Sainte-Anne de Beaupré*, n.d.: "In 1787 it was rebuilt almost entirely, the walls being torn down to the ground and reconstructed."

thus avoiding the troubles Bishop Laval had once experienced with a clocher on the Cathedral.

Our inquisitive traveller might then ask who was responsible for the design of these churches, which were already clearly influencing church building all over New France. It is, of course, an immensely important question in this connection, but until recently we did not know what the answer would have been. Laval had some theoretical knowledge of architecture, but not the kind of training required to draw up a working plan. Tradition ascribed the building of both the 1676 church of Sainte-Anne de Beaupré and the 1675 church of Ange-Gardien to Abbé François Fillion, which might suggest that he was responsible for the rest of Laval's churches; but so far as we know he had no practical architectural training either.[85] Now, however, M. Morisset's recent researches have disclosed not only that Fillion's church at Sainte-Anne de Beaupré was completely rebuilt in the years 1689–1695, but also that the man in charge of this operation, even to superintending the design of the clocher,[86] was Claude Baillif. And Claude Baillif, most famous architect in seventeenth-century New France, is precisely the sort of man we are looking for.

From 1684 Claude Baillif came into great prominence as an architect in Quebec, so much that we shall discuss his later works under a separate head; what building he did during his nine previous years in New France has always been something of a mystery. Now, I think, we have the answer—he was superintending Laval's programme of parish church building. At least, circumstantial evidence would point strongly to this conclusion.

In 1669 Laval began the first of his parish churches, Sainte-Famille; in 1671 he made a trip to Paris, and it would be only natural to assume that he sought advice on some of the practical building problems he had met with. Whether he actually met Claude Baillif on this trip is, of course, pure conjecture; all we know about Baillif's life in France is that he was born around 1635.[87] Baillif in 1671 must have been well established in his profession of master builder; if Laval invited him to New France at this time, he would have taken some time to think it over. At any rate, in 1675 he came, at the Bishop's express invitation, to teach in the so-called Ecole des Arts et Métiers—we would call it a Trades

---

85Cf. *Souvenir du pèlerinage de Sainte-Anne-de-Beaupré*, Sainte-Anne, c. 1925; Casgrain, *Histoire de la paroisse de l'Ange-Gardien*, p. 51. Fillion was born at Autun in Burgundy in 1629. Ordained twenty years later, he came to Canada in 1667 and served three parishes on the Beaupré coast. Late in 1678 he was recalled to the Seminary of Quebec, and he died there on June 14, 1679.

86The record states that the clocher was built in 1696, "according to the designs of Claude Baillif" by the carpenters R. Leclaire and Jean Marchand. *D.G.F.C.*, p. 409, lists a Jean Marchand, *charpentier*, baptized in 1646 in the bishopric of La Rochelle, who married Marie Hayot in Quebec in 1681 and had a numerous progeny. There is no mention of Leclaire.

87*A.N.F.*, pp. 127–128.

School—recently established by Laval in connection with the Seminary. Here, according to a contemporary document, "there is now being taught carpentry, sculpture, painting, gilding for church decoration, masonry, and woodworking."[88] Baillif may have taken a hand in many or all of these subjects, but he evidently came primarily to teach masonry, as the record of his arrival at Quebec calls him "Claude Baillif, stone-mason, engaged for three years, arrived at Quebec September 22, 1675."[89]

Baillif stayed in New France the rest of his life; he was drowned at sea in 1698 on his first trip back to France. For most of that time he was the leading authority on building in the colony; yet until 1684 there is little record of his activities, other than participation in a few lawsuits and a contract to build a house for Louis Joliette in Quebec.[90] It would seem unreasonable that Bishop Laval, who brought him to New France to teach masonry, would not have consulted him when building his parish churches, particularly when the church of Sainte-Anne de Beaupré which Baillif built resembled them so exactly. Therefore, despite the fact that Baillif is not mentioned in connection with any of Laval's parish churches, I think there can be little doubt that it was he who worked out their master plan. He would have been particularly well fitted to solve the problem of the clocher on the façade, for in all probability he came from Normandy,[91] a region where a tradition of clochers so located was very strong.[92] One further consideration: in his first important commission, rebuilding the Cathedral of Quebec from 1684 on, his work seems to have been unsatisfactory precisely because it looked so very like a large version of one of Laval's parish churches. But these later projects belong to a different phase in the development of church architecture in the Age of Laval; to them we shall now turn.

## BAILLIF AND SAINT-VALLIER

Ever since Pope Clement X had raised Notre-Dame-de-la-Paix to the rank of a cathedral church, in 1674, Bishop Laval had been nurturing plans for its enlargement and embellishment, as befitted a diocese embracing all of North

---

[88]According to Amédée Gosselin, *L'Instruction au Canada (1635–1760)*, Quebec, 1911, the school was founded in 1668. It had two branches: one connected with the Seminary at Quebec, and another which was particularly devoted to agriculture, at Saint-Joachim, a few miles down the river on the north shore. Interrupted by the English invasion of 1690, the school continued on in the eighteenth century, but after 1715 it became primarily a school of agriculture. It was virtually defunct by 1740. For the document quoted see Ramsay Traquair, *McG.U.P.*, no. 19.

[89]"Livre de Comptes," II (1674–1686), or "Grand Livre du Séminaire de Québec," 1675, p. 225.

[90]For the lawsuits see *Jugements et délibérations du Conseil Souverain*, Quebec, 1886, II, p. 188 ff. The contract is for 1683; see *Le Canada français*, Quebec, Sept., 1945, p. 67 f.

[91]According to M. Morisset, the name "Baillif" is a common one in Basse-Normandie. *A.N.F.*, pp. 127–128.

[92]See further chap. v.

America except New England. From time to time he brought the matter to Louis XIV's attention, in various ways, and finally in 1683 the King donated 4000 *livres* for a reconstruction programme. Laval began work the following year, whereupon the King gave another 2000 *livres,* and in 1685, 4500 more.[93]

Claude Baillif was put in charge of the work. The apse and transept of the old church had been repaired in the years 1665 and 1666 with "iron rods to support the vaults,"[94] so that they were left intact; it was decided to proceed first with construction of a tower beside the façade to support a new clocher, and then to enlarge the nave by some fifty feet. Two side aisles were also projected, but they were apparently not added until the middle of the eighteenth century.

While the work was underway, however, important changes were taking place in New France. In 1684 Bishop Laval's health had become so precarious that he no longer felt able to carry on the episcopacy with vigour; he therefore signified his intention to resign, and nominated as his successor Mgr Jean-Baptiste de Saint-Vallier. In 1685 Saint-Vallier came out to Canada as Laval's vicar-general; after surveying the situation in New France, he returned to Paris to be consecrated second Bishop of Quebec in the church of Saint-Sulpice on January 25, 1688.[95]

The change had very considerable effects on the development of church architecture. At the time of his nomination Saint-Vallier was only twenty-nine years of age (he was born in Grenoble in 1653) and already *aumônier ordinaire* to Louis XIV. As a precociously successful prelate, moving in the highest court circles of Paris and Versailles, Saint-Vallier naturally had certain ideas of appropriate magnificence which made him a considerable contrast to the ascetic Laval. These ideas were bound to influence the church architecture of New France, since Saint-Vallier inherited in full the authoritarian control which Laval had established for his office.

If Saint-Vallier had hoped to find a new cathedral mirroring the architectural glories of seventeenth-century France, however, he must have been sorely disappointed; Baillif's initial attempt at monumental architecture seems to have been not overly successful, to say the least. Charlevoix in 1720 wrote "The Cathedral would not be worthy of a good parish in one of the smallest towns of France. . . . Its architecture, its choir, its high altar, its chapels—all are exactly like the architecture of a country church. The most tolerable feature is a rather high tower, solidly built, which is fairly presentable from a distance."[96] Charlevoix was not always an impartial commentator (he seems to have had some private

---

[93]Gosselin, *Henri de Bernières,* pp. 158–159, 160.

[94]*Ibid.,* p. 158.

[95]For a convenient summary of Saint-Vallier's life, see *V.d.Q.,* I, pp. 453–454; for a more detailed account, Auguste Gosselin, *L'Eglise du Canada depuis Monseigneur de Laval jusqu'à la Conquête,* I, Quebec, 1911.

[96]R.P. de Charlevoix, *Journal d'un voyage . . . dans l'Amérique septentrionale,* quoted in *B.R.H.,* XXIX, 1923, p. 259.

dislike for the church in New France),[97] and the parts of the church he disapproves of belong to the old building; but his general impression of the church seems to be corroborated by what we know of it from other sources.

We know the old Cathedral of Quebec best from Short's two drawings of it in ruins in 1759; here it does not merit Charlevoix's description. (See Plates XI, XIX. The clocher as represented in Plate XI does not make sense, so we must rely on Plate XIX for this feature. Both drawings show the same architectural proportions, however.) But Short's drawings do not represent the Cathedral as Baillif built it, rather, as it was altered by the royal engineer Chaussegros de Léry in the years 1744–1748, just a decade before the siege. We know that this was a long and costly rebuilding, but from documentary sources it cannot be determined precisely what was done.[98]

There is in existence, however, a drawing which represents the front elevation of the Cathedral, and which carries the signature of Chaussegros de Léry (Plate X). This has been supposed to represent his plan for the rebuilding. If it does, certainly Traquair's estimate of de Léry is justified: "His knowledge and designing abilities were very slight indeed."[99] But a comparison of the drawing by Chaussegros de Léry and the Cathedral as represented by Short must make it apparent that one is not a plan for the other. The elevation does not correspond to the building Short saw in 1759. But it would, however, correspond very well with Charlevoix's uncomplimentary description of the cathedral that he saw in 1720—the building designed by Baillif in 1684.

Furthermore, it has considerable resemblances to the third church of Sainte-Anne de Beaupré, as designed by Baillif. Here may be seen the steep gable with the round-headed door and the single opening above, and the first transept crossing the main nave at the same roof level, which are salient features of Laval's parish church. The resemblance would explain Charlevoix's characterization of the Cathedral as a "country church," and point up Baillif's connection with Laval's parish church programme. In addition, this elevation corresponds exactly to the plan of the church as it appears on the plan of the Seminary of Quebec drawn in 1714 (Figure 4).

For these reasons, I think it entirely probable, if not sure, that this drawing, if it is by Chaussegros de Léry, represents the Cathedral of Quebec not as he

---

[97]Cf. P.-G. Roy, "L'Historien Charlevoix à Québec," V.d.Q., II, pp. 31–32.

[98]Chaussegros de Léry was perhaps the most important architect of the eighteenth century in New France. Born at Toulon in 1682, he came to Canada in 1716, and died at Quebec in 1756. (J. Daniel, Le Vicomte Chaussegros de Léry et sa famille, Montreal, 1867.) See further, chap. IV. For the rebuilding see V.E., p. 1 f.; Paul-V. Charland, "Les Ruines de Notre-Dame," Le Terroir, Sept., Oct., 1924.

[99]Ramsay Traquair, The Old Architecture of Quebec, Toronto, 1947, p. 94. Professor Traquair's remark refers not to the cathedral, but to "La Paroisse," for which de Léry designed a façade in 1722 which is, if anything, a somewhat better design than the one under consideration.

*left* it, but as he *found* it. And in this case we can sympathize with Charlevoix's view; the church was indeed something of a hodge-podge, a blown-up version of one of Laval's parish churches. And Saint-Vallier cannot have been pleased even with the tower which Charlevoix found "fairly presentable"; its location gave the building an oddly asymmetrical look, reminiscent of medieval tradition,[100] and certainly painful to one familiar with Louis XIV's architecture, while the clocher, made of oak from Batiscan by a carpenter named Lemire,[101] must have seemed equally clumsy to him.

Saint-Vallier was not slow to take action. Only a few weeks after his consecration as Bishop, on February 22, 1688, he wrote three identical letters from Paris to officials at Quebec,[102] advising them that he was sending out "a skilled and clever building contractor called Larivière, along with six masons and three carpenters, to work on Our cathedral and succursal church." "Put them to work quickly," he urged. "They cost me quite dearly, but I believe it will be worth it, provided they lose no time." One might suppose from this that Baillif was discredited, and the new Bishop's exhortations to haste indicative of a wish to at least end the programme with something presentable, but such does not seem to have been the case. Larivière supervised the final work on the Cathedral, notably the lengthening of its nave by fifty feet during the years 1687–1689, but he seems afterwards to have worked mainly as a surveyor, while Baillif continued to dominate the architectural field, being put in charge of the succursal church mentioned in Saint-Vallier's letter of 1688, and providing plans for rebuilding the important church of Sainte-Anne de Beaupré a year later.[103]

For Sainte-Anne, it is probable that Baillif used his old master-plan for Laval's parish churches; but for the succursal church of Notre-Dame-des-Victoires it seems clear that he was influenced by Saint-Vallier's more advanced architectural ideas. It was an old project of Laval's; as early as 1682 the first

[100]Cf. n. 48. It is improbable that a second tower was considered until Chaussegros de Léry's work in the mid-eighteenth century, which was inspired certainly by his previous undertaking for "La Paroisse" in Montreal.

[101]Jean Lemire, *maître charpentier* and a syndic of Notre-Dame, to which office he was elected in 1667, was born in 1626, and died in 1684. *D.G.F.C.*, p. 378. It is probable that he began the construction of the clocher (i.e., its wooden parts) on the ground, and that one of his numerous sons finished it.

[102]To de Maizerets, Denonville, and Champigny; "Inventaire des documents concernant l'Eglise du Canada," *Rapport de l'Archiviste de la Province de Québec pour 1939–40*, p. 283 f.

[103]Cf. Auguste Gosselin, *Henri de Bernières*, p. 160. Hilaire Bernard, Sieur de Larivière, was born in 1639; he died at Quebec in 1729. The *D.G.F.C.* (p. 44) calls him "notaire, arpenteur et architecte." According to J.-E. Roy, "La Cartographie et l'arpentage sous le régime français," *B.R.H.*, I, 1895, pp. 39–40, "Bernard de la Rivière, as well as being the busiest surveyor of this epoch, also acted as an architect. The number of contracts in which he figures is considerable." He often worked in association with François de Lajoue. *D.G.F.C.*, p. 168, lists Lajoue as a "maître tailleur de pierre, architecte, et bourgeois," born in 1656. See further, chap. IV.

Bishop had written to M. de Seignelay in Paris that "There will soon be space to construct a chapel, of which the Lower Town stands in great need."[104] Not until 1688, however, was the first stone laid, and the church dedicated to l'Enfant-Jésus.[105] While the building was under construction, Phips' attack on Quebec was repulsed, and the name changed to Notre-Dame-de-la-Victoire, in honour of the Virgin's miraculous help. When the Virgin intervened again, in 1711, to wreck Walker's invasion flotilla on the Lower St. Lawrence, the church was renamed Notre-Dame-des-Victoires, and the façade rebuilt by popular subscription. This rebuilding probably accounts for the three statues in niches, and the framing of the door with pilasters and entablature, which we see on the façade as drawn by Short in 1759 (Plate XIII).

Short's drawing is our major piece of evidence for the original appearance of Notre-Dame-des-Victoires. Its general outline, and the elements of its façade, recall with rather more elaboration Baillif's design for Sainte-Anne de Beaupré. But to the left of the façade appears a sort of lean-to, seemingly a rough equivalent of the construction seen to the left of the Cathedral. The latter is obviously intended as a base for the Cathedral's second tower, and the resemblance suggests that at least one tower was planned to flank the façade of Notre-Dame-des-Victoires in a similar manner. No semblance of a clocher remained when Short made his drawing of the succursal church. But in 1749 Peter Kalm observed that "it has a small steeple [clocher] in the middle of the roof, square at the bottom and round on top."[106] This remark suggests that the original clocher of Notre-Dame-des-Victoires, like that of the Cathedral, was not located directly over the façade, as it is in the present building. What evidence is offered by various contemporaneous views of Quebec seems to substantiate Kalm's description; evidently the clocher *was* in the middle of the roof.[107] This is a peculiar arrangement; from it and from the tower or towers evidently planned to flank the façade, it is apparent that while in general outlines Notre-Dame-des-Victoires may have been similar to Laval's parish churches, it was strongly influenced by the architecture of the religious orders, and thus presents a sort of prelude to the fusion of the craft and "academic" trends in the eighteenth century. The exact source of influence on the succursal church evidently was Jesuit; of this more will be said.

Neither Notre-Dame-des-Victoires nor the Cathedral was a particularly happy conception architecturally. In both, Baillif seems to have been thinking primarily in terms of simple stone parish churches. But following the completion

104P.-G. Roy, "Quelques Lettres de Mgr de Laval," *B.R.H.*, XLVI, 1940, p. 66 f.
105*V.E.*, pp. 47–51.
106*P.K.T.*, p. 428.
107Cf. Plate V; all representations of Quebec dating from the *ancien régime* seem to agree on this feature.

of the third parish church of Sainte-Anne de Beaupré, which was the last of
Laval's parish churches, strictly speaking, Baillif undertook with markedly
greater success the last work of his life. This was the Episcopal Palace, for
the construction of which Baillif signed a contract with Bishop Saint-Vallier
in January, 1693. Possibly his success in this work was owing to Saint-Vallier's
being finally free from the more ascetic influence of Laval, free to dictate to
the artist his own more advanced ideas of architectural design.

Preliminary work had already been begun when the contract was signed with
Baillif; among other specifications, a façade was called for to be twenty-four
and a half feet high, crowned by "a cornice, frieze, and architrave in the Tuscan
order . . . conforming to the plan which the parties have signed."[108] Baillif set to
work in 1694, and when Saint-Vallier returned from a trip to France in 1697,
the building was substantially complete.

The Episcopal Palace was probably the most elaborate building of seventeenth-
century New France. We can visualize it reasonably well, although it was completely rebuilt around 1830,[109] from a long description by Lapotherie and the
representation of it in a view of Quebec appearing in Lapotherie's book, and
from drawings by Richard Short.[110] Lapotherie writes: "There is a road from
the Lower to the Upper Town. . . . The Episcopal Palace is on the hill; it is a
large building of cut stone; the main body of it, with the chapel making up the
central section, faces the channel [i.e., the St. Lawrence River]. It has a wing
seventy-two feet long, with a pavilion at the end. . . ." In other words, the
plan—although irregular because of site—was that of a typical seventeenth-
century French *château*, a main body enclosing a *cour d'honneur*, with a wall
and ornamental entrance on the fourth side. The drawings show this very well
(Plates V, XII). "The chapel," continues Lapotherie, "is sixty feet long; its
façade is of the composite order, built of fine cut stone, which is a sort of rough
marble. Its interior is magnificent, by reason of its altar retable, the ornaments
of which are an abridgment [*un raccourci*] of that in the Val-de-Grâce. There
would be few episcopal palaces in France could rival it, if it were finished."
This last phrase refers to the second wing, never completed.

---

[108]The contract is quoted by Henri Têtu, *Histoire du palais épiscopal de Québec*, Quebec,
1896, pp. 26–27. The details read as follows: "corniche, frise, et architrave de l'ordre toscan,
l'arcade du dit portail bombée et formé de claveaux bien joints, taillés proprement, et
faits de la forme et manière conforme au dessin qui en a été signé par les parties. . . . Plus
fera ce qu'il conviendra faire de murailles pour l'enceinte du dit palais épiscopal, et ce de
la pierre du lieu, réservé le côté qui en sera exposé au nord-est, lequel sera de pierre de
Beauport."

[109]By Thomas Baillargé; cf. Gérard Morisset, "Thomas Baillairgé," *Technique*, Montreal,
XXIV, 1949, p. 471.

[110]Lapotherie's description is from his article in the *Dictionnaire universel de la France
ancienne et moderne* (Paris, 1726), q.v. It is quoted in *B.R.H.*, XXXII, 1926, p. 291. The
plate in question is from volume I of Lapotherie's *Histoire de l'Amérique septentrionale*,
p. 23a. Short made two drawings of the palace, front and rear.

Lapotherie may have been a trifle over-enthusiastic, but the Palace and chapel were magnificent enough for the time and place. His drawing shows that the body of the chapel was set into the Palace building at right angles, the façade and apse projecting. Short depicts the façade as a typical "Jesuit" type of the seventeenth century, in two stories joined by reversed scrolls, and articulated by pilasters and cornice. The small clocher appears in Lapotherie's drawing to be set in the middle of the roof of the Palace building; in form and location it suggests the one described by Kalm on Notre-Dame-des-Victoires. The semicircular apse which projects towards the river is a simple craft construction, however, in five panels. Thus again the exterior of this chapel shows a mixture of craft and "academic" forms.

The interior of the Episcopal Palace was evidently elaborate also; but all we know of it is Lapotherie's mention of the magnificent baldachin, an abridgment of that in the Val-de-Grâce in Paris. This, however, is significant. For in conjunction with the "Jesuit" type of façade and the location of the clocher, it suggests that the ultimate influence back of the more elaborate architectural forms evident in the Episcopal Palace was that of the Jesuits.

## THE RELIGIOUS ORDERS

*The Jesuits.* In 1666 the Jesuits began to build a church beside their college in Quebec, to replace the patched-up chapel they had been using since 1633. Father Beschefer's letter, already mentioned,[111] tells us that it was a hundred feet long by thirty feet wide, so that it was the largest church in the colony when built. Lahontan called it "fair, stately, and well lighted," and made especial note of the great altar "adorn'd with four great Cylindrical Columns of one Stone; The Stone being a sort of *Canada* Porphyry, and black as Jet, without either Spots or Veins." We are at once reminded of the baldachin in the Episcopal Palace, described by Lapotherie as an abridgment of that in the Val-de-Grâce. Of the exact appearance of this baldachin, we know nothing; it had disappeared when Short depicted the Jesuit church interior in 1759[112] (Plate XIV). However, it must have been quite elaborate, for contemporary writers commented on the magnificence of the interior as a whole on several occasions; Charlevoix, for instance, declared, "It is very much ornamented on the inside; the gallery is bold, light, and well-wrought, and surrounded by an iron balustrade of excellent workmanship, which is painted and gilded. The

---

[111]See p. 22, n. 31. The letter is quoted in *B.R.H.*, XXXV, 1929, p. 335. It also gives the date of the Jesuit church: "We have this year begun a church, which will be finished next year. . . ."

[112]R. G. Thwaites (ed.), *Lahontan's New Voyages to North-America*, Chicago, 1905, I, letter III, p. 39. It is conceivable, of course, that Lahontan is describing merely the altar which appears in Short's drawing against the end wall (Plate XIV). However, the Trois-Rivières altar, mentioned below, seems to me evidence of the early existence of a baldachin form in Quebec. See further, chap. IV.

pulpit is all gilt, and the work both in iron and wood is excellent. There are three altars, handsomely designed, and some good pictures. There is no vaulting [i.e., on the inside], but the flat ceiling is handsomely ornamented. . . ."[113]

Around 1730 this baldachin seems to have been copied by Augustin Quintal for the parish church of Trois-Rivières; his work survived until 1908, and is known through photographs (cf. Plate XXV). The Trois-Rivières baldachin is astonishingly like that in the Val-de-Grâce. Being on a smaller scale, and having four columns instead of six, it could very properly be described as an abridgment of the Parisian monument. We may presume that if its model were the altar in the Jesuit church, as is highly probable,[114] the latter represented a very advanced work for its time indeed.

The exterior of the Jesuit church was equally remarkable. As Short depicted it in 1759 (Plate XV), the façade was flanked by a single tower with an unfinished clocher; since the church adjoined the college directly, there was no room for a second. The façade was articulated with pilasters and entablature in two stories, which, however, appear to have been added later, around 1730, by Chaussegros de Léry. The walls were rather high, to accommodate interior galleries; there was a spacious transept, and a high clocher over the crossing which appears in exaggerated form in various views of Quebec (cf. Plate V). Unusual features included a sun-dial on the clocher and a slate roof.[115]

Even in smaller projects the Jesuits built ambitiously. In their mission chapel at Ancienne-Lorette, begun in 1674,[116] they went to the great trouble and expense of a supposed reproduction of the Santa Casa in Italy.[117] The attempt,

[113]F.-X. de Charlevoix, *Histoire et description générale de la Nouvelle-France*, Paris, 1744, III, p. 76.

[114]Cf. my article on this problem in *Culture*, XII, 1951, pp. 151–157.

[115]Kalm mentions the sun-dial; Charlevoix, the slate roof: "It . . . is the only [church] in Canada which has this advantage, all the buildings here being covered with shingles."

[116]This mission ministered to those Hurons who had escaped from Huronia following the *débâcle* of 1651. At first the mission was located on the Ile d'Orléans; later the Hurons were moved to Sainte-Foy, where a mission chapel was built in 1669; in 1673 the mission moved to a site on the Jesuit seigniory north of Quebec, called Lorette after Loretto in Italy; in the 1690's the mission moved again, a few miles to the east; the new location was called La Jeune-Lorette, to distinguish it from the 1673 site, henceforth known as Ancienne-Lorette. Cf. Lionel Saint-George Lindsay, *Notre-Dame de la Jeune-Lorette en la Nouvelle-France*, Montreal, 1900, *passim*.

[117]The idea of imitating the Santa Casa was that of Father Joseph-Marie Chaumonot, who had made two pilgrimages there; he in all probability designed the plans. *Ibid.*, p. 27. It is a moot point just how closely the chapel at Ancienne-Lorette resembled the Santa Casa. It was apparently thirty-seven years since Chaumonot had last seen the Italian building. Lindsay (p. 28) notes that the original Santa Casa was not in brick (this was apparently a misconception of Father Chaumonot's), but concludes that from the description of Horace Torsellini, an Italian historian writing in 1597, the disposition of the elements of the building at Lorette was similar to that at the Santa Casa. "For the rest," he says, "this difference [brick instead of stone] . . . would be amply compensated for by the acquisition of a statue sent from Loretto by Father Poncet, a statue exactly the same, except for the colour, as that attributed to St. Luke, and of a faience bowl similar to that of the infant Jesus, and designed to perform minor miracles by means of bread dipped in it and distributed to the poor."

while not very successful in imitating its prototype, did result in an example of brick construction unique in church architecture of the *ancien régime*. That the Jesuit experiment of building in brick was not repeated seems due both to an excessive cost of manufacture, and the fact that the bricks produced were evidently of poor quality.[118]

In sum, Jesuit building seems to have been the major influence, besides the craft tradition, on church architecture in seventeenth-century New France. The single tower built beside the Cathedral in 1684 apparently was suggested by the Jesuit church; not until the mid-eighteenth century, when Sulpician influence was felt, was a second, balancing, tower considered. The Episcopal Palace had a Jesuit façade, and its interior also was evidently conceived under Jesuit inspiration. The Jesuits apparently also were responsible for the location of clochers in the middle of the roof, or over the crossing. And, of course, the church of Notre-Dame-de-la-Paix, which seems to have been the prototype for Laval's parish churches, was built largely on Jesuit inspiration.

If we consider the cultural background of the Age of Laval, the predominance of Jesuit influence seems inevitable. The Society of Jesus was by far the largest, most powerful, and most influential order in the first century of New France's history; we have already noted that in the Heroic Age the Jesuits were responsible for five of the nine stone churches built. The Jesuits took their orders direct from Rome, and in theory were independent of the Bishop of Quebec. In practice, however, they and Laval, and later Saint-Vallier, worked closely together. Laval's entire education had been in Jesuit colleges in France, and throughout his and Saint-Vallier's time, the Bishop of Quebec and the Jesuits were in substantial agreement on every issue, including architecture. For the Jesuit system was precisely suited to conditions in seventeenth-century New France.

The Jesuits were expelled from France in 1594, the day after Jean Chastel's attempt on the life of Henri IV. They were allowed to return in 1604, and immediately embarked on a vast programme of propaganda, which included all the arts. How the Jesuits' programme affected architecture in France is succinctly told by Reginald Blomfield, and I shall use his words, pointing up the comparison with New France, although this is hardly necessary.[119]

"It was part of the policy of the Jesuits to standardize their methods, and it thus became essential to their purpose not only that there should be one recognized system of religion and education, but also a recognized environment, so that in all parts of the world the same regimen should prevail, and the same influences, external no less than internal, be brought to bear on their pupils and

[118]Only twenty years after its construction the building appears to have been in ruins. On the construction and subsequent history of the Ancienne-Lorette chapel, see further Appendix, p. 113.

[119]All the following quotations are from Reginald Blomfield, *A History of French Architecture from the Reign of Charles VIII till the Death of Mazarin*, London, 1911, II, chap. XII, "The Jesuits in France."

converts," writes Blomfield. Undoubtedly this would include their pupil François de Laval, first Bishop of Quebec, and their vast mission field in New France. "It is in this conception that we have the origin of what is called the Jesuit style in architecture. . . ." ". . . in most cases the municipalities made contracts with the Jesuits, agreeing to find certain sums of money for building and endowment, in consideration of the Jesuit fathers undertaking all the business of education." This again is quite close to the situation in seventeenth-century Quebec, where the Jesuit college was the first educational institution in the colony.[120] "The sums so found were by no means adequate. . . . The strictest economy had, therefore, to be observed." "The practice was for the architect of the Order to prepare designs and specifications, which were faithfully adhered to in essential points, whether the building took five years to build or fifty." Here again, it can be pointed out that the plans for Notre-Dame-de-la-Paix were drawn up in 1645, but the building was on a scale so disproportionate to the actual resources of the colony that it was not opened for regular services until 1657. "These plans and specifications were handed over to the local people for execution. The Jesuit architect visited the work from time to time to settle difficult points of construction or business, but does not appear to have superintended the work from start to finish. . . ." Thus, the Jesuits probably imported the three workmen named in the contract for Notre-Dame-de-la-Paix to assist in solving technical problems, and sent them back to France, probably to another project, before the Quebec church was quite completed.[121] For the Jesuit church of Quebec built in 1666, it is quite possible that the same plans were used as for Notre-Dame-de-la-Paix.

"The attitude of the Jesuits towards architecture," Blomfield concludes, was "that art was necessary to their system, accordingly they mastered it sufficiently for their purpose of keeping the control of it in their own hands, but there is no trace so far of their having studied it with the thoroughness of the professional architect. They were highly intelligent and able amateurs who, so far as details of business and construction were concerned, must have been much in the hands of their contractors, and in regard to design cut down architecture to certain standard forms, which could be reproduced anywhere with the least possible difficulty." And this, I think, also sums up very aptly the attitude of Bishop Laval to architecture in his diocese; he learned it from the Jesuits. The tendency towards standardization, towards homogeneity, which we found in Laval's parish churches, was undoubtedly a result of the Jesuit point of view. And the appearance of certain modifications of the Jesuit prototype, such as the clocher above the façade, would appear to have been the result of employing "contractors"— such as Claude Baillif—to supervise the actual construction.

120It was built in 1648 under Frère Liégeois. *V.d.Q.*, I, pp. 231–232.
121The three workmen named in the contract for this building (*B.R.H.*, VII, 1901, p. 269) were Denis Bochard, Jacob Desbordes, and Jean Garnier. None of these names appears in the *D.G.F.C.* See chap. II, p. 25.

But it is also possible that Jesuit influence on the church architecture of New France consisted of something more than a general line of approach; that there was, in fact, some direct inspiration from Jesuit buildings of Old France in the Jesuit church of Quebec and Notre-Dame-de-la-Paix. This is a matter it might be worth while to consider in some detail.

Perhaps the greatest Jesuit educational institution in France was the Royal College at La Flèche, founded by Henri IV as a gesture of goodwill towards the Society of Jesus upon their return to France in 1604. Here, in 1631, came the young François de Laval to study, and here he remained for ten years, until he was nineteen. During Laval's stay, the building of the college church was finally completed, and it was consecrated in 1637. This building, if not designed by Etienne Martellange, was built mainly under his supervision, and must reflect many of the ideas of this greatest Jesuit architect of his time in France, who was sent to La Flèche in 1612 by Louis XIII, to direct building operations there.[122] Martellange set the type for the Jesuit church in France, and here we see the first major example of it (Plate XVI). The fundamental inspiration is that of the Jesuits' home church, Il Gesù in Rome; from this prototype it derives the long nave with shallow chapels, and the round apse. To this basis are added the shallow transept, the high gables, and two clochers—one "in the middle of the roof," the other at the point of the apse. The latter features, Gothic reminiscences persisting through the French Renaissance, could have been added by local craftsmen filling in the broad outlines of Martellange's plan, as we have seen to be customary in Jesuit building. Precisely the same process could explain the design of Notre-Dame-de-la-Paix in Quebec and the Jesuit church of 1666. These had transepts, but in general lines must have looked rather similar to the Jesuit church at La Flèche.

The building upon which Etienne Martellange's fame chiefly rested was the Jesuit Noviciate in Paris. Its first stone was laid in 1630. Destroyed at the Revolution, it is well known from contemporary engravings (Plate XVIII). It was exactly the same type as the church of La Flèche, but with a fine "Jesuit façade"—recalling Il Gesù in Rome—and considerably more elaboration. Here again, typically French features such as the steep roof, large windows, and a little domed clocher have entered in to modify the basic scheme. Such a clocher, fused with the more vertical craft-type lingering on from the Middle Ages, was the direct ancestor of the *Québécois* type as we find it at Saint-Laurent and Sainte-Anne de Beaupré.[123]

In the Jesuit church of 1666 in Quebec, and probably in Notre-Dame-de-la-Paix also, cruder provincial forms did not disguise marked similarities to the Noviciate church, both in disposition—Latin-cross plan, round apse, clocher

---

[122]Louis Hautecœur, *Histoire de l'architecture classique en France*, I, pt. II, Paris, 1943, p. 210. Martellange was born in 1579 and died in 1641.
[123]See further, chap. V.

over the transept—and in details such as the hipped treatment of the roof above the main façade. The Noviciate church also helps to explain certain anomalies that appear in Short's drawing of the Jesuit church.

In the Jesuit chapel of La Flèche there was no dome, and in the Noviciate church in Paris it appeared only on the interior (Plate XVII). If we assume that these two churches represent the Jesuit tradition in France which was brought over to Canada, we can explain how it happens that no domed church is found in Quebec until the eclectic period of the later nineteenth century. A reminiscence of the interior dome of the Noviciate is perhaps preserved by the circular motif, circumscribing a flaming sun and Jesuit monogram, which appears on the ceiling of the Jesuit church in Short's drawing. Very probably it was of this that Charlevoix was thinking when, in describing the interior of the Jesuit church, he took occasion to say, "There is no vaulting"—a remark otherwise singularly gratuitous.

Again, the plan of the Noviciate explains a puzzling incongruity in Short's drawings of the Jesuit church in Quebec. If we look at the exterior, it would seem to be a simple Latin-cross plan. But if we compare this exterior with the interior view drawn by the same artist at the same time, we must realize that the plan cannot be a simple Latin cross—assuming, of course, that Short has not made a gross error in drawing. At first sight, the artist would seem to have made his drawing from a position in the nave just in front of the crossing. But the left lateral chapel, which we see in its complete depth, cannot possibly correspond to the long transept seen on the exterior. The plan of the Jesuit church, as we may deduce it from Short's two drawings, is thus an enigma. But if we compare this interior with the plan of the Noviciate church in Paris, a plausible solution presents itself. The artist actually made his drawing from a position in the centre of the crossing, and the transept chapels are off to the right and left. What at first sight appeared to be the transept is a small chapel flanking the choir, as we see it in the Noviciate plan. Once again it is evident how very closely the Jesuits in Quebec followed contemporary trends in France.

This very close tie with France made the Jesuits leaders in architectural design in seventeenth-century New France. When in the eighteenth century a spirit of independence manifested itself in the colony, the other orders—Récollets and Sulpicians—who were closer to the people, proved more influential. But in the Age of Laval, the Jesuit contribution counted for most; even the other orders drew upon it.

*The Récollets.* The Récollets, a French branch of the Franciscan Order, were the first missionaries to New France, arriving in 1615. They left the colony in 1629, and did not return until 1671. The Jesuits did not welcome them, looking on them as unwanted and unnecessary rivals, and Laval, close friend of the

Jesuits that he was, shared this feeling increasingly as time went on.[124] At first, however, he was glad to have them serve outlying French missions; as we have seen, many of the mission chapels erected in the Age of Laval were the work of Récollets.[125] Thus from the very first the Récollets moved among the people, and came to know them. They recruited for their Order among Canadians, in distinction to the Jesuits, who did not accept Canadians in their ranks.[126] Some of the Canadians accepted among the Récollets were craftsmen; hence Récollet building early showed a stronger craft influence than that of the Jesuits. But the Récollets also received support from many influential leaders of New France who welcomed the Récollet Order as a counterbalance to the somewhat despotic authority of Laval and the Jesuits. The Governors of New France in particular were almost unanimously pro-Récollet; they subscribed generously to the Récollets' church building, and enabled them to build on a much more elaborate scale than their vows of poverty could ever have permitted. Thus the Récollets were by circumstances in a position to combine the craft tradition of New France with the more elaborate traditions of architecture built with outside resources; this made them influential in developing an indigenous tradition of church architecture in Quebec during the eighteenth century.

Typical of the early appearance of the native craft element in Récollet architecture was the second parish church of Trois-Rivières. At the beginning of their stay in New France, Laval placed the Récollets in charge of the important parish of Trois-Rivières. Under them the settlement prospered, and in 1682 a new parish church was commenced; significantly, the contract for it was made with a carpenter, named René Pelletier. In it, Pelletier "has voluntarily contracted and promises . . . the inhabitants of Trois-Rivières . . . to demolish the large church located in the said town . . . and to build . . . a new one of timber construction . . ., in length sixty feet, and in width from twenty-five to twenty-six feet. . . ."[127] The rest of the contract goes on to describe in detail various features of the church, including a clocher "about forty-five feet high";[128] its height suggests a craft influence, harking back to medieval verticality.

[124]The best account of the Récollets in Canada is that of Odoric-M. Jouve, *Les Franciscains et le Canada*: *Aux Trois-Rivières,* Paris, 1934, p. 32 f.

[125]See p. 32, nn. 25–27.

[126]"The Jesuits who live here have all come from France. . . . The priests . . . of the order of St. Sulpicius all come from France, and I was assured that they never allow a native of Canada to come among them. . . . The Récollets . . . do not endeavour to choose the best fellows amongst them, but take all they can get. . . . Some of these monks come from France and some are natives of Canada. . . ." So Peter Kalm, writing in 1749. *P.K.T.,* pp. 451–454.

[127]Jouve, *Les Franciscains et le Canada: Aux Trois-Rivières,* p. 32 ff. *D.G.F.C.,* p. 471, lists a René Pelletier, *charpentier,* who married Marie Auvray in 1679. He came from the bishopric of La Rochelle.

[128]". . . auquel bâtiment il y aura une poutre qui divisera la sacristie, dans laquelle il y aura une porte et deux petites fenêtres, plus il y aura une autre poutre pour faire un

On the other hand, when given encouragement the Récollets built with considerable ostentation. When they returned to Quebec in 1671, one of the first arrivals was Frère Luc, a painter of some merit who had studied in Paris with Simon Vouet, and worked in Rome with Poussin and Claude; Roger de Piles was one of his pupils.[129] There are several pictures in Canada by him, and he was entrusted with architectural designing for the order, although presumably his knowledge of architecture was derived principally from his studies as a painter.

In November, 1671, Frère Luc and Bishop Laval took ship together for France, and en route they appear to have decided upon plans for building the Seminary of Quebec; it was begun in 1677 and finished in 1679. This structure was fairly elaborate; it is said to have had a "coffered vault," and an "ornamental cornice."[130] Whether a chapel was built at this same time is somewhat doubtful, however, because there is no mention of one until some twenty years later, when Jacques Leblond *dit* Latour undertook its decoration; in any event it was destroyed, along with all the other Seminary buildings, in a great fire in 1701.[131]

Frère Luc's other work, executed in 1671, still stands, although totally altered. It is the chapel in the Hôpital-Général in Québec,[132] which was originally built as part of the new establishment of the Récollets, dedicated like their former one to Notre-Dame-des-Anges, and located like it on the St. Charles River; in 1692 Mgr de Saint-Vallier purchased it for use as a general hospital, and all the interior furnishings were removed. We know that the chapel had a clocher, evidently located over the altar;[133] it was also noteworthy in that it terminated in a flat wall. In these features—and perhaps in the altar retable as well—the

---

jubé, et trois fenêtres rondes de chaque côté (de l'édifice) en forme de fenêtres d'église; plus, une fenêtre ronde dans le pignon de la dite église sur le jubé; plus il y aura une grande porte au bas de l'église, et un tambour par dehors de dix pieds de long et de six pieds de large par dedans. Item il y fera un clocher qui aura environ quarante-cinq pieds de haut."

Apparently the church when completed did not follow exactly the specifications of the contract, presumably because the Récollets were forced out of their parochial charge while the building was still under construction, having quarrelled with Laval over their building in Quebec's Upper Town. The *Plan général* of 1683 says the church was 50 feet long and 27 feet wide (thus following the two-to-one proportions of Laval's parish churches). *P.G.M.*, p. 124.

[129]See the monograph by Gérard Morisset, *Frère Luc,* Quebec, 1944.

[130]For the first feature see Auguste Gosselin, *L'Eglise du Canada depuis Monseigneur de Laval,* III, Quebec, 1914, p. 152, and for the second Ch. Rambure, "L'Art monumental au Canada," *Bulletin de la société de géographie de Québec,* VI, 1912, p. 45.

[131]*V.d.Q.*, I, pp. 287–288, and II, pp. 11–12.

[132]The standard reference work on this building is the anonymous *Monseigneur de Saint-Vallier et l'Hôpital-Général de Québec,* Quebec, 1882. Specifically on the architecture, see R. Traquair and G. Neilson, "The Architecture of the Hôpital Général," *McG.U.P.*, no. 31.

[133]The clocher was struck by lightning in 1713, and rebuilt in 1725. Since the same bolt also wrecked the altar and retable, it is to be presumed that the clocher was located over this end of the building.

Hôpital-Général chapel was the prototype for the Récollets' most important building effort in the Age of Laval, their church begun in Quebec in 1693.

The Récollet church of 1693 in Quebec was built over the violent objections of Laval and the Jesuits; it represented a successful challenge to Laval's authoritarianism presaging the new spirit of independence in eighteenth-century New France and the part the Récollets were to play in it.[134] The church existed until 1796; we know it primarily from interior and exterior drawings made by Richard Short in 1759 (Plates XIX, XX). According to Morisset, the architect was Juconde Drué, a Récollet, and pupil of Frère Luc.[135]

Charlevoix, writing about 1720, declared that the Récollet church was "large and beautiful," and that "it would do the Récollets honour at Versailles."[136] While it is apparent that Charlevoix is deliberately exaggerating here, to heighten the unfavourable contrast he is drawing with the Cathedral, at the same time we can see from Short's drawings that the church was quite elaborate. We know that Count Frontenac, the Governor of New France at this time, contributed towards its erection, and it is probable that the Récollets drew upon other outside sources as well. The interior, with its fine carving and vaulted roof, and the exterior with its ornamental door in cut stone and its niches, have the same spirit of ostentation that we have seen in the Jesuit church and the later buildings by Claude Baillif. It was a famous church; in it were buried Governors Frontenac, Callières, Vaudreuil, and La Jonquière.[137]

At the same time, many craft features are evident.[138] The clocher is located over the east end of the church, a placing which probably reflects Jesuit usage in New France; but it is thin, with a very high *flèche*, suggesting the one specified for the Récollets' Trois-Rivières church, and in form it is reminiscent of medieval

---

[134]The Récollets felt that their establishment on the St. Charles was too far from the centre of the city, and determined to move closer. In 1681 they acquired a plot near the Château Saint-Louis, and, according to Lahontan, "through the intercession of Count *Frontenac*, [they] obtain'd leave of the King to build a little Chappel (which I call a Church;) notwithstanding the Remonstrances of Mr. *de Laval* our Bishop, who, in concert with the Jesuits, us'd his utmost Efforts for ten years together to hinder it" (*V.d.Q.*, I, pp. 529-530, and Thwaites (ed.), *Lahontan's New Voyages to North-America*, letter III.) This first *hospice* was built in 1682; the Récollet church of 1693 replaced it. It in turn was used by the Anglican congregation of Quebec for a time after 1760, when the Récollets were forbidden to recruit and abandoned their church. Cf. P.-G. Roy, "Le Lieu de réunion des Anglicains à Québec, de 1759 à 1804," *B.R.H.*, XLII, 1936, p. 321.

[135]*C.O.A.*, p. 14. Drué was born in Paris in 1664, and died there in 1739.

[136]*Histoire et description*, III, pp. 74-75.

[137]*V.d.Q.*, I, pp. 529-530.

[138]They may perhaps have been introduced by Claude Pelletier (no relation to René), a Canadian born at Sainte-Anne de Beaupré in 1657, who joined the Récollets in 1680 as Frère Didace. Trained in traditional craftsmanship as a carpenter, Frère Didace travelled about doing carpentry on all the Récollet buildings in New France until his death in 1738. Cf. P.-G. Roy, "Didace Pelletier," *B.R.H.*, I, 1895, p. 27 f. Here it is stated that Pelletier died of a cold caught while working on the Récollet church of Trois-Rivières in 1699. But Antoine Roy, *L.S.A.*, p. 222, n. 4, establishes the later date. Cf. also *B.R.H.*, XVII, 1911, pp. 54-55.

survivals, without the more up-to-date cupola-like quality of the Jesuit clocher. The proportions of the church are likewise narrower and higher than in Jesuit building; the roof is very steep. The Récollet church of 1693 is already, in fact, a fusion of craft and "academic" features, presaging the development of the eighteenth-century parish church tradition in New France.

The interior disposition of the east end of this church was equally influential on parish church architecture of the next century. There are no transepts; the main altar is set back into the wall in a sort of niche, flanked by side altars. The niche is occupied by an elaborate retable composed of four columns on pedestals. The central pair of columns, framing a picture, carried an entablature and curved gable, and the tabernacle stood in front of them. This is the apse arrangement called by later writers *à la récollette*; designated as such, it was very popular in the eighteenth century for parish church interiors. Indeed, just as the Récollet fusion of craft and "academic" traditions in New France set the pattern for later parish church architecture, so the apse treatment *à la récollette* lived on into the nineteenth century to become a permanent contribution to the Quebec tradition of church architecture.

Where did the Récollets derive the ideas which are incorporated in their architecture? I suggest, from the Jesuits, at least in New France. The Récollets had no architectural traditions of their own, and their first architect, Frère Luc, was by training and profession a painter. When he came to try his hand at architecture, the best models were obviously the churches of the Jesuits. It is supposed that Frère Luc inaugurated the *récollette* retable in the Hôpital-Général chapel, repeating it, in all probability, in the Seminary chapel executed the same year. But the *récollette* retable, it seems to me, is already present in essence in the Jesuit church of 1666 (cf. Plate XIV). And certain of its more developed elements, as we see them in the Récollet church of 1693, are satisfactorily explicable as borrowings from the baldachin form in the Jesuit church; later *récollette* variants of the eighteenth century point up this source even more clearly.[139] The flat end-wall characteristic of Récollet building is anticipated in the Jesuit church and found in the Jesuit chapel at Ancienne-Lorette; so also the east-end location of the clocher.

Definitely, then, Jesuit influence was more vital to the church architecture of New France in the Age of Laval than that of the Récollets. Not so in the succeeding century; with the decline of the Society of Jesus as a whole, the Récollets came into their own as popularizers of the more "academic" forms of architecture borrowed from the Jesuits. And therein lay their lasting contribution to the *Québécois* tradition of church architecture.

[139]Notably, the Trois-Rivières altar of *c.* 1730, mentioned earlier, and the 1749 *récollette* altar of Sault-au-Récollet, which, although restored in the nineteenth century, is clearly reminiscent of a baldachin in relief.

*The Sulpicians.* Compared to that of the Jesuits or Récollets, the Sulpician contribution to the church architecture of New France in the Age of Laval was limited. Ultimately, however, their influence was of equal significance, and if we consider the persistence of the twin-towered tradition which, as we shall see, the Sulpicians established, perhaps their influence was the most permanent of all.

The Company of Saint-Sulpice was founded at Paris in 1642.[140] In 1657 the Sulpicians came to Montreal to direct that community's spiritual life, and from the first they quarrelled with the ecclesiastical authorities of Quebec. There is some evidence that the Sulpicians' first leader in Canada, the Abbé de Queylus, had been in Montreal as early as 1644;[141] certainly by 1645 the Sulpicians were interested enough in Canada to propose Abbé Thomas Legauffre as Bishop of Quebec. In January of 1657 the names of Laval and de Queylus were proposed almost simultaneously. The Sulpicians' candidate was favoured by Archbishop de Harley of Rouen, who had for years claimed jurisdiction over New France, and by the Bishop of Paris. The Jesuits, naturally, supported Laval. When the papal bull naming Laval Bishop of Petræa, with authority in New France, arrived in Paris in 1658, Laval was consecrated privately in the abbey of Saint-Germain des Prés, because the chapel there was not under the authority of the hostile bishops of Paris or Rouen. Throughout the whole era of Laval's administration there was never any good feeling between him and the Sulpicians, and relations worsened under Saint-Vallier. The historic rivalry between Quebec and Montreal begins in the seventeenth century, and a good part of it may be traced to the disputes between the Sulpicians of Montreal and the ecclesiastical authorities of Quebec. In church architecture, too, the style of Montreal has always been markedly different from that of Quebec.

Under such circumstances, the Sulpicians were naturally eager to express their claims in ostentatious church architecture, to rival the building programmes of Laval and the Jesuits. Their resources came originally from their home organization, centred in the church of Saint-Sulpice in Paris; but the phenomenal growth of Montreal assisted materially in carrying out Sulpician architectural ideas.

The population of Montreal, which was only 584 in 1665, had grown to 1500 by 1670, and by 1680 it was over 2000.[142] As early as 1662 the Sulpicians had realized that the parish church built next to the Hôtel-Dieu in 1656 would no longer satisfy the needs of this growing population, and appropriated land for a new building. Laval, however, did not give his permission to build until 1669, and not until 1672 was begun the second parish church of Notre-Dame—always colloquially known, like its successor of 1829, as "La Paroisse." Dollier

---

140*M.H.:S.-S., passim.*
141Laval's relations with the Sulpicians, as recounted here, are based on Maurault's source book cited in the previous note, and Scott, *Bishop Laval,* p. 65 f.
142C. Bertrand, *Histoire de Montréal,* I, Montreal, 1935, pp. 124 f.

de Casson, Superior of the Sulpician Order in Canada and one of the most remarkable figures of the Age of Laval, was the designer.[143]

Dollier de Casson was born in 1636, probably in Paris. He entered the Seminary of Saint-Sulpice in Paris in 1657. In 1666 he came to Canada, and almost immediately departed with de Tracy on an expedition against the Iroquois, as chaplain. A man of versatile interests, he wrote a history of Montreal in 1673, and was one of the earliest advocates of the Lachine canal, a fact of more than passing interest. The construction of the Lachine canal in the nineteenth century was a major factor in making Montreal the greatest inland seaport in the world; Dollier de Casson's early advocacy of this project suggests that he realized its ultimate consequences—the modern displacement of Quebec by Montreal as the economic centre of New France. This desire to promote Montreal above Quebec shows also in the parish church which Dollier de Casson designed for his city; it would seem that he was deliberately trying to outdo the Cathedral at Quebec.

La Paroisse, begun in 1672, was one hundred and twenty-nine feet long and thirty-eight feet wide, very considerably larger than Laval's Cathedral at Quebec.[144] It was entirely of stone, except, of course, for the roof. François Bailly *dit* Lafleur was the mason.[145] Charlevoix in 1720 noted that "the parish church of Montreal looks much more like a Cathedral than that of Quebec,"[146] which, I think, was the designer's intention (Plate XXVII).

La Paroisse was planned on such an elaborate scale that it was not opened for worship until 1683, and then, after eleven years' work, it still lacked aisles on the interior, and façade and clocher on the exterior.[147] Dollier de Casson was forced to demolish other buildings to obtain the necessary amount of building materials. Lahontan noted the bareness, but eulogized, "Their church is none the less superb. It is modelled after Saint-Sulpice in Paris, and the altar is isolated in the same way."[148]

[143]Olivier Maurault, "Dollier de Casson, sulpicien, premier ingénieur et architecte de Montréal," *Revue trimestrielle canadienne*, Feb., 1919.

[144]The main documentary source for this church is *A.V.M.*, I, pp. 345 f. Olivier Maurault's excellent monograph, *La Paroisse*, Montreal, 1929, is concerned in the main with its successor of 1829, but is also extremely valuable for the study of the 1672 building.

[145]François Bailly *dit* Lafleur arrived in Montreal about 1659. Around 1675 he became Sergeant-Royal and warden of the prison, posts which he held until 1683. He is also known to have designed a bakery, in 1683. He died in July, 1690. E.-Z. Massicotte, "Maçons, entrepreneurs, architectes," *B.R.H.*, XXXV, 1929, pp. 137–138. This article will hereafter be referred to as *M.E.A.*

[146]*Histoire et description*, III, p. 139.

[147]*A.V.M.* gives the date for completion as 1678. Maurault, *La Paroisse*, established the date 1683 from the archives of Notre-Dame.

[148]*La Paroisse*, p. 21. Olivier Maurault, recording this remark, comments: "This is a good deal to say, since we believe that the two churches resembled each other only in this isolation of the altar, which did not occur elsewhere here [in Canada]." However, in the present writer's opinion, Lahontan's remark is truer than when he made it; we discuss the question further in chapter IV, pp. 77–79.

And indeed, by the time Lahontan was writing, the efforts of Bishop Saint-Vallier, the Jesuits, and the Sulpicians to raise the architectural standards of New France were very evidently successful. In buildings like the chapel of Saint-Vallier's Episcopal Palace, the Jesuit church in Quebec, and La Paroisse in Montreal, which were reasonably good facsimiles of models in Old France, they had succeeded in transplanting in the colony advanced architectural ideas which were a considerable contrast to the craft traditions on which Laval's parish churches had so largely been based. In the following chapter we shall see how the two trends thus established in the Age of Laval were integrated in the developed parish church of eighteenth-century New France.

# IV

## NEW FRANCE BECOMES CANADIEN, 1700-1760

BY 1700 FRANÇOIS DE LAVAL WAS AN OLD MAN, AND THE TIGHT ecclesiastical control which he had established in New France was slipping; since 1688 he had been living in retirement. The new Bishop of Quebec, Mgr de Saint-Vallier, was absent from New France for long periods, a precedent followed by most of his successors. This situation, along with economic factors, hastened the development of a new self-reliance and a new spirit of independence in the parishes. And this in turn led to the appearance of a distinctively Canadian parish church architecture, created out of seventeenth-century elements, but essentially indigenous, no longer "colonial."

As we have seen, Laval made New France ecclesiastically a mission, with only a very few fixed curial charges. He had established the Seminary of Quebec, as he said, "to be . . . a body of reserve from which I may draw pious and able subjects and send them . . . into parishes . . . none of them being by special title particularly bound to any parish: but, on the contrary, my will being that they be rightfully removeable, revocable, liable to dismissal, according to the will of the bishop, or of the aforesaid seminary. . . ."[1] But already at the time of Laval's resignation there was a feeling of rebellion against such a system. In 1689 the Intendant Desmeules wrote to Louis XIV that "His Majesty can do nothing more glorious than to establish solidly several curial charges; . . . after having visited all the settlements, we have found that it was most vitally necessary to establish forty of them at once, and that by this means we shall ensure the curés having their eye upon their parishes. . . ."[2] But Saint-Vallier, certainly motivated in part by fear of gallicanism, hesitated to so weaken his authority. In 1708, the year of Laval's death, it was reported that only fifteen fixed curial charges had been established in New France, and of these only eight actually had incumbents. By 1720 only twenty parishes had been occupied by curés en titre.[3] Most of the trouble experienced by Saint-Vallier during his

[1]H. A. Scott, *Bishop Laval*, Toronto and London, 1926, p. 148.
[2]Quoted in J.-Charles Gamache, *Histoire de Saint-Roch de Québec*, Quebec, 1929, p. 30.
[3]Claude de Bonnault, "La Vie religieuse dans les paroisses rurales canadiennes au dix-huitième siècle," *B.R.H.*, XL, 1934, p. 648.

episcopacy[4] can be traced to this unrest and the prevalent dissatisfaction with the powers bequeathed him by the first Bishop. Finally, in 1721, he was forced to submit to popular demand, and agreed to the delimitation of the parishes in New France, and the establishment of fixed curial charges.[5]

M. Collet, the *procureur général* to the Conseil Souverain of Quebec, was commissioned on January 28, 1721, to ascertain suitable limits for each parish, his authority in this matter being publicly announced to all *habitants* and *seigneurs*. From January to September he travelled all over the colony, vehicles for his transportation being requisitioned on the Intendant's order at each place visited. He not only determined boundaries, but made notes on the condition of each parish, especially their church buildings. On September 20, 1721, Collet's report was adopted by the Council.[6] But not until the next year, and then only on the urgent advice of Intendant Bégon, did the ecclesiastical authorities authorize putting the report into execution.

The new parishes were in most cases coterminous with the old seigniories.[7] Forty-one parishes were created in the district of Quebec, twenty-eight in the district of Montreal, and thirteen in the district of Trois-Rivières—eighty-two in all. The creation of these parishes marked the end of the kind of episcopal control Laval had established. In many ways it was a most decisive event in the cultural life of New France.

The demand for greater parochial independence which resulted in the creation of the new parishes was also reflected by a growth in the numbers of native clergy. In the beginning, and throughout the seventeenth century, practically all clergy in New France had been born in France. But as the eighteenth century wore on, an increasingly large number of them were Canadians, trained in the seminaries of Quebec or Montreal, or in the Jesuit College of Quebec. By 1760, of 163 ecclesiastics living in Canada, 51 had been born in the colony.[8] These constituted a majority of the priests assigned to the parishes, and they contributed considerably to the growing nationalistic spirit.

Native elements in the Church were further strengthened after Saint-Vallier's death by the marked lack of interest in Canada on the part of his first three

[4]"His infinite zeal made Mgr de Saint-Vallier's episcopacy a long series of disputes with the civil authorities, the religious orders, and the priests of the diocese. Things came to such a pass that it was considered a relief when he had an enforced stay of thirteen years in England and France [during the war]. . . . Louis XIV, to ensure peace in the diocese of Quebec, twice tried to obtain Saint-Vallier's resignation but he would not yield. . . ." P.-G. Roy, "Mgr de Saint-Vallier, évêque de Québec," *V.d.Q.*, I, pp. 453–454.

[5]The best account of the delimitation of the parishes, and the events leading up to it, is found in Auguste Gosselin, *L'Eglise du Canada depuis Monseigneur de Laval jusqu'à la Conquête*, I, Quebec, 1911, p. 25 f.

[6]Cf. J.-E. Roy, *Histoire de la seigneurie de Lauzon*, II, Lévis, 1898, pp. 94–95.

[7]W. B. Munro, *The Seigniorial System in Canada*, New York, 1907, pp. 182–183.

[8]Benjamin Sulte, *Histoire des Canadiens-français*, Montreal, 1882–4, VII, pp. 73–74.

successors. De Mornay, who was Bishop from 1728 to 1733, never set foot in the country. The fourth Bishop, Dosquet, was in Quebec as Bishop for only one year, from 1734 to 1735; his successor, Lauberivière, died a few days after his arrival in Quebec in 1740.[9]

Such indifference was part of a general trend; as the eighteenth century wore on, the interests of Old and New France became more and more divergent. In the sophisticated courts of Louis XV and Louis XVI, Canada was no longer thought of as a field for earnest spiritual endeavour, but as an object of derisive amusement. Lahontan's *New Voyages*, which ran into twelve editions in several languages between 1703 and 1741, described with considerable ribaldry the choosing by benighted Canadian bachelors of wives "in all shapes and sizes" from among the newest consignment of girls sent out by the King—a theme taken up again in the mocking Parisian comedy of 1743 entitled *Les Mariages de Canada*. By Voltaire's time, the attitude of fashionable and intellectual circles in France towards Canada was well summed up in *Candide*: "These two nations [England and France] are at war over a few acres of snow in Canada. . . . They are spending in this fine war more than all Canada is worth"; the Peace of Paris reflects that attitude, ceding all Canada to Great Britain in barely more than a sentence.

At the same time, resentment of the supercilious French attitude towards Canada now became apparent in New France, abetted by a very considerable growth in prosperity which strengthened the colony's self-reliance and spirit of independence. Canada's real wealth increased so much, especially under the administration of Fleury,[10] that when Franquet visited the country in the last decades of the *ancien régime* he found marked evidences of prosperity even in the homes of the lower classes.[11] Thus there would seem to be something of an undertone of exasperation in a letter like the one Father Navières, curé of Sainte-Anne de Beaupré, wrote to a friend in France in 1734; he described his church as "one of the finest and best appointed in Canada," and saw fit to add, "If you think this does not mean much, you are mistaken; please understand that the parish churches of the countryside in France are not comparable to those where I live."[12]

Along with this change in the cultural climate of the colony, the complexion of its population was also changing. In the last half century of New France's existence, only four or five thousand persons came to it from France. And a majority of these, in contrast to those of the previous era, came of their own volition. Like the Puritans of New England, many of them were outcasts from their native French society. Some were prisoners from French jails, a few were Huguenots, some Swiss, and there were also a few English deserters.[13] By 1760

[9]*V.d.Q.*, II, pp. 117–118, 129–130, 161–164.
[10]*L.S.A.*, p. 212 f.
[11]*Voyages et mémoires sur le Canada, 1752–1753*, Quebec, 1889, p. 157 f.
[12]Quoted in *B.R.H.*, IV, 1899, p. 367.          [13]*D.G.F.C.*, Introduction.

the vast majority of the 60,000 people in New France were native Canadians. Thus the ties between Old and New France were not strengthened by immigration from the mother country.[14]

The new parishes created in 1722 best embodied the growing independence of spirit in Canada. They soon became the unit of Canadian social life, and the curé soon came to be a far more authoritative figure than the seignior. Besides providing spiritual leadership, he kept the civil records and usually acted as a lawyer also. The general assembly of parishioners, held under the curé and nearly always in the presbytery, became the instrument by which their wants were habitually made known to the authorities. In the assembly were named the *marguilliers* (wardens) of the parish, and the syndics, who were sometimes named in addition to the *marguilliers* to serve on special committees, especially for building churches and presbyteries. The *marguilliers* were usually three in number, elected in rotation, one a year. During their period of office they occupied a special pew, known as the *banc d'œuvre*, which was usually located against the wall of the church opposite the pulpit, at right angles to the rest of the pews; sculptors gave as much consideration to its decoration as they did to the decoration of the pulpit, so that some of the finest examples of the older Quebec schools of wood-carving are *bancs d'œuvre*. Curé and *marguilliers* together managed parish finances, selling pew space in the church, and buying needed equipment. With the syndics, they were responsible for handling special problems connected with the construction of new buildings.[15] Of course, ultimate authority for building still rested with the Bishop and Intendant, but their permission became more and more a formality. By mid-century, then, there was developing around the new parishes an essentially indigenous culture, derivative but substantially emancipated from Old France. And with it was developing what we can call the *Québécois* tradition of church architecture.

## FORMATION OF THE QUÉBÉCOIS TRADITION

About 1750, an anonymous draftsman compiled the *Carte générale des paroisses et missions établies des deux côtés du fleuve Saint-Laurent, depuis Rimouski au montant jusqu'au côteau des Cèdres.*[16] Here we see the churches of New France at the end of the *ancien régime*, dotted thickly along both shores of the St. Lawrence between Quebec and Montreal (Plate I). Visiting New France in 1749, Peter Kalm remarked that these churches constituted the most prominent single feature of the country. To him, it seemed that the country "could really be called a village, beginning at Montreal and ending at Quebec, which is a

[14]For a discussion of French elements in the Canadian population under the *ancien régime*, see Lionel Groulx, "Le Colon venu de France," in *La Naissance d'une race*, Montreal, 1919, pp. 11 ff.

[15]For a good short study of eighteenth-century parish life in New France, see Claude de Bonnault, "La Vie religieuse dans les paroisses rurales canadiennes au dix-huitième siècle," *B.R.H.*, XL, 1934, p. 645 f.

[16]On the date of this map, see Appendix, p. 152.

distance of more than one hundred and eighty miles. . . . The prospect is exceedingly beautiful. . . ."[17] The churches of this "continuous village" were mostly built after 1700.

As in the case of seventeenth-century architecture, few of them are now extant, and those remaining are very considerably altered. But we can reconstruct their appearance, as in the Age of Laval, by means of old descriptions, maps, and photographs. There are considerably more of the latter than for the Age of Laval, since a much higher proportion of church buildings of the eighteenth century survived long enough to be photographed.

The *Québécois* tradition of church architecture as it developed in the eighteenth century was pre-eminently embodied in parish churches. Other categories of church building became increasingly insignificant; however, they were not without influence. Indeed, we can hardly understand the final formulation of the parish church tradition without taking into account the contributions to it of both the mission and devotional chapels and the architecture of the religious orders.

*Contribution of the Mission and Devotional Chapels.* Typical of the trend of the times was the fact that in the eighteenth century devotional chapels tended to be attached to parish churches and built by the parishes, rather than by individuals, as commemorative chapels or processional chapels of a Calvary Road. Examples are the chapels at Oka,[18] Beaumont, and Neuville.[19] The last is typical (Plate XXI). Built with a beautiful simplicity and a fine sense of the use of materials, it is perfectly adapted to the country. It has thick walls of fieldstone, and a steep roof for shedding the snow. With its distinctive clocher, round-headed door, and tiny niche, it looks like a model of a parish church of the Age of Laval—except, of course, for the transept, which is omitted in such a small structure—just as the mission chapels of Laval's time, when prosperity was increasing, had come to resemble parish churches of the epoch before.

Very similar to the devotional chapels were the mission chapels, which were fairly numerous in the early years of the eighteenth century. Typical of the Montreal area were the chapels of Ile-Dupas, built in wood about 1704,[20] and Sainte-Anne au bout de l'Isle, built in 1703 of stone, and so small that it was said to have been lighted only from the roof.[21] In the Quebec area, the type is represented by the second chapel of Saint-François, I.O. Built in 1707 to replace the first chapel of *c.* 1683, it was unpretentious; the archdeacon Chartier de Lotbinière in 1730 found it near ruin and ordered its rebuilding in stone.[22] The first church of Nicolet, built about 1710, probably represents a mission chapel

---

[17]*P.K.T.*, pp. 416–417.
[18]Built *c.* 1740. *V.E.*, p. 119 f.
[19]*A.N.F.*, p. 65. Both chapels were built *c.* 1735.
[20]*A.V.M.*, I, pp. 1 f., 15.
[21]Désiré Girouard, *Lake St. Louis, Old and New*, Montreal, 1893, p. 153 f.
[22]R. Traquair and M. Barbeau, "The Church of St. François," *McG.U.P.*, no. 14.

of the Trois-Rivières area. Bellemare says it was a stone church;[23] but a more probable tradition describes it as "built of logs, later clapboarded, and covered with thatch."[24] Again, the *retardataire* character of this category of church buildings is evident; they resemble the poorer parish churches of Laval's time. Several more mission chapels of this type date from the wave of expansion in New France beginning about 1730: at Forges-Saint-Maurice near Trois-Rivières, a chapel built about 1735, apparently another example of log-cabin construction;[25] wooden chapels on Ile-aux-Coudres, built in 1748, Ile-aux-Oies, built about 1750, and Tadoussac, in 1747.[26] The latter is still extant, and despite very considerable alteration provides a good example of the clapboarded type of church building of colonial New France, surviving into a later era (Plate XXII).

The ultimate significance of the devotional and mission chapels to the developed parish church tradition was twofold. In the first place, it was in this type of structure, rather than in more pretentious churches, that the builders of New France first came successfully to grips with their environment and the new local materials—in a word, that the craft tradition became acclimatized. Gérard Morisset has pointed out how high was the incidence of mortality in the early church buildings of New France; very often such failures were caused by following techniques of construction inherited from France which were not suited to the climate and materials of Quebec.[27] Experience gained through experiment in smaller chapels played a large part in developing those more indigenous techniques which were the necessary basis for the Quebec tradition of church architecture.

Secondly, the building of these chapels represented a certain spirit of piety which has always characterized New France. In the seventeenth century, this piety had tended to be individualistic and somewhat fanatical, as in the case of Mlle Jeanne Le Ber, who lived for nineteen years as a recluse in a tiny cell

[23]J.-E. Bellemare, *Histoire de Nicolet, 1669–1924*, Arthabaska, 1924, p. 363.

[24]Cf. "Les Trois Premières Eglises de Nicolet," *B.R.H.*, XXXII, 1926, p. 15 f. See further Appendix, p. 134. The description suggests log-cabin construction, which would have been quite possible: there were Swiss settled in the vicinity who could very well have introduced the technique.

[25]Auguste Gosselin, *L'Eglise du Canada depuis Monseigneur de Laval*, III, Quebec, 1914, p. 160.

[26]Alexis Mailloux, *Histoire de l'Ile-aux-Coudres*, Montreal, 1879, p. 18; N.-E. Dionne, *Sainte-Anne-de-la-Pocatière et l'Ile-aux-Oies*, Quebec, 1910, p. 24; on Tadoussac, see *V.E.*, p. 179 f.

[27]Cf. *Les Eglises et le trésor de Varennes*, Quebec, 1943, pp. 6–7. Morisset attributes the high mortality to three causes: (1) The builders' inexperience, which caused the 1715 church at Cap Santé, for example, to fall into ruin within ten years after its construction; (2) failure to calculate the effects of rain and snow—for example, at Saint-François, I.O., Sault-au-Récollet, Longueuil, and Boucherville, the first stone churches practically dissolved; and (3) failure to take foundations into proper account.

A good example of the precautions against weathering taken by later builders is the contract for the clocher of Saint-Thomas de Montmagny, in 1736. Cf. Appendix, p. 136.

behind the altar of the chapel of Notre-Dame-de-Pitié in Montreal,[28] or as described in Lahontan's account of the atmosphere prevailing in that city: "You cannot imagine to what a pitch these Ecclesiastical Lords have screw'd their Authority. They prohibit and burn all the Books that treat of any other Subject but Devotion."[29] In the eighteenth century, Canadian piety was more constructively expressed by the centring of social and political life around the parishes, but it was no less strong; Peter Kalm could observe in 1749 that "It was said by all those who had been in France that people of both sexes in Canada were more devout than in France."[30] This, of course, is even truer today; the great churches still form the most conspicuous feature of the Quebec landscape. In them, the spirit represented by the missionary and devotional chapels of New France lives on.

*Contribution of the Jesuits.* From its dominant place in the Age of Laval, Jesuit church architecture during the eighteenth century declined steadily to the point of insignificance. Their buildings—a church in Montreal in 1719,[31] Indian chapels at Caughnawaga and Jeune-Lorette,[32] a façade on their church in Quebec —were not influential; in the case of the latter, even derivative (it was built by Chaussegros de Léry around 1730 in imitation of the façade of La Paroisse in Montreal; cf. Plate XV). Undoubtedly the reason was the prevalent change in cultural climate, which favoured those orders more closely identified with the people. What influence the Jesuits had on parish church architecture in New France during the eighteenth century was exercised through the Récollets, who as we have seen borrowed most of their architectural ideas from them.

*Contribution of the Récollets.* Most popular of the orders in Canada, the Récollets flourished everywhere in the eighteenth century. They built a fine church in Montreal in 1706;[33] but here they were overshadowed by the Sul-

[28]This chapel was begun in 1693. It was attached to the convent of the Sœurs de la Congrégation Notre-Dame. *A.V.M.*, I, p. 147 f.

[29]R. G. Thwaites (ed.), *Lahontan's New Voyages to North-America*, Chicago, 1905, Introduction. He continues (letter VIII, p. 89): "When I think of this Tyranny, I cannot but be inrag'd at the impertinent Zeal of the Curate of this City. This inhumane Fellow came one day to my Lodging, and finding the Romance of the Adventures of *Petronius* upon my Table, he fell upon it with an unimaginable Fury, and tore out almost all the Leaves. This Book I valued more than my Life . . . if my Landlord had not held me, I had gone immediately to the turbulent Pastor's House, and would have pluck'd out the Hairs of his Beard with as little mercy as he did the Leaves of my Book."

[30]*P.K.T.*, p. 541.

[31]C. Bertrand, *Histoire de Montréal*, I, Montreal, 1935, pp. 180–181; II, pp. 256–257. J. Douglas Borthwick, *Montreal: Its History*, Montreal, 1875, Plate p. 74, text p. 134 f. A rather more reliable depiction than the foregoing is that by John Drake in the Album de Jacques Viger (Bibliothèque Municipale de Montréal, archives of the Seminary of Quebec, and elsewhere).

[32]The chapel at Caughnawaga was built in 1717; that at Jeune-Lorette in 1730. For data, see Appendix, pp. 137, 145.

[33]It was begun in 1706; like the Jesuit church of Montreal, it replaced a chapel built around 1692, and the same architect was employed on both projects, Pierre Janson-Lapalme. A drawing by Drake in the Album de Jacques Viger shows the state of the church in 1828; in 1830, the central section of the façade of Notre-Dame, the parish church of Montreal,

picians. Around Quebec and Trois-Rivières, however, their influence, freed of restriction by the decline of the hostile powers of both the Bishop of Quebec and the Jesuits, was pervasive and permanent.

We have already suggested something of the influence exerted by the Récollet church of Quebec built in 1693. Its designer, Juconde Drué, remained for long in the region around Quebec; he was responsible for the so-called "Petit Hermitage" of 1694,[34] and probably also for the churches of Saint-Joseph (1721) and Saint-Nicolas (1728) on the Lauzon coast.[35] Drué was a pupil of Frère Luc, and as such followed the Récollet tendency to borrow more elaborate architectural forms, especially from the Jesuits—the façades for both the Lauzon churches were planned to be built in cut stone, with five niches for statues, like the Récollet church of Quebec, and recalling the "Jesuit façade" of the Episcopal Palace. A similar type of façade was designed for the Récollet church of Montreal, and may perhaps be taken as typical Récollet exterior design (Plate XXIII). The clocher and hipped roof represent evident borrowings from the Jesuit church of Quebec; the elements of the façade a much simplified version of the Jesuit façade. It was precisely this simplification, and the reliance upon craft tradition also apparent in such a design, which made Récollet architecture a natural vehicle for the fusion of craft and "academic" traditions in eighteenth-century parish church architecture.

On interior design, Récollet architecture had even more influence. We have already mentioned the popularity of the *récollette* form of apse as developed in the seventeenth century. It found its way into parish church architecture almost immediately; as early as 1693 a *récollette* altar, quite possibly designed by Juconde Drué, appeared in the church of Sainte-Anne de Beaupré.[36] In the succeeding century, its use was widespread. We may see a good surviving example of the *récollette* form (despite a considerable alteration in 1902) in the Ursuline convent in Quebec[37] (Plate XXIV). This altar was executed in the years 1734–1739 by

---

was transferred to the old Récollet church and it was used for services by the Irish Catholics of the city. A representation of the church with its new façade is to be found in Newton Bosworth, *Hochelaga Depicta*, Montreal, 1839. The original façade of the Récollet church was built in 1712. Cf. S. Lesage, "Les Récollets au Canada," *La Revue canadienne*, IV, 1867, p. 304; *M.H.:M.*, p. 149 f.; E.-Z. Massicotte, "Edifices transplantés," *B.R.H.*, XLVII, 1941, pp. 202, 324.

[34]In 1697 it is recorded that Drué was living in this little chapel, for which building permission was granted late in 1693; Drué was then acting as chaplain of the Hôpital-Général, and in all probability he designed the chapel. Cf. Gamache, *Histoire de Saint-Roch de Québec*, pp. 24–25; *V.d.Q.*, I, pp. 539–540; *C.O.A.*, p. 14.

[35]Drué was in Saint-Nicolas from November, 1718 to September, 1720; cf. J.-E. Roy, *Histoire de la seigneurie de Lauzon*, II, p. 96 f.

[36]Executed by Jacques Leblond *dit* Latour. Cf. *C.O.A.*, pp. 26–27, and Figure 3.

[37]The chapel was built in 1720 by a Parisian, François de Lajoue. *D.G.F.C.*, p. 168, lists Lajoue as a "maître tailleur de pierre, architecte et bourgeois." He was born about 1656. The Hôtel-Dieu convent in Quebec was begun under his direction in 1695 and finished late in 1698. Cf. *Histoire de l'Hôtel-Dieu de Québec*, Montauban, 1751, p. 280; P.-G. Roy, *A travers l'histoire de l'Hôtel-Dieu de Québec*, Quebec, 1939, p. 103.

Noël Levasseur (1680–1740), a Canadian much influenced by Juconde Drué;[38] in fact, Drué may well have provided the design for this altar also.

It was a pupil of Juconde Drué, Augustin Quintal, who designed the most imposing single Récollet work in New France, the interior of the third parish church of Trois-Rivières.[39] Quintal played an important role in the Récollet contribution to the parish church tradition. Born Joseph Quintal at Boucherville in 1686,[40] he was another native of the colony in the Récollets' ranks. He joined the order at Montreal in 1706 as Frère Augustin, and was ordained a priest in 1713. From 1724 to 1733 he served the parish of Yamachiche, and according to Morisset he designed the first church there.[41] In 1733 Quintal came to Trois-Rivières. Although the church had been started in 1710, the building programme had been long and costly, and the main decoration of the interior had only been under consideration since 1730. At Trois-Rivières, Quintal met Gilles Bolvin, a sculptor from Avesnes in France, who had been married at Trois-Rivières the year before Quintal arrived.[42] Bolvin was born about 1711 and died in 1766; together, he and Quintal formed what has been called the Trois-Rivières school of sculpture,[43] a school which incorporated into parish church architecture ideas of magnificent sculpture from the architecture of the orders.[44]

The main feature of the Trois-Rivières interior (Plate XXV) was a baldachin set on four twisted columns which, with due allowance for time and place, bore an astonishing resemblance to the baldachin in the Val-de-Grâce.[45] We have already suggested the probability that a baldachin in the Episcopal Palace in Quebec inspired the Trois-Rivières example, and the possibility that there was a baldachin in the Jesuit church of Quebec even earlier. In any event, it was unlikely that Quintal conceived the idea, and in the writer's opinion it must have been Drué who designed the Trois-Rivières baldachin. And in turn, since it was Drué's *récollette* altar in the Récollet church of Quebec which embodied the most outstanding example of that form, a connection between the baldachin and *récollette* forms is suggested, the *récollette* altar being essentially a simplified variant, in relief, of the baldachin. The one would be adaptable to smaller parish churches, the other to more ambitious works.

[38]C.O.A., pp. 27–28.

[39]*Ibid.*, p. 15; Benjamin Sulte, "L'Eglise paroissiale," *Mélanges historiques*, XIX, 1932, p. 29 f.

[40]*A.N.F.*, pp. 137–138, *C.O.A.*, p. 15.

[41]*Ibid.* N. Caron, *Histoire de la paroisse d'Yamachiche*, Trois-Rivières, 1892, p. 70 f., gives a date of *c.* 1735 for this, the first church of Yamachiche; *c.* 1730 would probably be closer.

[42]*D.G.F.C.*, II, p. 345.

[43]By Morisset, *C.O.A.*, pp. 14, 35.

[44]In Récollet sculpture in general, and the Trois-Rivières school in particular, a strong stylistic influence of late Flemish Baroque is apparent. This is explicable through Bolvin's probable training in Flanders, and the fact that Bishop Dosquet brought a number of Flemish workmen with him on arriving at Quebec in 1729. It is possible also that Quintal visited Flanders around 1712.

[45]See earlier, chap. III, p. 54.

Quintal and Bolvin executed designs of all degrees of elaborateness. In the Trois-Rivières interior their work was lavish, especially the pulpit and *banc d'œuvre*, ornate sculpture splendidly complementing the altar. At Lachenaie, Boucherville, and Sainte-Anne de la Pérade they worked on a more restrained scale,[46] but at the very end of the *ancien régime*, at Neuville, ostentation returned. The famous baldachined altar there (Plate III) is the sole intact survivor of their sculpture. Begun in 1766, the year of Bolvin's death,[47] its derivation from the Trois-Rivières altar is clear. This work, executed just after the Cession, carries the tradition of elaborate monumental sculpture of parish church interiors over into the new era. Quintal died in 1776, but the Récollet contribution lived on in the Quebec tradition of church architecture far into the nineteenth century.

*Contribution of the Sulpicians.* Dominant in the region around Montreal, the Company of Saint-Sulpice in the eighteenth century exerted a lasting effect on parish church building. In keeping with the changing spirit in New France, the Sulpicians' main emphasis in building shifted to parish churches.[48] Practically all parish churches built around Montreal in the eighteenth century were in some measure affected by Sulpician architectural ideas. Typical was the church of Saint-Sulpice.[49] The first church there was built in 1706, presumably of wood, since the Intendant ordered a new church to be built of stone in 1723. Both churches were built under the supervision of the Sulpicians, who settled the first colonists on that land, and who served the parish continually until 1776. Again, the church of Saint-Laurent (Ile-Jésus) was built in 1735 entirely at the expense of the Seminary of Saint-Sulpice.[50] In 1712, the first stone of the second parish church of Boucherville was laid by Vachon de Belmont.[51] Since the second church was replaced by the third, extant, church in 1801, it is idle to speculate on whether the Sulpician superior designed it, but his connection with this parish church is typical and significant.

The Sulpician Louis Geoffroy is of particular interest here. Geoffroy was born in Paris about 1661 and ordained in France; he came to Canada first at Laval's

[46]The contract for the altar at Lachenaie which states that it was designed by Quintal and was to be executed by Bolvin, is extant in the *Livre de Comptes* of Saint-Charles de Lachenaie. It is reproduced by Ramsay Traquair, *The Old Architecture of Quebec*, Toronto, 1947, pp. 313–314. No document connects the work at Boucherville directly with Bolvin and Quintal, but it is practically identical with the Lachenaie example. Cf. *ibid.*, p. 197. For Sainte-Anne de la Pérade, see Chanoine Rhéault, *Autrefois et aujourd'hui à Sainte-Anne-de-Lapérade*, Trois-Rivières, 1895, pp. 42–43.

[47]According to Morisset, *C.O.A.*, p. 14. The altar was completed after Bolvin's death, presumably. Most of the interior decoration of Neuville dates from the régime of Abbé Charles-François Bailly, curé from 1777 to 1794. *V.E.*, pp. 65–66.

[48]The Sulpicians built one mission chapel, at Oka (Lac des Deux-Montagnes) in 1721. *M.H.:S.-S.*, pp. 165 f, 205 f.

[49]See P.-G. Roy, *Inventaire des ordonnances des Intendants*, Beauceville, 1919, I, p. 248; A. Leclaire, *Le Saint-Laurent historique*, Quebec, 1906, p. 20.

[50]Armand Grou, "Les Origines de la paroisse Saint-Laurent," *La Revue canadienne*, VII, 1870, p. 721 f.

[51]*A.V.M.*, I, p. 279 f.; L. Lalande, *Une Vieille Seigneurie—Boucherville*, Montreal, 1890.

suggestion, in 1685. From 1686 to 1690 he conducted missions in Acadia; then, becoming thoroughly discouraged about the future of the colony, he returned to France, where he stayed until 1697. He then came back to Canada to become curé of Champlain the same year.[52] He seems to have had some training in architecture, for during his short stay in New France—he died at Quebec in 1707—he designed at least five buildings. The second church of the Hôtel-Dieu in Montreal, which he designed in 1702, was perhaps his most ambitious effort; it seems to have been a large structure with wings enclosing a court like the Episcopal Palace in Quebec or the Sulpician Seminary in Montreal. It was finished on the exterior in 1703, and on the interior in 1704, but unfortunately was totally destroyed in the great fire which ravaged Montreal on June 19, 1721.[53] In 1702 Geoffroy also designed a third convent building for the Sœurs de la Congrégation in Montreal.[54]

Geoffroy was at various times curé of Laprairie, Champlain, Contrecœur, and Boucherville. To him are attributed the designs of several parish churches in that area, notably the first church of Champlain, built in 1697,[55] the first church of Sorel, finished 1708,[56] and the first church of Contrecœur, finished 1711.[57] We have little evidence what these churches looked like, but it is important to note that a man like Geoffroy, a Sulpician with up-to-date ideas about architecture, should now be designing parish churches; it was by such men that ideas from the more monumental design of the orders were incorporated into parish church design.

Of all the Sulpicians' contributions to parish church architecture the most important was embodied in "La Paroisse"—Notre-Dame, the parish church of Montreal—begun in 1672. As we have seen earlier, it was built in stone, one hundred and twenty-nine feet long by thirty-eight feet wide, and had been planned on such an ambitious scale for the time and place that by 1683 it was finished only in bare essentials. In the eighteenth century, work was recommenced under the direction of Vachon de Belmont, Dollier de Casson's successor as superior of the Sulpicians in Canada, and a man noted for his interest in the arts.[58] In 1708 he initiated an elaborate programme for remodelling the façade, beginning

[52]The most complete biographical notice on Louis Geoffroy is that by Prosper Cloutier, *Histoire de la paroisse de Champlain*, Trois-Rivières, 1915–1917, p. 170 f.

[53]*A.V.M.*, I, p. 60.

[54]*M.E.A.*, p. 141.

[55]Replaced by the second church in 1808. Cloutier, *Histoire de la paroisse de Champlain*, p. 170 f.

[56]Replaced by the second church in 1732. *M.H.:S.-S.*, p. 201; A. Couillard-Després, *Histoire de Sorel*, Montreal, 1926, p. 175 f.

[57]Replaced by the second church in 1726. F.-J. Audet, *Contrecœur*, Montreal, 1940, p. 87. The attribution of this church to Geoffroy is made by Morisset, *A.N.F.*, p. 132.

[58]Born in 1642, he was ordained in Canada in 1681. He died in 1732. "From his youth he was interested in the fine arts, especially drawing and music." *M.E.A.*, p. 132 f.

a tower and clocher to the left,[59] but the tower never progressed beyond the lowest storey, and was converted into a chapel dedicated to Saint-Roch. In 1720 Vachon de Belmont tried again; once more the façade remained unfinished, but not before one tower and clocher had been completed, part of a Jesuit façade applied, and the outline of the whole drawn up by Chaussegros de Léry in a plan dated 1722 (Plates XXVI, XXVII).

The plan of this façade is of signal importance to the history of church architecture in New France. A Jesuit-type façade, as designed to ornament the gable and front of La Paroisse, was not new, but the twin towers flanking the façade were. Earlier buildings in New France may be cited which had single towers beside the façade—notably the Cathedral and the Jesuit church in Quebec; but in them the tower seems to have been a reminiscence of medieval asymmetry, and there is no evidence that twin towers were planned. The case of La Paroisse was different; twin towers were apparently planned from the first. They had a great influence on subsequent parish church architecture, and therefore it is of consequence to suggest their source. In my opinion, that source was the Sulpicians' home church, Saint-Sulpice in Paris.

Already in 1684, as we have seen, Baron de Lahontan had declared that La Paroisse was built on the model of Saint-Sulpice in Paris, although at that time he could point only to the isolation of the altar as proof.[60] However, Lahontan's remarks may well have been based not so much on what was actually standing when he saw the church, as on what he knew or had been told of the complete plans. For the building of a new church of Saint-Sulpice in Paris was actively in progress during the whole time Dollier de Casson was in the Seminary there, and to model La Paroisse after it would have been the most natural thing for him to do.

The first stone of the church of Saint-Sulpice in Paris was laid in 1646. Jean-Jacques Olier, founder of the Company, had at first intended merely to rebuild the medieval structure, but the rapid growth of his order changed his plans, so that he commissioned the architect Gamard to design a completely new building. Then came the Fronde, and work stopped. Construction was resumed in 1655, but in the meantime Gamard had died, and Louis Levau was called in. Whether Levau provided completely new plans, or radically modified Gamard's, is not certain; at any rate, it seems that Levau's ideas were not entirely acceptable, and in January, 1660, Daniel Gittard was commissioned to take over. Again, there is dissension among authorities as to whether Gittard drew up new plans or modified

[59]It is possible that Vachon de Belmont had a hand in the design of La Paroisse even earlier than this. He certainly assisted Dollier de Casson in the design of the Seminary of Saint-Sulpice, built between 1680 and 1685, and he also designed the chapel in the "Fort des Sauvages" at the foot of the Côte des Neiges. Cf. *M.H.:S.-S.*, p. 23 f.

[60]Cf. chap. III, p. 64.

Levau's, but certainly the bulk of the seventeenth-century construction on Saint-Sulpice was done under him;[61] it went on actively from 1660 to 1675, during which time the choir, the aisles, and the greater part of the left crossing were completed, and—of most significance in this connection—the façade was begun.[62] This means that the plans for Saint-Sulpice must have been substantially complete by 1660; hence that Dollier de Casson, who entered the Seminary of Saint-Sulpice in July, 1657, could have known them well. Furthermore, since he did not leave for New France until 1666, he must have seen at least the choir standing. That he copied the choir of Saint-Sulpice in La Paroisse is evident. Whether he took his ideas for a twin-towered façade from Saint-Sulpice also is more difficult to prove, but I think there is a good circumstantial case for it.

The present twin-towered façade of Saint-Sulpice was begun by Servandoni in 1733;[63] what was planned in the seventeenth century we do not know precisely, since the original papers appear to have vanished. But we do know that immediately following their work on Saint-Sulpice, both Levau and Gittard produced designs for twin-towered church façades, Levau for Saint-Eustache,[64] and Gittard for Saint-Jacques-et-Saint-Philippe.[65] The coincidence of both men producing a design so unusual for the time and place strongly suggests common inspiration, which very plausibly could have been a twin-towered façade planned for Saint-Sulpice. And if we take this probability for granted, it means that the plans for Saint-Sulpice provided the model for the twin-towered façade of La Paroisse.

However, exactly when the twin towers of La Paroisse were decided upon is a matter of considerable uncertainty. Dollier de Casson may already have had Levau's or Gittard's plans for Saint-Sulpice in mind when Laval approved the building of La Paroisse in 1669; this is my opinion. But the decision to build twin towers could also have been taken at some subsequent time; say, during the building of the Seminary between 1680 and 1685, when architectural matters were uppermost on the Superior's mind, or in 1708, when Vachon de Belmont

[61]Louis Hautecœur, *Histoire de l'architecture classique en France*, II, pt. I, Paris, 1948, pp. 94, 168.

[62]Guadet and Pascal (eds.), *L'Architecture françoise de François Blondel*, reprint, Paris, 1904–5, III, p. 37.

[63]The final construction programme of Saint-Sulpice was undertaken in 1719. Following completion of the transept façades, the nave was finished, and then the façade was begun in 1733. Two towers carrying clochers were planned to flank it. Only the northern one of these was ever fully completed, under Chalgrin in 1777; the sculptures of the second, built under Maclaurin in 1749, were not executed.

[64]Hautecœur, *Histoire de l'architecture classique en France*, II, pt. II, Paris, 1948, p. 96, and Figure 85. This design, which was apparently not executed, seems to have been presented immediately after Levau ceased connection with Saint-Sulpice.

[65]Guadet and Pascal (eds.), *L'Architecture françoise de François Blondel*, III, p. 74. This church was begun in 1630 but only the choir finished. Gittard began to build the nave and façade in 1675, the very year work was stopped on Saint-Sulpice.

began the first tower beside the façade of La Paroisse.[66] In the early 1720's the archives of La Paroisse record a curiously contradictory series of parochial assemblies in which plans for the façade and towers were debated; what sense one can make of them seems to indicate that Vachon de Belmont was trying to get the parishioners to agree to a twin-towered façade plan, but whether it was a new idea at that time, or one he had been pressing for some while, is not at all clear.[67]

Admittedly, then, derivation of the twin-towered façade of La Paroisse from Saint-Sulpice is speculative hypothesis; but for all that I think it is reasonable. No other explanation so adequately accounts for the appearance of this type of façade in New France. Twin towers are certainly not part of any craft tradition; they are not very common in seventeenth-century French architecture, and they are certainly not functional. They represent, in fact, a sort of Baroque exuberance seemingly so far beyond the resources of New France that most of the builders who planned them failed to execute their projects, as we shall see; even the second tower of Notre-Dame failed to get beyond the first storey, despite repeated projects for finishing it.[68] But the twin-towered façade evidently satisfied an expressional need in eighteenth-century New France, a liking for ostentation which reflected a new self-assurance. For the example of La Paroisse soon led to the twin-towered façade becoming an integral part of the parish church tradition of New France.

Most indicative of its popularity, perhaps, was the fact that Chaussegros de Léry was called on to repeat his design of 1722 for the Cathedral of Quebec in

[66]It may perhaps be of some significance to note that Pierre Janson-Lapalme, the mason Vachon de Belmont called in to execute this tower, came from the Saint-Sulpice district of Paris (*D.G.F.C.*, p. 318).    Vachon de Belmont, being a Canadian, would not have been familiar with the appearance of the church of Saint-Sulpice; Janson-Lapalme presumably was. Janson-Lapalme died at Montreal in 1743. He is recorded as working on La Paroisse in 1710; the Récollet church of Montreal in 1712; the third parish church of Varennes in 1718; and the Jesuit church of Montreal in 1719. Cf. *A.N.F.*, p. 133; *M.E.A.*, p. 136.

[67]On July 28, 1720, according to the records of La Paroisse (*A.V.M.*, I, p. 345 f.), there was held "une assemblée au sujet de la Tour du portail de l'Eglise. M. de Belmont promet de payer les ouvriers pour la façon de l'architecture. . . ." On August 4 it was resolved to build "un clocher capable de loger quatre cloches, le tout en pierre de taille, avec une flèche de charpente couverte d'ardoise." The citizens contributed 375 *livres* towards this project. It would seem that the clocher was to have been located in the position usual for a parish church, for on June 14, 1722, at an "assembly of *marguilliers* and citizens," it was decided "that the clocher should not be put on the front of the church, but to the south-east, and that one should be put to the right of the church similar to the first one." This appears to be the twin-towered project commemorated by Chaussegros de Léry's plan. At a meeting held on June 24, however, "it has been decided that the clocher on the south-east side shall not be executed, but on the north-west side," and there the single tower was finally built. Apparently Vachon de Belmont had been hoping that by introducing the parishioners to his large-scale project by degrees, it could be executed in its entirety, and for that reason he approved building a new tower and clocher instead of completing the tower begun in 1708.

[68]For the later history of La Paroisse, see Appendix, pp. 140–142.

1744, as part of a general refurbishing of that structure not yet completed in 1749.[69] Most of de Léry's work was concerned with the interior, which was widened by the construction of side aisles running between the transept chapels and the bases of the proposed twin towers.[70] This scheme made the twin-towered façade useful as well as ostentatious, and enhanced its appeal to parish church builders. However, though the side aisles were constructed, as we see in Short's drawings of the Cathedral in 1759 (Plates XI, XIX), funds ran out and the towers remained in substantially the same state as those of La Paroisse—one completed, the other built only to the first storey. Not until 1843 were the towers and the Jesuit façade for the central section finally completed, by Thomas Baillargé.[71] But already in the eighteenth century the twin towers appeared in parish church architecture, as the mature Quebec tradition developed.

### PARISH CHURCHES: THE "MAILLOU PLAN"

Long before delimitation of the parishes in 1722, the growth of prosperity and independence of spirit in New France was reflected in a tendency towards greater elaboration and the incorporation of more advanced architectural elements in parish church building. This process was hastened by the fact that so many of the leading architects in the colony concerned themselves with parish churches: besides Quintal, Drué, and Geoffroy, one might cite Pierre Janson-Lapalme, who worked on La Paroisse and the Jesuit and Récollet churches in Montreal and then, in 1718, built the elaborate second church of Varennes in 1718;[72] François de Lajoue, designer of the elaborate Ursuline chapel in Quebec, who gave advice to the parishioners of Sainte-Famille on the restoration programme for their church in 1702;[73] and Jean-Marie-Josué Boisberthelot de Beaucours, an engineer-in-chief of New France and successively Governor of Trois-Rivières and Montreal, who designed the first church of Sainte-Anne de Bellevue, about 1714.[74]

Typical of the more ostentatious sort of parish churches that began to develop

[69]Kalm writes in 1749: "The people were at present employed in ornamenting it. The organ had just been removed because of the improvements being made on it. . . ." *P.K.T.*, pp. 427–428.

[70]De Léry wrote, too optimistically, it would seem, in October, 1748, that "the cathedral . . . will be finished the 15th of next month. . . . It is two thirds as wide again as the old one; . . . it is built like those of France, with nave, side aisles, and galleries [*nef, bas côtés, et tribunes*]." H. Têtu and C.-O. Gagnon, *Mandements des évêques de Québec*, II, Quebec, 1888, pp. 5–6.

[71]It was evidently intended that the Cathedral should be completed with a Jesuit façade similar to that built by de Léry for the Jesuit church of Quebec around 1730 (cf. Plate XV).

[72]Cf. note 66, and Gérard Morisset, *Les Eglises et le trésor de Varennes*, Quebec, 1943, p. 9 f.

[73]J.-T. Nadeau, "La Sainte-Famille," *L'Almanach de l'Action Sociale Catholique*, 1925, p. 90.

[74]Born in 1662, he came to New France in 1688, and died at Montreal in 1750. *M.E.A.*, pp. 136–137. Cf. *catalogue raisonné*, 1713, Pointe-Claire, note 2.

in the eighteenth century was that of Lachine, consecrated in 1703[75] (Plate XXIX). In basic lines, it still closely resembled Laval's standard type, having its characteristic proportions (sixty feet long and thirty wide),[76] façade with two openings, and a clocher very similar to those we know from Sainte-Anne de Beaupré or the old church of Saint-Laurent, I.O. But the main door, framed rather elaborately in cut stone, with architectural elements such as pilasters and reversed scrolls in evidence, suggests inspiration from the more elaborate architectural ideas of the Sulpicians; indeed, a Sulpician monogram can be made out, cut into the keystone. Furthermore, the church ended in a flat wall, evidently treated *à la récollette* on the interior. In the case of another church, closely resembling that of Lachine—Saint-Augustin, Portneuf, begun in 1719—we have a contract stating explicitly that "the apse shall be flattened [*reduit*] in the manner of that in the church of the Récollet Fathers [i.e., their 1693 church in Quebec], which will provide space for two altars six feet wide, set into the body of the church. . . ."[77] In this case, a clocher fifty-four feet in height was specified, again suggesting inspiration from the Récollet church.[78] Something of the

[75]Désiré Girouard, *Lake St. Louis, Old and New,* p. 45 f., and line drawing p. 50. The church was demolished in 1869.

[76]This coincidence is not an isolated example. The first church of Pointe-Claire, in 1713, had the same dimensions. Cf. *ibid.,* p. 186. The contract for the church at Saint-Augustin, Portneuf (see further below), called for a church 80 feet long and 38 feet wide. These were exactly the dimensions of Laval's first cathedral, Notre-Dame-de-la-Paix.

[77]This church was replaced by the existing structure in 1809. The contract is cited by A. Béchard, *Histoire de la paroisse de Saint-Augustin, Portneuf,* Quebec, 1885, p. 43 f. It is made with a mason named Jean Aide-Criquy (or Aide-Créquy), born in 1661 at La Rochelle, married at Pointe-aux-Trembles (Quebec) in 1689, who died in 1726 (*D.G.F.C.,* p. 2). The contract reads, in part:

". . . La taille sera de Pierre blanche, comme la taille de l'Eglise de Ste. Foy, que lesd. entrepreneurs promettent avoir taillé et livrer sur la fin du caresme prochain 1720, affin qu'elle se puisse amener en traîne, moyennant seize sols le pied, toutte l'une portant l'autre, tant celle de la porte sa parure, et la niche, que celle de touttes les croisées ou fenêtres de l'Eglise.

"La grande porte aura huit pieds de large et douze de haut sous clef. La taille de la porte aura huit poulces (pouces) et autant de tableau, ny comprenant point le pied detaillé, qui en aura au moins douze. La feuillure aura trois poulces. La clef du ceintre de la porte pendera de doux pouces debordant quasy autant, pour en suitte estre creusée en façon de Quadre pour y graver le chiffre de l'année de la Bâtisse. Les deux Inpostes deborderons autant que lad. clef. La frize, ou espèce de capucine, qui sera audessus de la grande porte, debordera autant en la première arreste que la pierre du ceintre de la porte sur laquelle elle sera posée, ayant six à huit poulces d'épaisseur et autant de debordement sur toutte la parure de la porte. L'oeüil de bœuf qui se mettera audessus aura cinq pieds de diamêttre de jour. Sa taille sera semblable aux croisées, aussi bien que celle de la niche, qui aura cinq pieds de haut et deux pieds et trois poulces de large, et dix-huit poulces de profondeur. La Pierre du bas de la niche debordera de trois poulces, et elle sera taillée en talu par dessous."

"Suite du marché pour la toize de la massonne de l'Eglise, qui aura quatre vingt pieds de long et trente huit de large; la muraille aura vingt pieds d'hauteur de dessus le Raz de chaussée. Elle aura trois pieds depaisseur dans les fondements, et audessus des fondements elle aura doux pieds et demy qui se termineront à deux pieds ou plus en haut; le portail ou pignon se continuera jusqu'au feste (faîte)."

[78]Mention of the clocher comes in another document of 1724, cited by Béchard:
". . . Le Clocher a cinquante pieds de haut au dessus de l'Eglise sans y comprendre la croix.

original appearance of such a parish church interior was preserved until 1937 in the church of Pointe-aux-Trembles, Montreal, begun in 1705; it made a very considerable contrast with the simpler interiors of Laval's churches (Plates XXX, XXXI).[79]

Even more striking was the third parish church of Trois-Rivières, begun in 1710 and probably designed by Juconde Drué. The interior of this church, as we have seen, was a showpiece; the exterior, too, was elaborate enough (Plates XXXII, XXXIII), with its finely carved door and many openings in the gable, dormer windows in the roof, and high clocher. Perhaps the most striking difference from Laval's churches was its new sense of proportion and linear *élan*; indeed, the 1710 church of Trois-Rivières was already, in its fusion of craft tradition and advanced architectural elements, an example of the mature tradition of Quebec parish church architecture.

The appearance of churches like these put Bishop Saint-Vallier in something of a quandary. As we have seen, his own upbringing predisposed him in favour of more elaborate architectural ventures; but as we have also seen, he was uneasy about the growing spirit of independence in the parishes which they represented. He would have liked to preserve that homogeneity of parish church architecture which symbolized the firm ecclesiastical control of Laval's day; but Laval's simple parish churches satisfied neither the new *Québécois* spirit of self-reliance and parochial pride, nor his own tastes. The Bishop's solution was to commission a new standard plan which would incorporate more elaborate architectural features, but would still symbolize ecclesiastical control, and curb over-extravagant planning as well. The result is still extant in the archives of the Seminary of Quebec; it bears the signature of Jean Maillou, so that we may conveniently refer to it as the "Maillou plan" for a new standard type of Quebec parish church (Plate XXVIII).

Jean Maillou was typical of the new age. A Canadian, born at Quebec in 1668,[80] he was trained in the native craft tradition, beginning as a simple stone-cutter; in the *Livre de Comptes* of Charlesbourg his name appears as a workman, receiving payment "for work on the church."[81] But by 1702 a document refers

---

Il a au pied de sa racine, sur ses entrais, dix pieds huits poulces de diamettre, et se reduit à dix pieds au bas de son octagone. La flesche jusqu'à létoc avait 24 pieds de haut et 3 pieds d'étoc. Le clocher se trouve bien proportionné à l'Eglise . . . la croix avec le cocq ont environ 8 pieds de haut. Les fenêtre du clocher dans les deux octogones sont distante par en haut de deux pieds de la sablière, les fenêtres de la première octogone ont quatre pieds et demy de haut, et celle de la seconde nont que quatre pieds. L'Eguille de la fleche a six poulces en carré et ses cheuvrons nont que cinq poulces par enbas et quatre par enhaut."

The Gallic cock specified here to cap the *flèche* is interesting. It seems to have been a practically universal feature in the church architecture of New France; after the Cession, it became a particular symbol in the face of the English challenge.

[79]For data on this church, see Appendix, p. 132.

[80]He was the son of Pierre Maillou Desmoulins of Bourge-en-Brie. *D.G.F.C.*, p. 405. On the Maillou plan in general, see Gérard Morisset, *Le Cap Santé*, Quebec, 1944, pp. 13–14.      [81]I, 1695, p. 47.

to him as a "master-mason,"[82] and the *Livre de Comptes* of Saint-Laurent, I.O., for 1708 calls him "le sieur Maillou, entrepreneur de la maçonne de l'église."[83] This last refers to his work on Saint-Laurent in 1702; we had occasion in chapter III to mention this church as a typical example of a parish church of the Age of Laval, so that there is no doubt about the tradition in which Maillou was trained.

By 1716, however, Maillou had apparently become a full-fledged master in his profession, for the census of Lower Town, Quebec, in 1716 calls him "Jean Maillou, architect."[84] As was common at the time, he acted also as an engineer,[85] and he began to take apprentices to work with and for him.[86] By the time his second wife died in 1719, he was called "Jean Maillou, architect to the King."[87] In 1723 and 1724 we hear of him as "architect and contractor for the King's buildings in Canada."[88] And he continued to rise. In 1728 he received an imposing commission: "par Pierre Robineau, chevalier, seigneur de Bécancour, baron de Portneuf, Conseiller du Roi, grand-voyer en Toute la Nouvelle-France, au Sieur Maillou, architecte, pour faire les fonctions de grand-voyer en son absence, etc. . . ."[89] In the capacity of *grand-voyer*, Jean Maillou, the humble Canadian, was chosen partner of Chaussegros de Léry, nobleman, royal architect and engineer, in an inspection of the Bishop's Palace in Quebec in 1730; in 1742 it is Jean Maillou and several others, "tous experts," who are named to visit and make estimates for future repairs to the same building.[90] He is mentioned as an architect at Quebec in 1744 and again in 1747;[91] and at his death, his body was buried with great honour in the Cathedral of Quebec, on September 18, 1753.[92]

Exactly when the Maillou plan was drawn up is a matter of some uncertainty. But it so closely follows most of Laval's ideas that it cannot be much later than 1715; indeed, Maillou's commission for it may well have been responsible for

---

[82]P.-G. Roy, *Inventaire des concessions en fief,* IV, p. 165. This, and several other references to Maillou which I have not included as somewhat irrelevant here, may be found collected by Antoine Roy, *L.S.A.,* p. 225, n. 3.

[83]I, 1708–1709, p. 30. He was paid 900 *livres* at this time.

[84]L. Beaudet, *Recensement de la ville de Québec pour 1716,* p. 211.

[85]On July 19, 1721, he submitted plans "for repairs which are ordered for the road, ditches, and bridges around Charlesbourg." *Inventaire des jugements et délibérations du Conseil Supérieur de la Nouvelle-France,* I, p. 27.

[86]In 1717, one Charles-Etienne Camanne, "anglois de nation"; in 1720, Pierre Marcou. Marcou's contract states that Maillou is to provide his apprentice with room and board, pay him each year fifty *livres* "monnaye de France," and twenty-five for the last six months, "avec un marteau Et une truelle." *Archives judiciares de Québec,* Minuitier de Mtre Pierre Rivet; *ibid.,* Minuitier de Mtre Lacetièrre.

[87]The record of her interment in the Cathedral reads: "Marguérite Caron, wife of Jean Maillou, architect to the King." P.-G. Roy, *Les Cimitières de Québec,* Lévis, 1941, pp. 43, 50.      [88]*L.S.A.,* p. 225, n. 3.

[89]P.-G. Roy, *Inventaire des insinuations du Conseil Souverain,* Beauceville, 1921, p. 185.

[90]P.-G. Roy, *Inventaire des ordonnances des Intendants,* II, p. 55, and III, p. 32.

[91]*L.S.A.,* p. 225, n. 3.      [92]P.-G. Roy, *Les Cimitières de Québec,* pp. 43, 50.

the sudden upturn in his fortunes apparent after this date. From the parish churches of the Age of Laval the Maillou plan took its general two-to-one proportions, its round apse, and its type of clocher. But it was larger; on the back of the extant drawing we read: "church plan by Mr. Jean Maillou . . . this plan is not wide enough . . . it is only thirty feet [the width of parish churches built under Laval] . . . thirty-six are needed. . . ." And it was more elaborate—doors and window-openings treated with cut stone, architectural elements such as pilasters and scrolls if these could be afforded, and more elaborate interior sculpture. From all this it is clear that the Maillou plan did little more than confirm, and attempt to direct, a trend already established; a parish church like that of Lachine already embodied its essential characteristics.

Apparently a variant of the Maillou plan was permissible, whereby small lateral chapels could be added. This feature had great appeal, probably because it allowed for greater sculptural ornament on the interior; certainly the majority of Maillou plan churches have it. A typical early example is the famous pilgrimage church of Cap-de-la-Madeleine, begun in 1714 (Plate XXXIV);[93] others were the first church of Saint-Thomas de Montmagny, begun about 1715,[94] and the church of Saint-Pierre, I.O., begun in 1717.[95]

Delimitation of the parishes in 1722 provided a great opportunity for application of the Maillou plan on a large scale; during the decade 1720–1730, about twenty churches were constructed.[96] Typical of them were the churches of Saint-Charles de Lachenaie, built in 1724 and demolished in 1883[97] (Plate XXXV); Longue-Pointe, dating from 1727; Beaumont, built in the same year;[98] and Saint-François-de-Sales, I.O., begun in 1734[99] (Plate XXXVIII). In all of these,

[93]On later alterations to this church, see Appendix, p. 136.

[94]Its lateral chapels are attested by an extant contract assigning pews in them. Cf. F.-E.-J. Casault, *Notes historiques sur la paroisse de Saint-Thomas de Montmagny*, Quebec, 1906, p. 43 f., and p. 89 f.

[95]This church has been much altered in the passage of time; cf. R. Traquair and M. Barbeau, "The Church of Saint Pierre," *McG.U.P.*, no. 22, and Appendix, p. 137.

[96]The most important were: Saint-Augustin, Portneuf (begun 1719, finished 1724); Beauport (c. 1720); Saint-François-de-Sales (c. 1720); Saint-Antoine de Tilly (1721); L'Islet (1721); Saint-Joseph, Lauzon (1721); Berthier-en-Haut (1722); Ancienne-Lorette (1722); Saint-Sulpice (1723); Sainte-Geneviève, Batiscan (c. 1723); Longueuil (1724); Lachenaie (1724); Verchères (c. 1724); Repentigny (1725); Saint-Roch des Aulnaies (c. 1725); Contrecœur (1726); Longue-Pointe (1727); Kamouraska (1727); Saint-Nicolas (Lévis) (1728); Vaudreuil (1728).

[97]R. Traquair and G. Neilson, "The Old Church of . . . Lachenaie," *McG.U.P.*, no. 38, *passim.*

[98]The clocher of Beaumont was rebuilt in 1870 by Ferdinand Peachy, and the façade in 1922, by Lorenzo Auger. Auger attempted, however, to retain the old appearance as far as possible. *V.E.*, pp. 128–129; J.-E. Roy, "Saint-Etienne de Beaumont," *B.R.H.*, I, 1895, p. 129 f., and XIX, 1913, p. 238 f.

[99]*V.E.*, p. 159 f.; R. Traquair and M. Barbeau, "The Church of St. François," *McG.U.P.*, no. 14, *passim.* Both here and at Beaumont the interior is to all intents and purposes nineteenth-century; the *récollette* form of the retable at Saint-François dates from 1768.

# PLATES

I ANGE-GARDIEN, FIRST CHURCH. Begun 1675; original decoration early eighteenth century, restored on the plans of Thomas Baillargé, 1835-1838. Nave enlarged 1875, with general restoration of the interior. Destroyed 1931, except for the retable executed by Jacques Leblond *dit* Latour, *c.* 1700. (Livernois, Quebec)

I NEUVILLE, FIRST CHURCH, APSE. Built 1696, decoration mainly 1777-1794; baldachin begun 1766. (Ramsay Traquair)

IV FORT RÉMI IN THE SEVENTEENTH CENTURY, showing the first chapel of Lachine, built in 1676. Recc
struction by A. S. Brodeur. (From Désiré Girouard, *Lake St. Louis, Old and New*)

QUEBEC, GENERAL VIEW, *c.* 1700 (the Episcopal Palace is marked "H"). (From Lapotherie, *Histoire de L'Amérique septentrionale*)

VI SAINT-LAURENT, I.O.,
FIRST CHURCH. Begun in
1695; lengthened by the
façade constructed under
Jean Maillou in 1708.
Destroyed in 1864. (Red-
path Library, McGill
University)

VII SAINTE-ANNE DE
BEAUPRÉ, THIRD
CHURCH. A rebuild-
ing of the second
church of 1676, car-
ried out between 1689
and 1695 by Claude
Baillif. Restored in
1787; demolished
1878. (Inventaire des
Œuvres d'Art)

II SAINTE-ANNE DE BEAUPRÉ, THIRD CHURCH, CLOCHER. Built in 1696 on the plans of Claude Baillif by the carpenters R. Leclaire and Jean Marchand. Removed to the Commemorative Chapel at Sainte-Anne in 1878. (Inventaire des Œuvres d'Art)

IX MONT-TREMBLANT, SUMMER CHAPEL. Constructed as a replica of the old church of Saint-Laurent, I.O. (Plate VI), incorporating its clocher by Joseph Chabot, 1709. (Inventaire des Œuvres d'Art)

X CATHEDRAL OF QUEBEC, front elevation, as show
in a drawing made by Chaussegros de Lé
representing the Cathedral as designed by Clau
Baillif, 1684-1689(?). (From P.-G. Roy, *La Vi*
*de Québec*)

XI "A VIEW OF THE TREASURY AND
JESUITS COLLEGE" drawn in 1759
by Richard Short; detail, showing the Cathedral of Quebec
in ruins. (Public Archives of
Canada)

XII QUEBEC, THE EPISCOPAL PALACE, drawn by Richard Short in 1759. Begun 1694; restored *c.* 1765; completely altered beginning 1831. (Public Archives of Canada)

XIII QUEBEC, CHURCH OF NOTRE-DAME-DES-VICTOIRES, as drawn by Richard Short in 1759. Begun 1688; façade 1711. (Public Archives of Canada)

XIV  QUEBEC, JESUIT CHURCH, INTERIOR, as drawn by Richard Short in 1759.  Begun 1666; restored *c.* 1765
destroyed 1807. (Public Archives of Canada)

XV  QUEBEC, JESUIT CHURCH, EXTERIOR, as drawn by Richard Short in 1759.  Begun 1666; façade adde
*c.* 1730 by Chaussegros de Léry; destroyed 1807. (Public Archives of Canada)

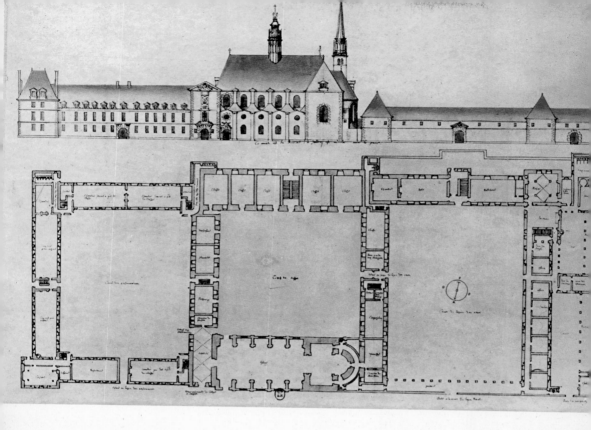

XVI La Flèche, Jesuit college and chapel, begun 1612. The chapel was probably designed by Etienne Martellange; consecrated 1637. (Bibliothèque Nationale, Paris)

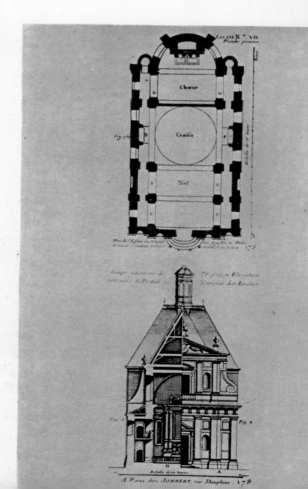

XVII Paris, Jesuit Noviciate church, plan and section. (From François Blondel, *L'Architecture française*)

XVIII PARIS, JESUIT NOVICIATE CHURCH, from an engraving by Marot. Begun 1630 by Etienne Martel lange, Jesuit; destroyed at the Revolution.

XIX QUEBEC: *left*, RÉCOLLET CHURCH (built in 1693 by Juconde Drué, Récollet); *right*, CATHEDRA From a drawing by Richard Short, 1759. (Public Archives of Canada)

XX Quebec, Récollet church, interior, as drawn by Richard Short in 1759. (Public Archives of Canada)

XXI Neuville, processional chapel. Built c. 1735. (Inventaire des Œuvres d'Art)

XXIII MONTREAL, CHURCH AND RESIDENCE OF THE RÉCOLLETS, from a sepia by John Drake in the "Album de Jacques Viger." Begun 1706; façade added in 1712 by Pierre Janson-Lapalme. (Inventaire des Œuvres d'Art)

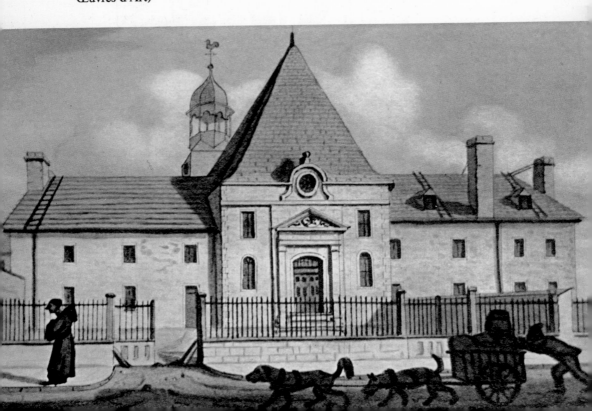

XXIV QUEBEC, CHAPEL IN THE SECOND URSULINE CONVENT. Built between 1720 and 1722 on the plans of François de Lajoue; altar ensemble by Noël Levasseur, 1732-1737. Photograph taken before the alteration of the chapel in 1902. (Inventaire des Œuvres d'Art)

XXV TROIS-RIVIÈRES, THIRD PARISH CHURCH, INTERIOR. Begun 1710; ensemble designed by Augustin Quintal, Récollet, and executed by Gilles Bolvin, c. 1733-1737. Destroyed by fire, 1908. (Inventaire des Œuvres d'Art)

XXVI Montreal, PARISH CHURCH OF NOTRE-DAME. Proposed appearance of the façade, as designed by Chaussegros de Léry in 1722. Drawing by John Drake, from the "Album de Jacques Viger." (Inventaire des Œuvres d'Art)

XXVII Montreal, La Paroisse, as it was at the end of the *ancien régime*; restoration in part conjectural.

XVIII PLAN AND ELEVATION FOR A PARISH CHURCH, signed by Jean Maillou; early eighteenth century. Preserved in the archives of the Seminary of Quebec. (Inventaire des Œuvres d'Art)

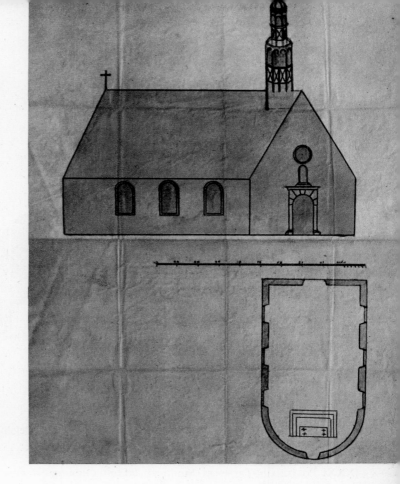

XXIX LACHINE, FIRST CHURCH. Begun 1702; clocher rebuilt 1718; destroyed 1869. (From Désiré Girouard, *Lake St. Louis, Old and New*)

XXX POINTE-AUX-TREMBLES (Montreal), SECOND CHURCH. Begun 1705; lateral chapels added 1740; destroyed 1937. (Redpath Library, McGill University)

XXXI POINTE-AUX-TREMBLES (Montreal), SECOND CHURCH, INTERIOR. Much later addition and restoration. (Ramsay Traquair)

XXII TROIS-RIVIÈRES, THIRD CHURCH. Begun 1710; façade and clocher rebuilt *c*. 1773; destroyed by fire 1908. (Inventaire des Œuvres d'Art)

XXXIII TROIS-RIVIÈRES, THIRD CHURCH, side view. (Inventaire des Œuvres d'Art)

XXXIV CAP-DE-LA-MADELEINE, FIRST CHURCH. Begun 1714; now a chapel attached to the pilgrimage church. Original lines preserved through considerable alteration and restoration. (Inventaire des Œuvres d'Art)

XXXV LACHENAIE, FIRST CHURCH, EXTERIOR. Begun 1724; demolished 1883. (Inventaire des Œuvres d'Art)

XXXVI LACHENAIE, FIRST CHURCH, INTERIOR, showing the tabernacle by Augustin Quintal and Gilles Bolvin. (Redpath Library, McGill University)

XXXVII SAINTE-FAMILLE, I.O., SECOND CHURCH. Begun 1743; flanking clochers rebuilt 1806; central clochers added 1843. (Inventaire des Œuvres d'Art)

XXXVIII SAINT-FRANÇOIS-DE-SALES, I.O., FIRST CHURCH. Begun 1734 by Thomas Allard, mason, of Quebec; many subsequent alterations. Clocher rebuilt 1821 and 1864. (Inventaire des Œuvres d'Art)

XL REPENTIGNY, SECOND CHURCH, EXTERIOR. Begun 1725; towers built 1737-1749; clochers restored 1838-1839. (Inventaire des Œuvres d'Art)

XLI CAP SANTÉ, SECOND CHURCH, INTERIOR. Begun 1754; details largely nineteenth century.

XLII PARIS, CHURCH OF SAINT-ETIENNE-DU-MONT. (Giraudon, Paris)

XLIII CAP SANTÉ, SECOND CHURCH. Begun 1754; finished in 1768. Façade refurbished in imitation stone, late nineteenth century. (Inventaire des Œuvres d'Art)

XLIV Armenonville-les-Gatineaux, Chapel, façade. Begun 1658; clocher rebuilt 1676.

XLV Armenonville-les-Gatineaux, chapel, exterior, side and apse.

XLVI *Top*. ARMENONVILLE-LES-GATINEAUX, CHAPEL, INTERIOR, looking west.

XLVII *Lower left*. ARMENON-VILLE-LES-GATINEAUX, CHAPEL, INTERIOR, looking east.

XLVIII *Lower right*. ARMENON-VILLE-LES-GATINEAUX, CHAPEL, detail of ceiling.

XLIX Saint-Laurent, I.O., first church, façade. (Redpath Library, McGill University)

Honfleur, chapel of Notre-Dame-de-Grâce. Founded eleventh century; rebuilt *c.* 1660. (Giraudon, Paris)

LI Nogent-le-Roi, church of Saint-Sulpice. (Giraudon, Paris)

the original lines of the Maillou plan may easily be discerned through later additions and restoration.

But in all of them too—and this is significant for the temper of the times—there is evidence of considerably more elaboration than the Maillou plan warranted. Saint-Charles de Lachenaie, for all its exterior simplicity, had an interior boasting a splendid tabernacle executed by Bolvin on the plans of Augustin Quintal (Plate XXXVI). The interior of the church at Longue-Pointe was even more ostentatious; its source of inspiration is suggested by a contract made with Antoine Cirier, a Montreal sculptor, for a vault and pulpit in 1731, the pulpit to have "a twisting stairway like that in the Récollet church of Ville-Marie [Montreal]."[100] And so with practically all the rest. The liking for ostentation in Quebec parishes was too pervasive; each parish wanted to vie with its neighbours in building as splendid a church as it could. And the feeling of independence was strong enough that parish builders chafed under the restrictions of the Maillou plan, and evaded its limitations wherever possible. Saint-Vallier's idea was simply too anachronistic; the building clock could not be turned back to Laval's time. Indeed, the very career of Jean Maillou himself showed how the times were changing; that a simple Canadian mason should become a royal architect was a thing impossible in Laval's day, and that an eighteenth-century bishop could direct church building as Laval had done was equally unfeasible. This was not the last time such an attempt was made by the Bishops of Quebec; we find the same thing occurring after the Cession, with the "Conefroy plan." But in 1715, as later, it was a futile effort. The Maillou plan remained in force for some twenty years, although as is evident its prescriptions were never followed too exactly; after that, it was ignored, and the parish church tradition of the *ancien régime* came to its climax.

## PARISH CHURCHES: THE DEVELOPED TRADITION

The first major departure from the Maillou plan took place in the parish church of Repentigny. When originally begun in 1725, this church must have looked much like that of Longue-Pointe (Plate XXXIX); the same man, Antoine Cirier, executed both interiors.[101] But in 1737 twin towers were begun to flank the façade; they were completed in 1749,[102] the first to be successfully carried

---

[100]A. Bellay, "L'Eglise de Saint-François d'Assise de la Longue-Pointe," *La Revue canadienne*, XXIX, 1893, p. 423 f.; O. Maurault, *Saint-François d'Assise de la Longue-Pointe*, Montreal, 1924, *passim*.

[101]*V.E.*, pp. 97–98.

[102]The *Livre de Comptes* of Repentigny records the completion of clochers in 1749, which presumably means the towers went with them; the main programme of building at Repentigny, aside from the structure, seems to have begun around 1735, when Antoine Cirier commenced work on the interior.

out in New France[103] (Plate XL). Without doubt, inspiration for the Repentigny design came from La Paroisse in Montreal, but it was not long before the example was followed all over New France.

In 1743 the church of Sainte-Famille, I.O., was begun with twin towers, completed in 1746[104] (Plate XXXVII). This building, one of the best known of all churches in the Province, is also one of the most important from the point of view of church architecture. In 1669, the first church of Sainte-Famille had been Bishop Laval's first major essay in parish church architecture; the 1743 church was an equally significant landmark in the evolution of a mature parish church style.

While its twin towers undoubtedly represent Sulpician inspiration, in general the church of Sainte-Famille rested solidly on the traditions of the Quebec area. The two towers, rather small, were built out from the gable and connected with it only at the corners,[105] like the single tower flanking the 1666 Jesuit church in Quebec, while the five niches of the façade recall Juconde Drué's designs for the façades of the Récollet church in Quebec and Saint-Nicolas, Lauzon.[106] Furthermore, the type of transept found at Sainte-Famille—large chapels, with a common ridge-pole crossing the nave at the same height as the main ridge—is that found in Laval's parish churches. Thus the church of Sainte-Famille provides a resumé of the evolution of parish church design from the type developed by Laval to the more monumental building at the end of the *ancien régime*.

Several other even more elaborate parish churches were projected around this time, most notably the first church of Sainte-Geneviève, Pierrefonds, consecrated in 1751, where twin towers on a grand scale were planned.[107] But outbreak of the Seven Years' War in 1756 postponed construction of the towers, and not until 1772 was the first one built; the other was never completed. The war and subsequent cession had a generally disastrous effect on the development of church architecture, interrupting its most flourishing phase; but fortunately,

[103]The church of Saint-Louis, Terrebonne, begun in 1734, may have been intended to have twin towers. The present single central tower was built in 1784, but the curious design of the central section of the façade—scalloped, reminiscent of de Léry's design for La Paroisse—suggests a completion with twin towers, as we find it in the very similarly designed church of Châteauguay, begun in 1775. Cf. C.-A. Gareau, *Aperçu historique de Terrebonne,* Terrebonne, 1927, p. 26 f.

[104]*V.E.*, p. 171 f.

[105]Cf. the plan as presented by R. Traquair and M. Barbeau, "The Church of Sainte Famille," *McG.U.P.,* no. 13, and Traquair, *The Old Architecture of Quebec,* p. 156. Traquair believed that the towers were not added until 1807. According to Morisset, however, the towers were part of the original building. In 1807 the lantern and *flèche* of the clochers were rebuilt. *A.N.F.,* p. 50, n. 2. The third clocher of Sainte-Famille was added in 1843, by Thomas Baillargé.

[106]J.-E. Roy, *Histoire de la seigneurie de Lauzon,* II, p. 96 f. The statues now to be seen in the five niches of the Sainte-Famille façade are replicas of the originals which have been removed to museums.

[107]J.-E. Roy, "Sainte-Geneviève de Jacques-Cartier," *B.R.H.,* IV, 1898, p. 321; P.-G. Roy, "Sainte-Geneviève de Pierrefonds," *B.R.H.,* XLVI, 1940, pp. 378–379.

before that happened, the developed tradition was embodied in one imposing building that still stands, the second parish church of Cap Santé.

This church was one of the most ambitious buildings ever erected in New France (Plates XLI, XLIII). It forms the subject of one of Gérard Morisset's excellent monographs, and there may be found a complete account of the history of church building in this parish.[108] The present church was the more remarkable in that the parish of Cap Santé, while among the older Quebec parishes (being founded around 1650), was certainly not one of the largest or most important when its second church was begun.

A contract signed with masons Pierre Renaud and "Aide-Créquy of Neuville" set the date for completion of the church of Cap Santé in 1758. The author of the plan is not recorded; but it is improbable that either of these masons designed the church.[109] The curé, Joseph Fillion, whose inspiration figures prominently in the Cap Santé records, may have drawn upon the Seminary of Quebec for help in designing the church, and Jean Maillou, most prominent of the then available architects (he died in 1753), may well have worked on the plans; Maillou seems the man most capable of producing such an ambitious work, and the craft quality so unfortunately evident in it is explicable in that case.

M. Morisset believes that Cap Santé was modelled upon the church of Sainte-Famille, and certainly there is influence from that source; the gable treatment shows definite resemblances: the three niches above, with statues, plus the two round windows below, correspond roughly in arrangement to the five niches on Sainte-Famille. But no single prototype predominates at Cap Santé. The towers, set back with their front faces parallel to the gable, suggest influences from de Léry's plan for Notre-Dame in Montreal. The body of the church, with its small transept chapels, seems to recall the Maillou plan. And the interior is a splendid elaboration of the *récollette* scheme, in two stories, with the end wall convex on the interior in a manner reminiscent of the Jesuit church of Quebec. The designers attempted to make the church of Cap Santé the largest in New France,[110] and they did more—they attempted to create in it a great synthesis of all the trends in Quebec church architecture. Into a framework which depended on the basic craft tradition of New France they built elements embodying the contributions of all the orders—Jesuit, Récollet, Sulpician.

Their synthesis could have been handled better; on the exterior the design is

[108]Gérard Morisset, *Le Cap Santé,* Quebec, 1944.

[109]Jean Aide-Créquy of Neuville, contractor for the 1719 church of Saint-Augustin, Portneuf (cf. note 77), had two sons, both born at Pointe-aux-Trembles (Quebec): Louis, born in 1695, and Antoine, born in 1716. The latter is most probably the man mentioned in the Cap Santé records, since Louis died in 1755. Morisset in his monograph does not mention the elder Aide-Créquy, and seems to consider Renaud the designer.

[110]The dimensions given by Morisset are: height, 35 feet (on the south side, 40 feet, the difference caused by sloping terrain); width, 45 feet on the interior. The length is not given. The work was so ambitious that it was not completed until 1763. The clochers were rebuilt in 1807.

marred by somewhat barn-like, ungainly proportions, and the interior also gives a clumsy effect in places.[111] But for all that, the church of Cap Santé is a landmark—thoroughly Canadian, a work of completely indigenous style. Little sense of historical development is needed to realize that here a mature tradition is on the point of emergence. Just at this point the development was broken off by the war, and when we pick up the history of church architecture in the Province of Quebec after 1760, there is a definite reversion to older, simpler, forms; but the final evolution of a mature and characteristic parish church architecture was merely delayed, not ended, and was to be revived in the early nineteenth century with the genius of Thomas Baillargé. That, however, is another story.

[111]On the various periods of work on the interior, see Morisset, p. 32 f. Until very recently, the interior was also disfigured by a huge black stove and stovepipes, installed, as in most Quebec churches, in the first half of the nineteenth century. Before 1800, the only warmth available in *Québecois* churches came from portable *chaufferettes*—small lampstoves used by officiating priests to keep the wine from freezing, or stones heated through and wrapped in cloth which parishioners would place under their feet. (Cf. Charlevoix: ". . . In winter . . . you are pierced with cold [in the churches]," chap. II, above, n. 48.) There are a few references to stoves in houses during the *ancien régime* (collected by E.-Z. Massicotte, *B.R.H.*, XXII, 1916, pp. 334–335), but not until after 1800 did large heating stoves come into use in churches. Since there was no attempt to make them fit their setting, many curés objected to having them installed, both because of their unsightliness and because of a fear that heat and smoke would damage the gilding. (Cf. Charles-P. Beaubien, "Le Chauffage de nos églises autrefois," *B.R.H.*, V, 1899, p. 57; B. Sulte, *Histoire des Canadiens-français*, III, p. 118 f.) Fortunately, the old type of disfiguring stove is today fast disappearing from Quebec churches.

# V

# FRENCH ORIGINS OF THE QUEBEC PARISH CHURCH TRADITION

THAT THE ARCHITECTURAL TRADITIONS OF QUEBEC DERIVE FROM French sources is obvious. But in the case of only a few churches are we able to suggest definite prototypes,[1] and for the parish church tradition in particular surprisingly little precise evidence of origin is available. There is practically nothing in the way of documents. Comparisons between churches in France and Canada made by contemporaneous writers are both vague and contradictory;[2] and, while we know of a number of French books on architecture that were available in New France,[3] there is no significant evidence for the direct use of any of them.[4] Thus it becomes apparent that any investigation of the origins of church architecture in Quebec must depend primarily upon stylistic comparisons with buildings in France.

Most commonly, these origins have been held to be in the regional craft traditions of Brittany and Normandy. Among early writers in the field, this idea is so fixed as to be practically a dogma. Writing around 1875, Sulte could say

[1]E.g., the Jesuit church in Quebec; La Paroisse in Montreal. Cf. chap. III, pp. 57 ff.; chap. IV, pp. 77 ff.

[2]E.g., Jesuit Father Thierry Beschefer, writing in 1666, says "the churches here are like those in the good towns of France" (quoted in *B.R.H.*, XXXV, 1929, p. 335 f.); Father Joseph Navières of Sainte-Anne de Beaupré in 1734 says, "The parish churches of the countryside in France are not comparable to those where I live [i.e., are better]" (cf. Benjamin Sulte, "Un Voyage à Nouvelle-France en 1734," *La Revue canadienne*, 1886, pp. 15–35); but Charlevoix in 1720 saw little to admire in Canadian churches, declaring that the cathedral of Quebec "would not be a good parish church in one of the smallest places in France" (*Histoire et description générale de la Nouvelle-France*, Paris, 1744, III, p. 74).

[3]Inventories of private libraries taken around 1740 contain references to *L'Architecture françois des bastiments particuliers* by Savot, *Le Cours d'architecture* by d'Aviler, and *Les Lois des bâtiments* by Desgodets (cf. *L.S.A.*, p. 63 f.). And we also know that "pocket Vignolas" (i.e., convenient abridgments of Vignola's writings and plans) were used by some Quebec artisans during the *ancien régime*; it is probable that the *récollette* retables of the eighteenth century owe many of their details to Vignola via this source, although their over-all composition is not attributable to him.

[4]About the only such evidence is a door in the Petit Séminaire de Saint-Joachim, which may be from Vignola; it is mentioned by P.-G. Roy, *Vieux Manoirs, Vieilles Maisons*, Quebec, 1927, p. 357.

without hesitation of the parish church of Trois-Rivières, "It all has the appearance of antiquity, but that is part of the Norman style, which was already old in 1715."[5] Similarly Lalande in 1890 remarked unquestioningly that for the typical Quebec parish church "Brittany, they say, furnished us the models."[6] And, although somewhat modified now, this theory is still taken for granted in many cases.[7] But to prove it, two further assumptions must be verified: first, that the Norman element formed the largest single part of the population of New France in its earliest period, and therefore Norman craftsmen had the greatest influence upon building traditions; second, that marked affinities can be demonstrated between the architecture of the Normandy-Brittany region of France and that of French Canada.

A good case can be made for the first assumption. During the first thirty years of New France's existence, the population seems to have been about half Norman—i.e., of 296 recorded immigrants, 178 were from Normandy or the vicinity.[8] In 1663 Bishop Laval specifically asked Louis XIV for Norman immigrants;[9] and by 1700 censuses show Normans and Bretons forming about one-fifth of the population, still a substantial proportion. And such names of craftsmen as have come down to us tend to confirm the corollary of these population figures. François Boivin, the earliest church builder to whom we have specific reference in New France, was a Norman, baptized in 1616 in the diocese of Rouen.[10] Jean Bourdon, first engineer-in-chief of New France and the most notable builder of the colony's early days, also came from Rouen.[11] Claude Baillif, leading architect of New France in the later seventeenth century, was most probably a Norman, as we have seen.[12] Michel Lefebvre, son of Pierre Lefebvre of Rouen, is another example.[13] Breton craftsmen figure hardly at all in the records; but certainly dominance of Norman builders in seventeenth-century New France seems clearly substantiated by documentary evidence.

[5]*Mélanges historiques*, XIX, 1932, p. 28.

[6]L. Lalande, *Une Vieille Seigneurie—Boucherville*, Montreal, 1890, p. 257. See above, p. 6.

[7]The best and most succinct summary of the main points of this theory is that of William Sener Rusk, "The Influence of Norman Architecture in French Canada," *Bulletin de l'Institut français de Washington (D.C.)*, XIII, December, 1940, p. 11 f.

[8]The table of immigration compiled by Stanislaus-A. Lortie, *Bulletin du parler français*, 1903–4, p. 18, forms the basis of most discussions of population in early New France. It is used by Georges Vattier, *Esquisse historique de la colonisation de la Province de Québec*, Paris, 1925, and by Lionel Groulx, *La Naissance d'une race*, Montreal, 1918.

[9]H. A. Scott, *Bishop Laval*, Toronto and London, 1926, p. 193.

[10]Cf. *D.G.F.C.*, p. 64, and chap. II, pp. 19–20.

[11]Cf. chap. II, note 20.

[12]Cf. chap. III, p. 47 and note 91.

[13]He was born in Canada but presumably was raised in the Norman craft tradition by his father. He worked on the 1682 parish church of Trois-Rivières (cf. chap. III, p. 59) and the first church of Lachine in the years 1702–1703. Cf. O.-M. Jouve, *Les Franciscains et le Canada: Aux Trois-Rivières*, Paris, 1934, p. 34; Désiré Girouard, *Lake St. Louis, Old and New*, Montreal, 1893, p. 45 f.

When we come to look for actual Norman or Breton churches which re-semble the Quebec type, however, nothing significant appears. Some features of the Quebec parish church tradition may be found in small churches and chapels of Normandy and Brittany, it is true—the steep roof, which tends to be splayed out at the eaves; the Latin-cross plan; a location of the clocher above the front gable; apses built in panels; the practice of arranging the elements of the clocher so as to have solids, rather than voids, on the axis. (Cf. Plate L.) But all these features are mere generalities, common to late medieval survivals all over seventeenth-century Europe; they offer no proof of the specific region from which the Quebec tradition came.

Realizing this, some later critics, notably Antoine Roy and Gérard Morisset,[14] have tended to abandon any theory of specific Norman or Breton origins, pre-ferring instead the idea that *Québécois* architecture sprang simply from the late medieval architectural traditions of Europe in general, and France in particular. But on this evidence I think it would be premature to conclude, with Ramsay Traquair, that "One would search France vainly for a Quebec parish church."[15] For that depends on what we are looking for.

We must remember, first of all, that the essential elements which the Quebec parish church tradition derived from France were all established in the colony by 1700. In the eighteenth century, as we have seen, the Quebec tradition not only received nothing new from France, but proceeded to develop along inde-pendent lines. Hence any Quebec parish church we may expect to find in France will look like those now vanished churches of the Age of Laval, not like any standing today. And secondly, there is strong evidence that the Quebec parish church of the Age of Laval represented a peculiar fusion of late medieval craft elements with more advanced elements from the "academic" trends of seventeenth-century French architecture. If that is so, we should not expect to find a Quebec parish church in a region of France where one local craft tradition predominated, as in Brittany or Normandy; the place to look would be in a region where there was in the seventeenth century a fusion of architectural elements parallel to that in New France. And there are several such, the most obvious being the general area of the Ile-de-France.[16]

It was in this region, of course, that Laval, Saint-Vallier, and Dollier de

[14]*L.S.A.*, p. 175 f.; *A.N.F.*, introduction.
[15]*The Old Architecture of Quebec*, Toronto, 1947, p. 135.
[16]Newer Renaissance elements were also being combined with late medieval traditions around La Rochelle and in French Flanders, and we might expect to look there with some profit. The architecture of Normandy and Brittany was very *retardataire* in the seventeenth century; Renaissance elements begin to appear there in strength only in the later eighteenth century. And, significantly in our connection, it is only then, when any possibility of influence on church architecture in New France is out of the question, that we find Norman and Breton churches with any close resemblance to the Quebec type (a typical example is the late eighteenth-century church of Bois-Normand, illustrated in Bonnenfant's *Eglises rurales de l'Eure*, Paris, 1937).

Casson all picked up their architectural ideas,[17] and that the specific buildings
we can cite as having influenced architecture in New France—the Jesuit Noviciate
and Saint-Sulpice in Paris, the Jesuit college at La Flèche—were all located. But
more significant than these possible coincidences, it was in the Ile-de-France
region that the sixteenth-century kings of France first introduced Renaissance
forms into French architecture, and that an architectural style based on a fusion
of late medieval and academic elements had already appeared by the early
seventeenth century. Typical of that style was the façade of Saint-Etienne-du-
Mont in Paris, built between 1610 and 1625; it already shows a certain resemblance to the church architecture of New France (Plate XLII). Not that there
is or was any church in Quebec which looked like Saint-Etienne; what is common is a combination of classical Renaissance elements and traditional late
medieval structure—niches, keystone arches, and pediments applied to an
essentially late medieval church with steep gable and rose window; a clocher
still medieval in its asymmetrical location and verticality, but Renaissance in its
cupola and semi-circular lantern arches. Another example, showing similar
parallels in spirit to New France, is the Gothic church at Nogent-le-Roi which
was finished off in the sixteenth century in a more or less Renaissance way
(Plate LI). On its heavy medieval tower was erected a clumsily classical clocher,
the lower part consisting of a belfry which could be described no better than as
a squared dome, with the S-curve silhouette common on Renaissance cupolas in
France; practically the same construction caps the one tower finished on the
1666 Jesuit church of Quebec, and de Léry's drawing of the clocher on the
1684 Cathedral of Quebec shows a markedly similar conception (Plates X, XV).

But among the larger seventeenth-century churches of the Ile-de-France region
we find none which resemble to any specific degree the typical Quebec parish
church of Laval's time. There is a reasonable explanation: the more mature
fusion of medieval craft traditions and Renaissance principles which the later
seventeenth century would normally have brought, and which was actually
accomplished in a provincial way in Laval's New France, never materialized in
the monumental architecture of the Ile-de-France; Louis XIV's academies of
art and architecture, which proscribed medieval forms and imposed strict ad-
herence to the classical, prevented it. However—and this is the significant point
—a development parallel to that of New France could have taken place in buildings close enough to the Ile-de-France to be affected by the academic ideas
radiating from it, yet unimportant and out-of-the-way enough to be constructed
by local craftsmen. In short, conditions roughly duplicating those which shaped
the formation of the Quebec tradition were possible in outlying parts of the
Ile-de-France region in the mid- and later seventeenth century. There would
be the place to look for a Quebec parish church; and if we could find one, it would
provide visible evidence which would impressively support the literary evidence

[17]Cf. chap. III, pp. 57, 48, 64.

for our thesis that the Quebec tradition of church architecture was not local late medieval craftsmanship simply, but a peculiar fusion of that with up-to-date seventeenth-century French trends.

With this in mind, I spent some time searching the Ile-de-France countryside. Small parish churches dating from the seventeenth century are not too common in France, but in the little hamlet of Armenonville-les-Gatineaux (Eure-et-Loir), about ten miles north of Chartres, I did find a Quebec parish church. A complete *Livre de Comptes* was located in a nearby house. In size (about sixty feet long and twenty feet wide), in date (rebuilt beginning in 1658), and in almost every other detail this building concurs exactly with what we know of the parish church architecture of New France in the Age of Laval.

Like Laval's parish churches, the church of Saint-Pierre-et-Saint-Paul of Armenonville-les-Gatineaux was built by local craftsmen working under the direction of a man familiar with academic architectural ideas from contacts at the royal court—Messire Charles Fleuriau, "conseiller et sécretaire du Roy, maison, et couronne de France."[18] In 1649, Fleuriau bought "the land and seigniory of Armenonville with all thereto pertaining,"[19] which included a decrepit chapel built in 1206, in the reign of Philip Augustus. He at once set about building a "château" (or, as it would have been called in New France, a "manoir"); then, in 1658, he determined to provide his seigniory with a new church, just as so many of the seigniors of New France began to do in the next decade. First, "the chapel was entirely repaired [= rebuilt], since formerly it had been neither clapboarded nor paved, and very dark . . .";[20] the next year, interior furnishings were provided,[21] and in 1660 a sacristy was added, the façade built, and a presbytery erected.[22] In 1667 "un nommé Jacques Monnoye, sculpteur" provided statues of Saints Peter and Paul to occupy the niches which flanked the doorway of the new façade.[23] By 1671 the building was sufficiently improved to be raised to the status of a parish church; but as a result "the said

[18]These and the following quotations are all from the *Livre de Comptes* of the Armenonville church. The account of Fleuriau's work was apparently written by the first curé, shortly after 1676. It is perhaps of interest to note that Fleuriau's wife is mentioned throughout the record as actively assisting him in his work on the chapel.

[19]"La terre et seigneurie d'Armenonville avec les circonstances et dépendances."

[20]"La chapelle fut entièrement reparée, car auparavant elle n'estoit ny lambrissée, ny pavée, et fort obscure; et on la mist en L'Estat où elle se voit aprésent."

[21]"M. et Mme. Fleuriau firent faire le grand autel avec celuy de la Sainte Vièrge, et les Lalustrées, où le temps et largent ne furent point espargnes pour que le tout fust mieux et de plus long durée." Unfortunately, all these interior fittings were destroyed at the time of the Revolution.

[22]"Ils firent faire la sacristie [illegible], le pignon de Lad. chapelle, et y firent placer de grandes auremoires pour mettre toute sorte d'ornements pour l'office divin."

[23]Monnoye's statues were probably destroyed at the Revolution; it would be incredible if the interior furnishings had been destroyed and the statues left intact. Thus in all likelihood the present figures represent folk art of the early nineteenth century, with a Baroque flavour. However, it is conceivable the statues could have been removed to a safe place during the Revolution; certainly there is nothing about their style to preclude a seventeenth-century date.

church being found too small, M. Fleuriau had it lengthened by about 3 *toises* [roughly twenty feet]," an operation which probably involved moving the façade forward and inserting an extra section of wall. The seignior took this opportunity "to have a clocher built, which everyone finds a very handsome piece of architecture."[24] The enlarged chapel was ready by 1673, and a regular curé duly appointed. In 1676 a gilded tabernacle was installed and the new clocher provided with bells;[25] unfortunately, lightning struck the clocher the very next year, and it had to be rebuilt. But from that time until now, the Armenonville chapel has remained substantially unchanged,[26] and in it we may see all the essential features of the Quebec parish church tradition as we know it from the Age of Laval. (Plates XLIV, XLVI, XLVII.)

There are a few differences. The churches of New France did not have apse buttresses, of course; but those at Armenonville (Plate XLV) are easily explained as vestiges of the older thirteenth-century building on the site.[27] And

[24]"La dite église s'estant trouvée trop petite . . . M. Fleuriau la fist acroistre d'environ 3 toises, et en même temps firent faire un clocher que tout le monde trouve d'une architecture très jolie."

There is nothing in the record about the façade being moved, but a good deal of evidence points to this conclusion: (1) the sections of the interior walls nearest the front of the church are treated differently from the rest, having a pair of pilasters which help the last two cross-beams support the weight of the clocher: it is a fair assumption that they were added later, and in building them provision was made for the clocher being planned at the same time; (2) the plate breaks off at the pilasters, indicating that the wall originally projected only to the point where the pilasters now are; (3) the two last cross-beams are square in shape, the others hexagonal, indicating that they date from different periods of construction; (4) the fenestration of the south wall of the church is irregular—after four windows spaced at regular intervals, the fifth, nearest the west end, is set off at quite a distance from the rest, between the pilasters, suggesting that this section of wall was added later (cf. Plates XLV, XLVI).

[25]"Lorsque l'Eglise nestoit encore que chapelle, elle avait deux cloches placées dans le haut du pignon d'icelle [Peter Kalm described the church at Baie-Saint-Paul in New France, built about 1675, as having a clocher of this sort, with a bell "fixed above the roof, in the open air"; *P.K.T.*, p. 483] dont l'inscription faisoit voir qu'elles estoient de plus de deux cents ans; on les suspendit dans le nouveau clocher. . . ." Unfortunately, in the process one bell was broken; it was thereupon decided to melt both the old bells down and cast a new one, to which was added a second.

[26]The records in the *Livre de Comptes* show an increasing decline in the parish life of Armenonville after Fleuriau's time, and it is this neglect which undoubtedly accounts for the survival of the building. After the first curé's enthusiastic account of the founding of the parish and the building of its church, there follow increasingly perfunctory and routine entries by one or two of his successors, up to 1740; then they break off for a century. In 1850 another priest adds several pages to bring the record up to date; he describes the Revolution, during which the church was plundered so that only the walls, clocher, and roof remained intact. He then extols Bonaparte's support of the Church, and describes how the destroyed furnishings were restored in the early nineteenth century. From 1850 until World War II the Armenonville church remained secure; then, during the German occupation of France, a nearby munitions dump was blown up by bombers, and the explosion blew out the glass of the church and shook some plaster loose from the walls. In 1944 the church was looted by retreating German soldiers; in 1950 the damage had not yet been repaired, but plans for restoration were being considered.

[27]There were probably side buttresses as well, which would explain why the thirteenth-century chapel was described as "fort obscure."

there is nothing in New France comparable to the ceiling treatment at Armenon-ville, either in its exposed timber framing, or its curious painted patterns[28] (Plates XLVI, XLVIII). However, since no really reliable evidence for the ceiling treatment of Laval's parish churches survives, it is quite possible that the Armenonville ceiling preserves something of their original appearance; this is a point we have dealt with elsewhere.[29] Such painted patterns may well be what Lapotherie is describing in 1695 for the chapel of the "Fort des Messieurs" in Montreal: "The walls are adorned with panelling, on which are [painted?] orna-ments, such as urns, niches, pilasters and pedestals having the appearance of red marble, white-veined."[30]

But the similarities are overwhelming. The practice of clapboarding, so common in early New France, was evidently found at Armenonville.[31] At Armenonville the apse was roofed in seven panels, exactly the construction specified in an extant contract for a church at Trois-Rivières between 1645 and 1650.[32] The sacristy added to the Armenonville chapel in 1660 may have been intended as one arm of a Latin-cross plan; however, there is no evidence that the balancing chapel was ever begun, and the plan as it now stands resembles that of several churches in New France, in particular Bonsecours chapel in Montreal as built in 1675 (Figure 5). Most striking of all are the similarities in façade and clocher (Plate XLIV). Compare the façade of Armenonville, as begun in 1660 and apparently rebuilt in the years 1671–1673 to facilitate enlargement of the church, with those of Saint-Laurent, I.O., or Sainte-Anne de Beaupré (Plates XLIX, VI, VII); the medieval elements of steep gable and rose window (or *œil de bouc*, as it would have been called in Canada) are combined with academic features such as niches and keystone arch in exactly the same way.[33]

[28]There is no documentary evidence that these patterns at Armenonville were painted in the seventeenth century. However, such a date is indicated both by stylistic considerations and by the fact that practically nothing in the way of repairs or embellishment seems to have been done to the chapel after Fleuriau's time.

[29]Cf. chap. III, p. 43.

[30]Quoted in P.-G. Roy, *Vieux Manoirs, Vieilles Maisons*, p. 5.

[31]At some later time the clapboarding seems to have been removed from the Armenonville church and replaced by a coat of plaster and whitewash. It is unfortunate that there is no record of when this was done, because it might help to fix the date of parallel development in New France. It was probably sometime in the early eighteenth century in New France; the first reference I have been able to locate to this practice occurs in the records of the first church of Saint-Augustin, Portneuf, begun in 1719 and completed in 1724: "Cette même année 1724, le premier jour de juillet, on a commencé à renduire l'Eglise, pour la blanchir en suitte" (A. Béchard, *Histoire de la paroisse de Saint-Augustin, Portneuf*, Quebec, 1885, p. 66). Whitewash and plaster seems to have been a more economical substitute for clapboards; in New France, the practice also fulfilled the function of clapboards in protect-ing the walls against frost.

[32]Cf. chap. II, p. 20.

[33]The combination of fieldstone construction with cut-stone framing of door and oculus at Armenonville corresponds remarkably with Mère Marie de l'Incarnation's description of the construction of the 1641 Ursuline convent in Quebec: "Quand je dis que nos maisons sont de pierres, je ne veux pas dire qu'elles soient de pierres de taille; non, il n'y a que les

And the clocher of the Armenonville church, in arrangement and proportion of drum, lanterns, and flèche, is precisely the characteristic clocher of the Quebec tradition—essentially a fusion of Renaissance cupola and Gothic spire. In proportion to the building, the Armenonville clocher is somewhat larger than those with which we are familiar in New France; but clochers of this proportion are not unknown there, particularly in the Montreal area. As for some minor differences in handling the elements of the clocher, we shall deal with them in a moment.

For the present, it is clear that the church of Armenonville-les-Gatineaux is to all intents and purposes a Quebec parish church of the Age of Laval. And this fact, I suggest, has three important consequences. First, as we have discussed, its very presence in a place where, following the premises of our thesis, it ought to be, strongly tends to confirm that thesis. We may take it as reasonably established that the Quebec tradition of parish church architecture was no simple offshoot of some regional French school, but from earliest times something complex and relatively advanced.

However, the existence of a Quebec parish church at Armenonville is in no way to be taken as proof that the Quebec tradition originated in the Ile-de-France region. What we are actually dealing with is something more in the nature of a coincidence; the fusion of craft and academic elements that took place in the Ile-de-France is a parallel to the development in New France, not its origin. And this becomes evident, I think, when we examine certain discrepancies in detail between the church at Armenonville and the Quebec type. At Armenonville there is no real distinction between the lower lantern of the clocher and the drum on which it rests; the lantern roofs have a decidedly domical form; and the side chapel or sacristy is considerably lower than the main body of the church. In the Quebec tradition we find that the lower lantern and drum of the clocher are clearly separate elements;[34] the lantern roofs are customarily splayed out at the bottom; and lateral chapels, certainly in the Age of Laval, are almost invariably the same height as the nave. Now these are minor points; they do not affect our central thesis of the origin of the Quebec parish church in a fusion of traditions. But they are of great significance in one respect, because they are the kind of details for which a local craft tradition is responsible, and

encognures qui sont d'une espèce de marbre presque noir qui se tire par coupeaux assez bien faits. Les encognures étant de cette sorte de pierre sont très belles; mais elles coûtent à tailler à cause de la dureté." Letter dated August 26, 1644, quoted by Antoine Roy, *L.S.A.*, p. 164. Roy points out that "encognures" here does not mean "quoins." The earliest evidence of quoins in New France known to me is on Chaussegros de Léry's drawing of the Cathedral of Quebec, assuming it represents that building as of 1684 (Plate X). After that date, they become common in the church architecture of Quebec; cf. the 1689 church of Sainte-Anne de Beaupré (Plate VII), the 1710 parish church of Trois-Rivières (Plate XXXII), the Récollet church of Montreal, begun 1712 (Plate XXIII), etc.

[34] Although isolated examples similar to Armenonville occur; cf., e.g., the Récollet church of Quebec in 1693 (Plate XIX).

the divergence between Armenonville and the Quebec type in them therefore implies that the local craft tradition of the Ile-de-France was not the one that went into the architecture of Quebec. For that we evidently must look elsewhere, and the place to look is obvious; we have seen both that literary evidence indicates a predominance of Norman craftsmen in early New France, and that in all these details under consideration the craft tradition of Normandy and Brittany parallels that of Quebec. I suggest, then, that the second significance of the Armenonville church is this: it enables us to understand the true nature of Norman-Breton influence on the architecture of French Canada. That influence was not responsible for the whole of the Quebec tradition—but it was the main source of the craft root of it. To this extent, the older chroniclers of Quebec are borne out.

And finally, these two conclusions lead us to the point where we can give a fuller significance to that later statement, "One would search France vainly for a Quebec parish church." It is true; there were regions in France, like the Ile-de-France, where a fusion of tradition similar to that which produced the parish church of Quebec took place, but nowhere was the combination of elements exactly the same. The parish church tradition of Quebec is in this sense entirely indigenous, entirely unique; one of which French Canada can most justly be proud.

# APPENDIX

## A *CATALOGUE RAISONNÉ* OF CHURCH ARCHITECTURE IN NEW FRANCE, 1615-1760

*"Churches" and "Chapels."* Properly speaking, a "church" (*église*) would be a building used for regular services and celebrations of the Mass in a specific parish, by a priest attached to that parish. A "chapel" (*chapelle*) would be a building used for intermittent services and occasional celebrations of the Mass by an itinerant priest or missionary. In documentary designation, however, this distinction does not appear ever to have been observed with any strictness. From 1608 to 1721 all New France was ecclesiastically considered as a mission; Notre-Dame de Québec was not erected as a parish until 1664. Hence, no structure in New France of the period between the foundation and 1664 could properly be called a "church"; yet this appellation occurs often in early documents. For example, a contract of 1649 calls for a "church" (*église*) to be built at Trois-Rivières, although this was certainly not a fixed parish. And the *Plan général de l'état présent des missions du Canada fait en l'année 1683* seems to use the terms "church" and "chapel" indiscriminately.

It is possible that in early New France a "church" generally meant a building provided with a permanent altar and other necessities for the Mass, in distinction to a "chapel" where the officiant brought his own. But in Mgr de Saint-Vallier's letter of 1687 describing the state in which he left the Church in Canada in that year, he specifically mentions "churches" on the Beaupré coast which lacked sacred vessels, ornaments, robes, and baptismal fonts. Again, the so-called "Chapelle Saint-Jean" of 1650 near Quebec was served regularly by a priest—the Abbé de Saint-Sauveur—who lived with Jean Bourdon and his family, the builders; it undoubtedly must have had a permanent altar and other fixtures.

In compiling the following list, I have therefore followed whatever seems to have been the current usage in the nomenclature of each building. Generally speaking, a "chapel" would indicate a small building, and a "church" a larger one. This distinction, unsatisfactory though it is in the case of those structures which were neither very small nor particularly large, seems about the only one possible.

*"Eglises consacrées" and "Eglises bénies."* Another distinction, more strictly observed perhaps by earlier writers than later ones, is that between an *église consacrée* and an *église bénie*. This is a fine distinction, generally not followed in English usage, which translates both *consacrée* and *bénie* by "consecrated." An *église consacrée* is a church which has been formally consecrated by a special ceremony of the Roman Catholic Church, and so set apart from ordinary churches. Any church, however, before the Mass may be celebrated in it, must be *bénie*. The first *église consacrée* in New France was Notre-Dame de Québec, in 1666, followed by the Ursuline chapel, which was *consacrée* in 1667. The whole question is lucidly presented by Pierre-Georges Roy in the *Bulletin des recherches historiques,* I, 1895, pp. 90–91.

In compiling the *catalogue raisonné,* I have made no distinction between *consacrée* and *bénie,* following general English usage.

## 1615-1665 (CHAPTER II)

1615    Quebec, first parish chapel. Built by the Récollets, and dedicated to l'Immaculée-Conception de la Sainte Vierge.[1] The Récollets, or Ordre des Frères Mineurs (Franciscans), were the first missionaries in New France. They arrived at Tadoussac, with Champlain, on May 25, 1615, and established themselves at Quebec a few days later. Father Jean Dolbeau said the first Mass in the chapel on June 25, 1615.[2] Since the chapel took only a month to be ready for services, it was likely of the simplest design. It served, however, as a parish church until 1629, when it was destroyed by the Kirke brothers, who captured the city of Quebec in that year.[3]

   1. Odoric-M. Jouve, "Les Titulaires des deux premières églises de Québec," *B.R.H.,* XLIV, 1938, pp. 257–273 and 289–301. Jouve's article is a refutation of two previous articles by Hugolin Lemay, in *La Revue franciscaine* (Montreal), Oct., 1936, and July, 1937, which would claim that both the chapel in question and the Récollet church of 1621 were dedicated to Saint-Charles-Borromée. His primary source of proof is Bertrand de La Tour, *Mémoire sur la vie de M. de Laval,* Cologne, 1751.
   2. *V.d.Q.,* I, pp. 51–52.
   3. *Ibid.,* pp. 53–54. Roy's source is primarily Chrétien Leclercq, *Le Premier Etablissement de la foi dans la Nouvelle-France.* The latter work is available in an English translation by J. G. Shea, published in New York, 1881. Leclercq (fl. 1641–1695) spells the name of the first officiating father in the church "d'Olbeau."

1617    Tadoussac, first chapel. Built of *écorce* (bark) by Father Le Caron, Récollet, as combined residence and chapel, it was a typical primitive structure. In 1629, when the Récollets left New France, the chapel was abandoned to ruin.[1]

   1. *V.E.,* p. 179.

1618    Trois-Rivières, first chapel. Similar to the Tadoussac chapel, it too was built by a Récollet missionary, Father Paul Huet. Abandoned in 1619.[1]

>    1. Benjamin Sulte, *Histoire de la ville de Trois-Rivières,* Montreal, 1870, p. 42 f.

1621    Quebec, church of Notre-Dame-des-Anges. Built by the Récollet fathers, beside their residence of the same name. From a letter written by Father Denis Jamet in 1620, we learn that the Récollets used half of the lower floor of this residence as a chapel "while waiting better," i.e., the completion of their church.[1] The first stone of this church, marked with the arms of France and those of the Prince de Condé, viceroy of New France, was laid June 3, 1620, by Father Dolbeau, who may have designed the church in its broad lines. Finished, it was dedicated to Notre-Dame-des-Anges on May 25, 1621. The English under Kirke ruined the building in 1629, and there is some confusion about its subsequent history. Apparently it was repaired and used by the Jesuits after 1632.[2] A letter by the Jesuit Father Thierry Beschefer in 1666 describes "the little chapel . . . we are using at present" as "very well ornamented with fine decorations, large silver chandeliers, lamps, and all the rest"; this may be the same one.[3] In 1666, however, the Jesuits were building their own church, and upon its completion, Notre-Dame-des-Anges was allowed to fall into decrepitude. When the Récollets returned to Quebec in 1670 they decided their old chapel was beyond repair, and began to construct a new building.

>    1. *V.d.Q.,* I, pp. 75–76.
>    2. *V.E.,* pp. 17–18.
>    3. Quoted from the *Jesuit Relations* in *B.R.H.,* XXXV, 1929, p. 335.

1626    Quebec, Jesuit chapel of Notre-Dame-des-Anges. The Jesuits arrived at Quebec June 15, 1625, coming on the invitation of the Récollets. They lived at first in the Récollet house of Notre-Dame-des-Anges; in August, 1625, they began work on a building of their own.[1] This structure was finished in April, 1626, and contained a small chapel dedicated, like the Récollet church, to Notre-Dame-des-Anges. The Jesuit house and the chapel were destroyed by the English in 1629. In 1632, on their return to Quebec, the Jesuits repaired the Récollet house and church of Notre-Dame-des-Anges; Father Le Jeune, writing in the *Jesuit Relation* for 1632, describes the same arrangement—chapel occupying half of the lower storey of the house—as the original one described by Father Jamet in 1620.[2] In 1648 the Jesuits built a new residence, in stone, under the direction of Frère Liégeois. It contained no chapel, the Fathers continuing to use the Récollet church of 1621, and serving in the church of Notre-Dame-de-la-Paix (1647).[3]

>    1. *V.d.Q.,* I, pp. 85–86.
>    2. *Ibid.,* I, pp. 141–142.
>    3. *Ibid.,* I, pp. 231–232.

1633    Quebec, parish church of Notre-Dame-de-Recouvrance. Built by Champlain, fulfilling a vow he made on condition Quebec were returned to France. It was the only parish church in Quebec from 1633 to 1640, when it was destroyed by fire (June 15). Champlain was buried in Notre-Dame-de-Recouvrance in 1635.[1]

1. *V.d.Q.*, I, pp. 117–118; N.-E. Dionne, "Notre-Dame-de-Recouvrance," *Kermesse* (Quebec), 1892–1893, p. 165.

1634    Trois-Rivières, second chapel. Built by the Jesuits who came with Champlain when he founded a strong post at Trois-Rivières in 1634, it was dedicated to l'Immaculée-Conception-de-Marie. The *Jesuit Relation* for 1635 contains a report on this chapel as follows: "Notre maison, en ce premier commencement, n'était que quelques bûches de bois jointes les unes auprès des autres, enduites par les ouverture d'un peu de terre, et couvertes d'herbes; nous avions en tout douze pieds en quarré pour la chapelle et pour notre demeure, attendant qu'un bâtiment de charpente qu'on dressait fut achevé."[1]

1. Benjamin Sulte, *Histoire de la ville de Trois-Rivières,* Montreal, 1870, p. 69.

1635    Beauport, first chapel (?). The only reference to this structure known to me occurs in an article on the church of Beauport in *L'Action Catholique* for February 10, 1923. This states only that the first chapel at Beauport was built in 1635. Since Champlain had re-established himself at Quebec only two years before, this chapel must have been of the smallest and most primitive sort, built at the time of the first settlement of the locality. Replaced by a stone church in 1672.

1636    Quebec, "Champlain's Chapel." Champlain's body was buried in Notre-Dame-de-Recouvrance in 1635. The following year, Governor de Montmagny built a chapel to his memory which was called indiscriminately "La Chapelle du Gouverneur" or "La Chapelle de Champlain." Presumably located near Notre-Dame-de-Recouvrance, it existed until about 1665.[1]

1. *V.d.Q.*, I, pp. 147–148; Ernest Myrand, "La Chapelle de Champlain," *B.R.H.*, IV, 1898, p. 290.

1638    Quebec, chapel of the Hôtel-Dieu begun. Three sisters of the order of Sœurs Hermites de Saint-Augustin, of Dieppe, were sent out to Canada in 1639, to take charge of the Hôtel-Dieu of Quebec.[1] The foundations of this building, which was to be financed by a grant from the Duchesse d'Aiguillon, were laid August 12, 1638. Work progressed only slowly, however, and in 1640, while waiting for its completion, the Sisters decided to go to Sillery. In 1644 Governor de Montmagny, believing it unfeasible to fortify both Quebec and Sillery against the Iroquois, requested the Sisters to return to the capital, whereupon work on the Hôtel-Dieu was pushed to completion in the fall of that year.[2] Lahontan in 1684 especially commended the Sisters of the Hôtel-Dieu, "who take a particular Care of the Sick, tho' themselves are poor, and but ill lodg'd."[3] In 1696, however, this situation was rectified with a new building, which was finished in 1698.

1. *B.R.H.*, L, 1944, p. 33.
2. *V.d.Q.*, I, pp. 159–160.
3. R. G. Thwaites (ed.), *Lahontan's New Voyages to North-America*, Chicago, 1905, letter III, p. 39 f.

*circa*
**1638**
Sillery, Jesuit chapel dedicated to Saint-Joseph. The Jesuit residence of Saint-Joseph de Sillery was begun in 1637, and the church attached to it some little time after.[1] A Jesuit father at Trois-Rivières, writing in 1640, declares, "We have a church for the savages at Trois-Rivières, which, since it is not as old as that of Sillery, is not yet as flourishing"; the church must therefore have been in existence at that time.[2] In 1663, when a declaration of lands held by the Jesuits at Sillery was made, the establishment was prosperous: "The aforesaid Fathers have had a stone fort, flanked by four turrets, constructed; here the Indians take refuge, living in security with the Fathers, who have built in the fort a chapel, as well as a house in which they live."[3] The date of the destruction of this chapel is uncertain; the present buildings are mainly nineteenth century in date, although some vestiges of the original construction may survive.

1. "La Maison des Jesuites à Sillery," *B.R.H.*, XXXI, 1925, p. 241.
2. Benjamin Sulte, *Chronique trifluvienne*, Montreal, 1879, p. 6.
3. H.-A. Scott, *Notre-Dame de Sainte Foy, 1541–1670*, Quebec, 1902, p. 393 f.

*circa*
**1640**
Trois-Rivières, third chapel. Mentioned by a Jesuit father writing in 1640. A new church was projected between 1645 and 1650, but was not built until 1664.[1] A detailed contract for the projected new church is extant in the Archives de la Province de Québec;[2] the contract is quoted above, in chapter II.

1. Benjamin Sulte, *Chronique trifluvienne,* Montreal, 1879, pp. 6, 123 f.
2. See the text in *B.R.H.*, XXXI, 1925, p. 192.

**1640**
Quebec, chapel in the house of the Compagnie des Cent-Associés. Following the destruction of Notre-Dame-de-Recouvrance by fire in 1640, a chapel in this building was fitted out and used for services until the completion of Notre-Dame-de-la-Paix in 1647. Despite its makeshift character, it was rather grandiloquently styled "l'église de la Conception de la Bienheureuse Marie à Québec" by Father Vimont, who officiated in it.[1]

1. *V.E.*, p. 1.

**1641**
Tadoussac, second chapel. In 1640 the Jesuits came to Tadoussac to re-establish the mission abandoned by the Récollets. Father de Quen in the *Jesuit Relations* for 1641 wrote: "The savages express general rejoicing over my arrival. They are erecting for me a *cabane* separate from theirs, to serve at once as chapel and residence."[1] This would imply a rough wooden structure; but the same source records Father de Quen's mention

of "bricks carried up, that had been brought for building the house at Tadoussac."[2] Auguste Gosselin, speaking of churches in existence in 1660, described the Tadoussac chapel as a "pretty little stone church."[3] He may, however, have been referring to the 1661 building at Tadoussac, which definitely was of stone. Whatever the character of this second chapel, it was replaced by a third building in 1661.

1. *V.E.*, p. 179 f.
2. R. G. Thwaites (ed.), *The Jesuit Relations and Other Documents*, XXVI, Cleveland, 1898, p. 119.
3. Quoted by R.-E. Casgrain, *Histoire de la paroisse de l'Ange-Gardien*, Quebec, 1902, p. 40.

1641    Quebec, chapel in the first Ursuline convent. The Ursulines arrived in Quebec in 1639, and established themselves in a house in Lower Town while awaiting the building of a convent. The first stone of this building was laid in the spring of 1641; on November 21, 1642, the Ursulines moved into their new quarters.[1] This convent is described in some detail in a letter from the Mother Superior of the Ursulines to her son in Paris.[2] In December, 1650, there was a fire in the convent, also described by the Mother Superior;[3] apparently, however, the stone walls of the building remained intact. The damage was not fully repaired until 1667.

1. *V.d.Q.*, I, pp. 165–166.
2. Benjamin Sulte, *Lettres historiques de la Vénérable Mère Marie de l'Incarnation*, pp. 29, 64, quoted by Ramsay Traquair, *The Old Architecture of Quebec*, Toronto, 1947, p. 10.
3. Quoted by P.-G. Roy, *V.d.Q.*, I, pp. 211–212. Cf. p. 40, n. 71.

1642    Montreal, first parish chapels, dedicated to Notre-Dame. Maisonneuve and
1643    his companions founded Montreal, which they named Ville-Marie, in 1642, and in that year built a primitive *cabane d'écorce* to serve as a parish church.[1] This structure was replaced the next year by a more solidly built chapel of wood. This latter building was known as the "Chapelle du Fort," to distinguish it from the little *oratoire* of 1644 attached to the Hôtel-Dieu, where services were also held. The "Chapelle du Fort" existed until 1656.[2]

1. *A.V.M.*, I, p. 315.
2. *Ibid.*, p. 340 f.

1644    Montreal, chapel of the Hôtel-Dieu. The Hospitalières de Saint-Joseph, an order of nursing sisters, was founded at La Flèche in 1636.[1] Their leader, Jeanne Mance, went to Paris in 1640 seeking support for her project to establish the Hospitalières in Canada.[2] Finding a wealthy patron in Mme de Bullion, she embarked for Canada in 1641, arriving at Quebec in the autumn of that year. In 1642 she came to Montreal. By an agreement signed January 12, 1644, the Hospitalières were established at Montreal, and in that year the first building of the Hôpital de Ville-Marie was erected. Beside it was built a little stone *oratoire* 9 or 10 feet square (?) wherein services were held conjointly with those of the "Chapelle du Fort".

The second chapel or church of Notre-Dame in Montreal, built in 1656, was erected beside the Hôtel-Dieu, and replaced both the parish chapel of 1643 and the *oratoire*.[3]

1. *A.V.M.*, I, p. 59, notes 1 and 2.
2. *A.V.M.*, II, p. 8 f; C. Bertrand, *Histoire de Montréal*, I, Montreal, 1935, p. 35 f.
3. *A.V.M.*, I, p. 59 f.

1647    Quebec, church of Notre-Dame-de-la-Paix. The decade 1640–1650 was a particularly hard time for New France, and it was not until 1645, five years after the destruction of Notre-Dame-de-Recouvrance, that plans were drawn up for building a new church, and then only with the liberal assistance of the Jesuits, who were very largely responsible for the project. The corner-stone was not laid until September 23, 1647, but the name decided upon in 1645, Notre-Dame-de-la-Paix—celebrating a treaty concluded with the Iroquois in that year—was retained. The slow progress of the building attests not only the troubled times in the colony, but that it was a sizable structure. A contract signed September 20, 1648, which copies earlier contracts of 1646 and 1647 with the craftsmen in charge, shows that at this stage the work was still far from complete. It names as masons Denis Bochard, Jacob Desbordes, and Jean Garnier; as carpenter, Nicolas Pelletier.[1] When completed, the church was 80 feet long and 38 feet wide, on a Latin-cross plan, with a wooden clocher over the transept.[2] The first Mass in the church was celebrated on Christmas Eve, 1650, but regular services were not inaugurated until 1657.[3] This church was consecrated as a cathedral church in 1666 by Laval, at which time it underwent considerable repairs. Between 1684 and 1687 it was thoroughly remodelled, and became to all intents and purposes a new church.

1. The text of this contract is published in part in *B.R.H.*, VII, 1901, p. 269 f. Cf. chap. II, pp. 25–26.
2. Auguste Gosselin, *Henri de Bernières*, Quebec, 1902, p. 158 f.
3. *V.E.*, p. 1 f.; *V.d.Q.*, I, pp. 179–180.

1650    Quebec, the "Chapelle Saint-Jean." In the summer of 1634 Jean Bourdon, a native of Rouen, came to Quebec, and in 1637 established himself outside the city, in a locality known as the *Coteau Sainte-Geneviève*, where he had been granted fifteen *arpents* of land. He prospered; in 1659 another twelve *arpents* were granted him, and the two grants were consolidated as a fief by an act of the Compagnie des Cent-Associés dated March 19, 1661. In the Acte de Foi et Hommage which he made the year before he died, on December 16, 1667, it is stated that there is in his fief "a large building [*corps de logis*] and a small one in which there is a chapel. . . ."[1] This chapel was built by Bourdon for the use of his family in 1650. It was consecrated by Father Ragueneau, the Superior of the Jesuit missions in Canada, in November of 1650. Being regularly served by the Abbé de Saint-Sauveur, who lived with the Bourdon family, it came to be looked on as a parish church by those living in the neighbourhood; Mgr de Laval mentions it as such in his report to the Holy See in 1660. After Bourdon's death in 1668 it apparently lapsed into ruin; when his fief was sold in 1677, the existence of a chapel is not mentioned in the contract.[2]

1. *B.R.H.*, XXVII, 1921, p. 101. According to J.-E. Roy, "La Cartographie et l'arpentage sous le régime français," *B.R.H.*, I, 1895, pp. 17, 18, Jean Bourdon, engineer, surveyor, *procureur-général au Conseil Supérieur,* for thirty years (1634–1668) directed most of the important construction projects of New France.
2. *V.d.Q.*, I, pp. 203–204.

1656    Montreal, second parish church. Proposed by Maisonneuve to replace the "Chapelle du Fort" in 1654, the first stone was not laid until August 28, 1656. Financial difficulties handicapped the building throughout; it was finally built largely at the personal expense of the seigniors of Montreal and with help from the Hôtel-Dieu. It was built of wood, and finished in 1659. Located beside the Hôtel-Dieu on St. Paul Street, it replaced in function both the 1643 parish church and the little *oratoire* built in 1644 beside the Hôtel-Dieu. The church was about 50 feet long, and had a clocher "de forme régulier et élégant, avec deux cloches."[1]

1. *A.V.M.*, I, p. 343 f.

1657    Montreal, project for a chapel to Notre-Dame-de-Bonsecours. The first religious order founded in Canada was the order of the Sœurs de la Congrégation Notre-Dame, which was ecclesiastically recognized April 30, 1658.[1] It was organized by Mère Marguerite Bourgeoys, declared Venerable December 7, 1878. In 1657 Mère Bourgeoys gathered materials for the erection of a devotional chapel to the Virgin, but M. de Queylus, leader of the Sulpicians, who had arrived in Montreal to take charge of the city's ecclesiastical life in 1657, withheld his consent to the building. Internal difficulties in Montreal caused further delays; the project was finally abandoned, and the assembled materials dispersed.[2]

1. *B.R.H.*, L, 1944, p. 3.
2. *V.E.*, p. 25.

1658    Sainte-Anne de Beaupré, the "Chapelle des Matelots." A small devotional shrine, replaced by a church in 1660.[1]

1. "La 'Chapelle des Matelots' à Sainte-Anne de Beaupré," *B.R.H.*, XXIX, 1923, p. 141. This is based upon a study which was made by Father Georges Bélanger in the *Annales de la Bonne Sainte-Anne de Beaupré*, April, 1923.

1658    Château-Richer, first church. Dedicated to the Visitation, it was begun in 1658 by Abbé de Queylus. It was apparently in wood, for the Bishop of Quebec, following his policy of consecrating only solid and durable structures, refused to dedicate it for worship until 1685.[1] At this time it was apparently rebuilt in stone.[2]

1. Laval's policy in this matter is referred to in the well-known letter of

Duchesneau to Seignelay, November 13, 1681, *Correspondance générale*, vol. 275, quoted by W. B. Munro, *The Seigniorial System in Canada*, New York, 1907, p. 185, n. 3.

2. "Notes historiques sur la paroisse de Château-Richer," *B.R.H.*, XXXIX, 1933, p. 716 f.

1659    Cap-de-la-Madeleine, first chapel. In a communication to the Holy See in 1661 Bishop Laval writes, "The Jesuits had a residence on the Cap, and two years ago a wooden church was built and dedicated to Sainte-Marie-Magdeleine; the savages came to it from all over in great numbers."[1] This chapel, or church, was about 20 feet square. In 1661 a second church was built in stone,[2] serving as a parish church for French settlers.

1. E.-Z. Massicotte, "Notes diverses sur le Cap-de-la-Madeleine," *B.R.H.*, XXXV, 1929, p. 390.
2. *V.E.*, p. 57.

1660    Sainte-Anne de Beaupré, first church. Already in 1665 Mère Marie-de-l'Incarnation was writing: "A sept lieues de Québec il y a un bourg appelé le Petit-Cap, où il y a une église de sainte Anne dans laquelle Notre Seigneur fait de grandes merveilles en faveur de cette sainte Mère de la Sainte Vierge. On y voit marcher les paralytiques, les aveugles recevoir la vue, et les malades, de quelque maladie que ce soit, recouvrer la santé." Replaced by the second church in 1676.[1]

1. "La 'Chapelle des Matelots' à Sainte-Anne de Beaupré," *B.R.H.*, XXIX, 1923, p. 141.

1661    Tadoussac, first church. Built to replace the 1641 chapel under the direction of Father de Quen, who by this time was Superior of the Jesuit Missions in France. Unfortunately, however, the new church was gutted by fire only three years later. Not until 1747 was another church built at Tadoussac. In 1720, a writer noted that the stone foundations and gable of the 1661 church were still visible.[1]

1. *V.E.*, p. 179 f.

1661    Cap-de-la-Madeleine, second chapel. Two years after building the first chapel at Cap-de-la-Madeleine, the governor of Trois-Rivières had it moved to a more defensible position and rebuilt on a somewhat larger scale. This second chapel, although only 30 feet long by 18 feet wide, served as a parish church until 1719, when it was replaced by the extant church begun in 1714.[1]

1. *V.E.*, p. 57 f.

1664    Trois-Rivières, first church. A church to replace the 1640 chapel had been projected as far back as 1645, but interminable delays intervened. *Marguilliers* (wardens) for the new church were elected in 1661, and ground for building was acquired in 1663.[1] Finally in 1664 the church was built, but again it was only a wooden structure.[2] It was replaced by another wooden church in 1682.[3]

1. Benjamin Sulte, *Chronique trifluvienne*, Montreal, 1879, p. 123 f.

2. Benjamin Sulte, "L'Eglise paroissiale," *Mélanges historiques,* XIX, 1932, p. 33 and n. 10.

3. Odoric-M. Jouve, *Les Franciscains et le Canada: Aux Trois-Rivières*, Paris, 1934, p. 32 f.

## 1665–1700 (CHAPTER III)

1665    Chambly, chapel in the fort. Typical of many early settlements, Chambly was a combination of military fort, trading post, and mission station. The 1665 fort was built *en pieux*: the chapel, served by the Jesuits, was of wood.[1] Rebuilt in stone in 1710, the fort always had a garrison and resident priest.[2]

1. Jacques Viger, *Archéologie religieuse du diocèse de Montréal,* Montreal, 1850, p. 9.

2. F.-A. Baillargé, "Le Fort de Chambly," *B.R.H.,* XV, 1909, p. 32.

1666    Quebec, second Jesuit church (Plates XIV, XV). The first Jesuit church, Notre-Dame-des-Anges, was built in 1626 and destroyed in 1629. From 1633 on, the Jesuits occupied the old Récollet residence of Notre-Dame-des-Anges, repaired it, and used its chapel. This latter is the building referred to as the church of the Jesuits by Asseline de Rouval, *Voyage de Canada en la Nouvelle-France* (1662).[1] Since the Jesuits also served in and were associated with the building of the parish churches of Notre-Dame-de-Recouvrance and Notre-Dame-de-la-Paix, it should be noted that these structures also are at times referred to as the "Jesuit church." The distinction between these two parish churches, and the two seventeenth-century churches connected with the Jesuit residence in Quebec, should be kept in mind. The second Jesuit church was begun in 1666, as we learn from Jesuit Father Thierry Beschefer's letter of 1666:[2] "We [the Jesuits] have this year begun a church, which will be finished next year. . . . It is 100 feet long by 30 feet wide." Being the largest church built up to this time in New France, the Jesuit church was an outstanding feature of the little city. Lahontan, who saw it in 1684, called it "fair, stately, and well lighted," and made especial note of the great altar, "adorn'd with four great Cylindrical Columns of one Stone; The Stone being a sort of *Canada* Porphyry, and black as Jet, without either Spots or Veins."[3] Even the usually critical commentator Charlevoix, who claimed that the Jesuit college "disfigures the city," was forced to concede that the church had a "handsome steeple; it is entirely roofed with slate, and is the only one in all Canada which has this advantage: all the buildings here being generally covered with shingles." He also remarked that the church was "very much ornamented on the inside: the gallery is bold, light, and well wrought, and is surrounded with an iron balustrade, painted and gilt, and of excellent workmanship: the pulpit is all gilt, and the work both in iron and wood excellent: there are three altars handsomely designed, some good pictures, and it is without any dome or cupola, but a flat ceiling handsomely ornamented. It has no stone pavement, in place of which it is floored with strong planks, which makes this church supportable in winter, whilst you are pierced with cold in the others."[4] It was described also by Lapotherie as "very handsome. The ceiling is in compartments of squares, filled with various figures and symmetrical ornaments."[5] The exterior was restored around 1730 by Chaussegros de Léry, who added a Jesuit-type façade. Probably at this time also the sun-dial, described by Peter Kalm as "the only one in all Canada," was built. Kalm also commented on the interior: "very fine, but has no seats."[6] Restored c. 1765, the Jesuit church was demolished in 1807, but the College beside it survived until 1877, when it was removed to make way for the present City Hall.[7]

1. Quoted in *B.R.H.*, XXXV, 1929, p. 276.
2. Dated October 4, 1666, this letter is reproduced in the *Jesuit Relations* for 1664–1667, and quoted in *B.R.H.*, XXXV, 1929, p. 335.
3. R. G. Thwaites (ed.), *Lahontan's New Voyages to North-America*, Chicago, 1905, letter III, p. 39 f.
4. Quoted by Alfred Hawkins, *Picture of Quebec*, Quebec, 1834, pp. 192–193.
5. *Ibid.*
6. *P.K.T.*, p. 448.
7. J. M. Lemoine, *Picturesque Quebec,* Montreal, 1882, p. 131; *V.d.Q.*, II, pp. 141–142.

*circa*    Quebec, second chapel in the Ursuline convent. Replacing the 1642 chapel
1668    which was gutted by fire in 1651, the new chapel had been begun in 1656, but the work proceeded very slowly until Governor de Tracy donated 2500 *livres* to the Ursulines, whereupon the work was pushed to a speedy completion. The building was dedicated August 17, 1667, by Laval, "avec une magnificence extraordinaire. Tout y fut ravissant, et les cérémonies y furent exactement à la Romaine." Burnt out again in 1686, this chapel was completely rebuilt in 1720.[1]

1. *V.E.*, p. 145 f. The description of the dedication is that of Mère Marie de l'Incarnation.

*circa*    Laprairie, first chapel. Laprairie was granted to the Jesuits as a seigniory in
1668    1647.[1] From 1667 on they began to colonize it,[2] and in 1668 built a wooden chapel, near the Sault-Saint-Louis. This first chapel was replaced by a second in 1687.[3]

1. "Les Seigneuries des RR. PP. Jésuites," *B.R.H.*, XLI, 1935, pp. 509–511.
2. E.-Z. Massicotte, "Une Page de l'histoire de Laprairie," *B.R.H.*, XXII, 1926, pp. 615–616.
3. Jos. Chevalier, *Laprairie, notes historiques*, Montreal, 1941, p. 49 f.

1668    Gentilly, first chapel, in Fort La Présentation. Connected with an Indian mission at Gentilly, it was adandoned in 1686. The fort was abandoned about 1691.[1] In the report of 1683 it is listed as a *chapelle domestique*.[2]

1. Désiré Girouard, *Lake St. Louis, Old and New*, Montreal, 1893, p. 61 f.
2. *P.G.M.*, p. 123.

1669    Sainte-Foy, first chapel. Built by the Jesuits for their Huron converts. Driven from Huronia (the Georgian Bay region of Ontario) by the Iroquois about 1651, the Christianized Hurons were first settled on the Ile d'Orléans; thence they moved to Sainte-Foy. The inhabitants of this region had previously used the Jesuit church of Saint-Joseph at Sillery; when they began to use the Indian chapel, the Jesuits moved their charges away again, this time to Ancienne-Lorette.[1]

> 1. H.-A. Scott, *Notre-Dame de Sainte-Foy, 1541–1670*, Quebec, 1902, *passim*; Ramsay Traquair, "The Huron Mission Church . . . of Notre Dame de la Jeune Lorette," *McG.U.P.*, no. 28.

1669    Sainte-Famille, I.O., first church. The Ile d'Orléans was for long a dependency of the Seminary of Quebec, since the Bishop of Quebec was also seignior of the Island. The date for the construction of this first church on the Island was established by Marius Barbeau from an examination of the parish archives.[1] In the report of 1683 the parish of Sainte-Famille is recorded as having 51 families, 384 people in all, making it one of the largest in the colony. Its church, too, was impressive, being in stone, 80 feet long by 36 feet wide, although at that time it was "covered in thatch which is worthless and needs repair."[2] Programmes of restoration were carried out in 1702 and 1734. Replaced by the second church, 1743.[3]

> 1. R. Traquair and M. Barbeau, "The Church of Sainte Famille," *McG.U.P.*, no. 13, *passim*.
> 2. *P.G.M.*, p. 117.
> 3. *V.E.*, p. 171 f.

1670    Boucherville, first church. The report of 1683 lists it as in wood, 50 feet long by 25 feet wide, and says "it is not yet finished."[1] This must refer to repairs or alterations, since by 1663 when Pierre Boucher wrote his *Histoire véritable et naturelle des mœurs et productions du pays de la Nouvelle-France,* his seigniory was noted for its prosperity, and certainly Boucher possessed the resources to finish his church begun in 1670. The date of 1670 was established by Huguet-Latour,[2] and followed by Lalande.[3] This church was replaced in 1712.

> 1. *P.G.M.*, p. 126.
> 2. *A.V.M.*, I, p. 275 f.
> 3. L. Lalande, *Une Vieille Seigneurie—Boucherville*, Montreal, 1890.

1670    Montreal, first chapel of Notre-Dame-de-Bonsecours. In 1657 Mère Marguerite Bourgeoys had collected materials to build a small votive chapel, but she was unable to bring the project to completion until 1670, when a diminutive wooden structure was erected. In 1672 Mère Bourgeoys was given a miraculous statue of the Virgin by Pierre Chevrier, Baron de Fancamp, first seignior of the Island of Montreal. The statue was of wood, and rested on a wooden base in which was a relic of Saint-Blaise. Her little chapel speedily became a place of pilgrimage, and in 1675 she was able to replace it with a stone chapel.[1]

> 1. *V.E.*, p. 25 f. For further bibliography, see under the second chapel, 1675.

*circa*   Charlesbourg, first chapel. In 1674 a *habitant* of Charlesbourg made up his
1670      church dues by providing straw for the roof of this building.[1] This is the
          only other reference to what is described in the report of 1683 as "a
          little chapel dedicated to Saint-Charles, which is constructed only *de pieux*
          and is near collapse."[2] Replaced by the first church, in 1695.

> 1. Claude de Bonnault, "La Vie religieuse dans les paroisses rurales cana-
> diennes au dix-huitième siècle," *B.R.H.*, XL, 1934, p. 645 f.
> 2. *P.G.M.*, p. 118.

1671–     Quebec, second Récollet church, now the chapel of the Hôpital-Général. The
1673      Récollet church of Notre-Dame-des-Anges, consecrated in 1621, was in a
          state of ruin when the Récollets returned to Canada after their protracted
          absence, in 1670. The new head of the Récollets in Canada, Father Allard,
          decided upon a complete rebuilding, and Frère Luc drew up the plans.[1]
          The first stone of the new church, like the old one dedicated to Notre-
          Dame-des-Anges, was laid June 22, 1671, by Intendant Talon, and the
          church was consecrated in the summer of 1673. In 1677 Governor Fron-
          tenac added a residence for the Récollets to the church, at his own expense;
          in 1678 a chapel with an apse was added, and in 1679 a sacristy.[2] In 1692
          the church and residence of the Récollets was sold to Mgr de Saint-Vallier
          for use as a hospital. The new Hôpital-Général was intended for invalids and
          other persons permanently afflicted with disease, while the Hôtel-Dieu took
          care of incidental maladies. The contract was signed jointly by Frontenac
          and Mgr de Saint-Vallier, the second Bishop of Quebec. The Récollets on
          leaving the buildings took with them practically everything movable, so
          that the interior had to be completely redecorated. The hospital was
          officially opened April 1, 1693, with four nursing sisters in charge; they
          proceeded with plans for redecoration, which were carried out from 1697
          on.[3] There was a good deal of work done on the chapel during the first
          half of the eighteenth century,[4] and after the cession a very complete
          reconstruction was undertaken in 1769, to repair the damage suffered
          in the siege. The major part of the present interior decoration seems to
          date from this period, and is the work of Pierre Emond.[5]

> 1. Gérard Morisset, *La Vie et l'Œuvre du Frère Luc,* Quebec, 1944, *passim.*
> 2. *Monseigneur de Saint-Vallier et l'Hôpital-Général de Québec,* 1882,
> *passim.* The anonymous author of this work, the basic study of the hospital,
> was Mère Saint-Félix, according to an article in *B.R.H.*, XXXIV, 1928, p. 462 f.
> She was born of Irish parents named O'Reilly who died on arrival at Quebec
> during a cholera epidemic; orphaned, she was taken into the hospital and
> ultimately became a member of the nursing order.
> 3. "Tableau chronologique des principaux faits touchant l'histoire de l'Hôpital-
> Général de Québec." *B.R.H.*, XXXIII, 1927, p. 457 f.
> 4. This work is carefully enumerated by R. Traquair and G. Neilson, "The
> Architecture of the Hôpital Général," *McG.U.P.*, no. 31, *passim.*
> 5. See further on the Hôpital-Général, Ramsay Traquair, *The Old Architec-
> ture of Quebec,* Toronto, 1947, p. 18 f.; *V.d.Q.*, I, pp. 527–528; *V.E.*, pp. 17–19.

1672      Beauport, first church. The report of 1683 lists it as in stone, 60 feet long
          by 28 feet wide.[1] It was replaced by a second stone church built between
          1720 and 1723.[2]

1. *P.G.M.*, p. 118.

2. "Nos Eglises: Beauport," *L'Action Catholique* (Quebec), February 10, 1923.

1672–
1678

Montreal, third parish church. Built by the Sulpicians, who came to Montreal to direct the community's spiritual life in 1657.[1] Already by 1662 the Sulpicians felt that the second parish church, built in 1656 and used simultaneously by the parish and the Hôtel-Dieu, was inadequate, and land was appropriated for the new church.[2] The building programme was authorized by Bishop Laval in 1669, but difficulties as to site forced a postponement of operations until 1672, the first stone being laid on June 6.[3] The plans were drawn by Dollier de Casson, Superior of the Sulpician Order in Canada. The contractor, and superintendent of the work, was the master mason François Bailly *dit* Lafleur.[4] On October 30, 1678, the Bishop of Quebec erected Notre-Dame de Montréal as a parish with a fixed incumbent. In the act, he states that he found the church "almost finished."[5] The church was consecrated and opened for worship in 1678,[6] whereupon the 1656 church was torn down. According to the report of 1683, the new church was "built of stone, 129 feet long by 38 feet wide, dedicated to the Holy Virgin under the title of her Immaculate Conception."[7] In 1708 the church was remodelled by Vachon de Belmont, the new Superior of the Sulpician Order in Canada.[8] He enlarged the whole church by about 24 feet, and began a tower and clocher on the south-west corner of the façade, which, however, was never completed.[9] The lower part of this unfinished tower was turned into a chapel dedicated to Saint-Roch. In 1722 a large-scale remodelling of the church was undertaken.

1. The Sulpician Order was founded in Paris, January, 1642, by Jean-Jacques Olier. Four Sulpicians came to Montreal in 1657, viz.: Abbés de Queylus, Souart, Galinier and Dallet. *B.R.H.*, L, 1944, p. 1; *M.H.:S.-S.*, *passim*; Henri Gauthier, *La Compagnie de Saint-Sulpice au Canada*, reviewed in *B.R.H.*, XVIII, 1912, p. 61.

2. *A.V.M.*, II, p. 662: "Il y a longtems que les habitans du dict lieu auroient faict un fonds des deniers apartenant à leur communauté pour bastyr une église paroissale au dict lieu . . . celle où se faict à present Le service diuin apartenant à l'hospital Saint-Joseph nestant qun emprunt, ils nous [i.e., Paul de Chambly, Governor of the Island of Montreal] requeroient de leur desliurer pour ce subject une place La plus conuenable pour la commodité du public pour y faire bastyr la ditte esglise. . . ." Then follows the Governor's grant of four acres for the purpose.

3. *A.V.M.*, I, p. 345 f., says the foundations were begun June 21, 1672, and the five first stones laid June 30. The date of June 6 is from the parish archives, "Actes de position de la première pierre le 6 juin 1672," cited by C. Bertrand, *Histoire de Montréal*, I, Montreal, 1935, pp. 123–124.

4. Dollier de Casson entered the Seminary of Saint-Sulpice in Paris July 13, 1657; he arrived in New France September 7, 1666. Following sundry travels, he settled definitely in Montreal in 1671. About 1673 he wrote his *Histoire de Montréal.* Besides designing the 1672 church of Notre-Dame, he was co-planner of the city of Montreal, and designer of the old Seminary on Notre-Dame Street. He died September 27, 1701. *M.H.:M.*, p. 33 f.

François Bailly *dit* Lafleur arrived in Montreal in 1659; about 1675 he became "sergent royal, géolier et concierge de la prison," posts which he held until 1683. He is also known to have designed a bakery, in 1683. Died July, 1690. *M.E.A.*, pp. 137–138.

5. Bertrand, *Histoire de Montréal*, I, pp. 123–124.

6. This is the date given by *A.V.M.*, I, p. 345 f. Olivier Maurault, *La Paroisse*, Montreal, 1929 (the best source book on Notre-Dame), has discovered by consulting the parish archives that the church was not used for regular services until 1683.

7. *P.G.M.*, p. 127.

8. Vachon de Belmont was born in 1642. Ordained in Canada in 1681, he rose to be Superior of the Sulpicians in Canada and of the Sœurs de la Congrégation, and Vicar-General of Montreal. From his youth he was interested in the fine arts, especially drawing and music; besides his work on Notre-Dame, he also assisted Dollier de Casson in designing the old Seminary on Notre-Dame Street. He died May 22, 1732. *M.E.A.*, p. 132 f.

9. *A.V.M.*, I, p. 351.

1674    Ancienne-Lorette, Jesuit chapel for the Hurons. The Hurons moved from Sainte-Foy, where the Jesuits had built a chapel for them in 1669, to Lorette, named after Loretto in Italy, in 1674. The new chapel was built in brick. It is quite minutely described in a letter of Father Martin Bouvart, dated March 1 and 2, 1675, as "similar to the true Loretto . . . forty feet long by twenty wide and twenty-five feet high. It is pierced by three doors, a chimney and two windows. There is a steeple [clocher] above that of the lower gable. . . ."[1] In the 1690's the Hurons moved again, this time to Jeune-Lorette; a deed dated January 7, 1698, gives the brick church, with four acres of ground, to the French settlers at Ancienne-Lorette.[2] Apparently this act was void, for a letter of Father de Couvert dated October 18, 1700, declares that "the ruins of the chapel [at Ancienne-Lorette] will serve to build the new one [at Jeune-Lorette],"[3] and it appears that the first church for French settlers at Ancienne-Lorette was a primitive structure, not replaced by a stone church until 1722.

1. R. Traquair, "The Huron Mission Church . . . of Notre Dame de la Jeune Lorette," *McG.U.P.*, no. 28. See also R. G. Thwaites (ed.), *The Jesuit Relations*, LVIII, Cleveland, 1899, p. 147; *L'Abeille* (Quebec), January 30, February 6, 13, 27, March 20, April 10, 24, 1879.

2. L. St-G. Lindsay, *Notre-Dame de la Jeune-Lorette en la Nouvelle-France*, Montreal, 1900, p. 32.

3. "La Chapelle des Hurons à la Jeune-Lorette," *B.R.H.*, XXXI, 1925, p. 351.

1674–   Pointe-aux-Trembles, Montreal, first church. The report of 1683 calls it a
1678    chapel, gives the dimensions as 36 feet long by 24 feet wide, and the information that it was dedicated to l'Enfant-Jésus.[1] Projected in 1674, work began in 1675 under François Beau and Laurent Archambault, and the church was opened March 13, 1678.[2] In 1684 a bell was acquired;[3] the church therefore must have had a clocher of some kind. The first church on the Island of Montreal outside the city, it was replaced by a second church in 1705. Adair presumes the chapel was of wood, but the length of time in building, and the presence of a pair of workmen—suggesting a carpenter and a mason—give room for speculation that it may have been partly of stone.

1. *P.G.M.*, p. 128.

2. *A.V.M.*, I, p. 209 f.

3. E. R. Adair, "The Church of L'Enfant-Jésus, Pointe-aux-Trembles," *B.R.H.*, XLII, 1936, p. 411 f.

1675–  Ange-Gardien, first church (Plate II). The work was under the direction of
1676      curé François Fillion, who came to the parish about 1667. The actual date
of construction is not certainly established.[1] Casgrain dated it on the basis
of a letter from curé Fillion to Bishop Laval preserved in the Archives de
l'Archevêché de Québec.[2] This letter, illegible in parts, would seem to give
the date for commencement of work as June 7, 1675, and of consecration
as St. Bartholomew's Day, 1676. The report of 1683 lists it as in stone,
60 feet long by 30 feet wide, dedicated to Les Saints Anges.[3] The original
interior decoration dated from the régime of curé Dufournel (1694–1749).[4]
Like the other churches on the Beaupré coast, it was badly damaged in
1759 during the siege of Quebec.[5] Restored 1835–1838 on the plans of
Thomas Baillargé, and altered again in 1875, when the nave was enlarged.
According to Casgrain, the apse was not touched during this alteration,
but to judge from photographic evidence and on stylistic grounds, the
interior decoration of the apse was probably altered at this time also. The
church was destroyed by fire in 1931; all that remains of it is a retable
made around 1700.[6]

> 1. A date of 1667 is proposed by the author of "Notes historiques sur la
> paroisse de Château-Richer," *B.R.H.*, XXXIX, 1933, p. 716. It seems hard to
> believe that this church would have been begun before that of the much more
> populous parish of Sainte-Famille, I.O., in 1669.
> 2. René-E. Casgrain, *Histoire de la paroisse de l'Ange-Gardien*, Quebec, 1902,
> *passim.*
> 3. *P.G.M.*, p. 117.
> 4. *V.E.*, pp. 33–36.
> 5. In a mémoire written by Mgr de Pontbriand, sixth Bishop of Quebec, to
> the King of France at the end of 1759, he declares, "The whole Beaupré coast
> and the Ile d'Orléans were destroyed before the siege ended. . . . The churches,
> to the number of ten, have been saved; but the windows, doors, altars, statues,
> and tabernacles have been broken." The text of this document, dated at
> Montreal, November 5, 1759, is found in H. Têtu and C.-O. Gagnon, *Mande-
> ments des évêques de Québec, 1647–1800*, II, Quebec, 1888, p. 6 f.
> 6. See p. 30, n. 17.

1675   Contrecœur, first chapel. According to the report of 1683, it was "a wooden
chapel, 30 feet long by 20 wide, dedicated to La Sainte-Trinité."[1] Replaced
by the first church in 1711.[2]

> 1. *P.G.M.*, p. 125.
> 2. Mathieu-A. Bernard, "Sainte-Trinité de Contrecœur," *B.R.H.* IV, 1898,
> p. 193; Ovide-M.-H. Lapalice, *Histoire de la Seigneurie Massue*, n.p., 1930,
> pp. 377–378.

1675   Montreal, second chapel of Notre-Dame-de-Bonsecours. The little wooden
chapel of 1670 soon became too small to accommodate the pilgrims
attracted to it by the miraculous statue of the Virgin, and in 1675 Mère
Bourgeoys was able to replace it by a stone chapel. This chapel stood until
1754 when it was destroyed by fire. It was in ruins until after the Cession;
a third chapel, utilizing the old walls, was begun in 1771.[1]

> 1. *V.E.*, p. 25 f.; Felix Martin, *Manuel du pèlerin à Notre-Dame-de-
> Bonsecours*, Montreal, 1848, *passim*; *A.V.M.*, I, p. 22, n. 1; *M.H.:M.*, p. 189 f.;
> O. Lapalice, "Les Pierres angulaires de la chapelle de Notre-Dame-de-Bonsecours,
> à Montréal," *B.R.H.*, XXXVI, 1930, p. 499.

circa 1675    Baie-Saint-Paul, first chapel. Exact date of construction uncertain, but Peter Kalm in 1749 described it as "reckoned one of the most ancient in Canada." Kalm further comments on its "bad architecture and want of ornaments, for the walls are formed of timbers, erected perpendicularly about two feet from each other, supporting the roof. Between these pieces of timber, they have made the walls of the church of black slate [rubble fill]. The roof is flat. The church has no steeple, but a bell fixed above the roof, in the open air."[1] This is probably the church mentioned in the 1683 report as at Saint-Paul *"du colombage,* very badly roofed, 50 feet long and 20 feet wide."[2] Replaced by a church begun in 1798.[3]

> 1. *P.K.T.,* p. 483,
> 2. *P.G.M.,* p. 118.
> 3. "Notes historiques sur la Baie-Saint-Paul," *L'Abeille,* November 10, 19, 28, December 6, 15, 22, 1859.

circa 1675    Nicolet, first chapel. A Récollet mission destroyed in the 1680's, probably before 1683, since it is not mentioned in the report of that year.[1]

> 1. J.-E. Bellemare, *Histoire de Nicolet, 1669–1924,* Arthabaska, 1924, p. 363.

circa 1675    Lauzon, first church of Saint-Joseph de la Pointe de Lévy. In 1675 King Louis XIV gave a grant of 4000 *livres* to curés and priests of the Seminary of Quebec to aid in building churches. The inhabitants of Lauzon received a considerable share of the royal bounty and began their church in that year.[1] It was completed in 1677; the report of 1683 records it as in stone, 45 feet long and 29 feet wide.[2] It was completely rebuilt and enlarged in 1721.

> 1. J.-E. Roy, *Histoire de la seigneurie de Lauzon,* I, Lévis, 1897, p. 264 f. Roy assumes that the date of 1677 given for this church by Bertrand de La Tour, *Mémoire sur la vie de M. de Laval,* Cologne, 1751, refers to the consecration of the church, not to its commencement.
> 2. *P.G.M.,* p. 120.

circa 1675    Lanoraie, first chapel. Built by Sieur Dautray following the concession of the seigniory to him in 1672, and served by a priest from Sorel. In 1689 the settlement at Lanoraie was annihilated by the Iroquois.[1]

> 1. "Notes historiques sur Lanoraie," *B.R.H.,* XXVI, 1920, p. 337 f.

1676    Lachine, first chapel (Plate IV). Built in the enclosure of Fort Rémi. Fort Rémi, built in 1671, was called Fort de la Chine until 1676 when the chapel was built in it, after which it was known as the Fort de l'Eglise until 1694, when the name was changed to Fort Rémi in honour of the first priest of the parish. The report of 1683 lists it as a chapel, 36 feet long by 36 feet wide (*sic?*), dedicated to Les Saints Anges.[1] Girouard gives as the builder one Pierre Gaudin *dit* Chatillon (1632–1700), a farmer and carpenter living near the Sault-Saint-Louis.[2] There is extant, however, a contract deeding land for this chapel on which the name of F. Bailly appears as a signer.[3] This may possibly be that François Bailly *dit* Lafleur who was the contractor for the 1672 parish church of Montreal.[4]

The first chapel at Lachine, however, seems to have been an exceedingly primitive structure, and an early replacement was planned from the first. However, all that was done was to shingle the roof, and to lay a stone foundation in 1686.[5] It was replaced by the first parish church begun in 1702.

1. *P.G.M.*, p. 128.
2. Désiré Girouard, *Lake St. Louis, Old and New*, Montreal, 1893, p. 45 f. See further p. 32, n. 29.
3. "La Première Eglise de Lachine," *B.R.H.*, XXXIV, 1928, pp. 26–27.
4. *M.E.A.*, p. 135.
5. Girouard, *Lake St. Louis.*

*circa*
1676

Sainte-Anne de Beaupré, second church. The first church of 1660 was almost immediately too small to accommodate the pilgrims crowding to the place of miraculous healing, and before its completion a programme of rebuilding was commenced under Abbé François Fillion, who was also connected with the 1675 church at Ange-Gardien.[1] According to the report of 1683, the new church was built in stone, 80 feet long and 28 feet wide, and in that year "one side of this church is ruinous and needs repair."[2] These repairs were begun in 1689, and the work went on through 1695; the result was an almost completely new church.[3]

1. *Souvenir du pèlerinage de Sainte-Anne-de-Beaupré*, Sainte-Anne, *c.* 1925.
2. *P.G.M.*, p. 116.
3. See further under the third church of Sainte-Anne, 1689.

*circa*
1676

Saint-Pierre, I.O., first church. Exact date uncertain. A document in the archives of the Seminary of Quebec records a payment to Robert Choret[1] in 1673, and later payments to André Coutdeau, *masson*,[2] and Jacques Chapelaine, *menuisier*.[3] On this basis, Traquair and Barbeau would date this first church *c.* 1676.[4] However, in the report of 1683, the church is listed as *de colombage*, 50 feet long and 22 feet wide, with a vault "not yet finished."[5] Roy would therefore date it 1680.[6] Replaced by the second church begun in 1718.[7]

1. Robert Choret, "seigneur de Bonsecours de Sainte-Croix, charpentier," was born in 1648. He married twice, in 1674 and again in 1686. *D.G.F.C.*, p. 128.
2. Tanguay lists no Coutdeau, but there is an André Coutron, baptized in 1646 in the diocese of Limoges, and married in 1681, whose occupation is recorded as that of a mason. *D.G.F.C.*, p. 147.
3. Baptized at Saint-Didier, bishopric of Poitiers, married at Quebec in 1666, professional carpenter. *D.G.F.C.*, p. 114.
4. R. Traquair and M. Barbeau, "The Church of Saint Pierre," *McG.U.P.*, no. 22.
5. *P.G.M.*, p. 118.
6. *V.E.*, pp. 79–80.
7. David Gosselin, *A travers Saint-Pierre, I.O.*, Quebec, 1923, *passim*.

1677–
1679

Quebec, Seminary buildings. The Seminary of Quebec was founded in 1663 by Bishop Laval.[1] In November, 1671, Laval and Frère Luc embarked together on a ship for France, and in the course of the voyage plans for the

Seminary buildings were determined; they were begun in 1677 and finished in 1679. Probably the chapel also was built at this time, but its decoration was not undertaken until some twenty years later, by Jacques Leblond *dit* Latour and his assistants.[2] It was the object of much contemporary admiration,[3] but unfortunately was totally destroyed, along with the other Seminary buildings, in the fire of November 15, 1701.[4]

1. *V.d.Q.*, I, pp. 287–288.
2. Communication of M. Morisset from the files of the Inventaire des Œuvres d'Art, December, 1952.
3. *V.d.Q.*, I, pp. 421–422.
4. *Ibid.*, II, pp. 11–12.

1679    Saint-Thomas de Montmagny, first chapel. Opened for worship August 24, 1679; replaced by the second chapel in 1685. In wood, located at the Pointe-à-la-Caille.[1]

1. F.-E.-J. Casault, *Notes historiques sur la paroisse de Saint-Thomas de Montmagny*, Quebec, 1906, pp. 17–18 and pp. 82–83.

1679    Repentigny, first church. The seigniory of Repentigny was established in 1676, the first seignior being Pierre Le Gardeur (d. 1736), who built the first church. It was replaced in 1725.[1] The report of 1683 calls it "a wooden chapel, 40 feet long and 22 feet wide."[2]

1. *V.E.*, pp. 97–98.
2. *P.G.M.*, p. 125.

1679    Neuville, first church. Listed in the report of 1683 as a "*Chapelle de colombage* dedicated to Saint-François-de-Sales, covered in thatch, 30 feet long and 22 feet wide."[1] Replaced by the second church, 1696.[2]

1. *P.G.M.*, p. 121.
2. *V.E.*, p. 65.

*circa* 1680    Montreal, Sulpician fort and chapel, foot of the Côte des Neiges. Known as the "Fort des Sauvages," it was built by Vachon de Belmont,[1] and dedicated to Notre-Dame-des-Neiges. Vachon de Belmont wrote to his superior in Paris that the chapel was "well-vaulted, and clapboarded [*lambrissée*] with shingled boards . . . well ornamented."[2] In 1694 the chapel was destroyed by fire. The mission was removed to Sault-au-Récollet in 1696,[3] where a chapel had been built five years before. The fort, however, was rebuilt in stone by Vachon de Belmont *c.* 1695.

1. *M.E.A.*, p. 132 f.
2. *M.H.:S.-S.*, p. 23 f.
3. R. Traquair and M. Barbeau, "The Church of the Visitation, Sault-au-Récollet," *McG.U.P.*, no. 18.

*circa* 1680    The following small chapels are mentioned in the report of 1683 as extant in that year:

1. Batiscan, "a wooden chapel 45 feet long by 22 feet wide, dedicated to Saint-François-Xavier." *P.G.M.*, p. 122.

2. Sainte-Anne (de la Pérade), "a wooden chapel, 20 feet long by 15 feet wide." *P.G.M.*, p. 122.

3. Champlain, "a wooden chapel 55 feet long by 25 feet wide." *P.G.M.*, p. 122.

4. Saint-Ours, "a little chapel *de pieux* dedicated to la Conception de la Sainte-Vierge, 30 feet long by 20 feet wide." *P.G.M.*, p. 125.

5. Laprairie (de la Madeleine). "There is a chapel in the mission of the Jesuit Fathers, and another on the *côte Saint-Lambert*, which is 25 feet long by 20 feet wide." *P.G.M.*, p. 127.

*circa*
1680

Château-Richer, second church. The report of 1683 lists at Château-Richer a stone church, 60 feet long and 30 feet wide, dedicated to "la Sainte Vierge sous le titre de la Visitation."[1] The 1658 church was almost certainly of wood, since it was never consecrated by Mgr de Laval; the new stone church which must have been built about 1680 was consecrated by the bishop in 1685. This church was destroyed in 1759.[2]

> 1. *P.G.M.*, p. 117.
> 2. "Notes historiques sur la paroisse de Château-Richer," *B.R.H.*, XXXIX, 1933, p. 716 f.

*circa*
1680

Sorel, first chapel. Abbé Ferland, writing in 1683, declares "There is a chapel at Sorel, 30 feet long and 12 feet wide, without a presbytery; the priest lives there."[1] According to the report of 1683, this chapel was dedicated to Saint-Pierre, and "the *habitants* have promised to repair it, until such time as they can build another."[2] However, this chapel was not replaced by a stone church until 1708.[3]

> 1. *A.V.M.*, I, p. 10.
> 2. *P.G.M.*, p. 124.
> 3. *M.H.:S.-S.*, p. 201.

1682–
1684

Trois-Rivières, second church. In 1682 René Pelletier, carpenter, contracted to tear down the 1664 church at Trois-Rivières and build another in wood, "de pièces en pièces."[1] According to this contract, which is quite detailed, the church is to be 60 feet long and 25 or 26 feet wide; it is to have a *jubé* (gallery) and a clocher resting on a *tambour* 10 feet long by 6 feet wide. Apparently these dimensions were not followed exactly, since the report of 1683 lists the church at Trois-Rivières as in wood, 50 feet long by 27 feet wide; it also adds that the church is not yet finished.[2] However, the building was complete by the next year, and in 1686 Mgr de Saint-Vallier noted in a letter: "I visited on my way [to Montreal] all the churches . . . on both sides of the river; that of the little town of Trois-Rivières, which is built *de pieux*, was the only one that gave me any satisfaction."[3] Replaced by the first stone church, begun in 1710.

> 1. The contract is cited by Odoric-M. Jouve, *Les Franciscains et le Canada: Aux Trois-Rivières*, Paris, 1934, p. 32 f. Cf. chap. III, n. 128.
> 2. *P.G.M.*, p. 124.
> 3. *Lettre de Monseigneur l'Evêque de Québec, où il rend compte . . . de l'état où il a laissé l'Eglise et la colonie*; see H. Têtu and C.-O. Gagnon, *Mandements des évêques de Québec*, I, Quebec, 1887, p. 191 f.

*circa* 1682   Longueuil, first chapel. The report of 1683 lists a chapel at Longueuil 40 feet long and 20 feet wide, dedicated to St. Anthony of Padua.[1] A description of the seigniorial establishment at Longueuil in the seventeenth century describes it as in a stone fort built by Sieur Le Moyne, and calls it "a very fine church."[2] It is difficult, however, to determine whether this refers to the same church cited in the 1683 report. Traquair dates the manorial establishment at Longueuil "between 1685 and 1690";[3] it may be that Le Moyne built the chapel in stone to replace an earlier wooden one, although there is no evidence either way. In any event, it is certain that there was a chapel built at Longueuil in the 1680's. The functions of this chapel were taken over by the parish church begun in 1724; the building itself was burned in 1792 and demolished in 1810.[4]

> 1. *P.G.M.*, p. 127.
> 2. *B.R.H.*, VI, 1900, p. 76. Cf. chap. III, p. 39.
> 3. R. Traquair, *The Old Architecture of Quebec*, Toronto, 1947, p. 37.
> 4. A. Jodoin and J.-L. Vincent, *History of Longueuil*, Montreal, 1889, *passim*.

*circa* 1683   Saint-Jean, I.O., first church. The report of 1683 describes it as *de colombage*, 45 feet long and 20 feet wide, and says it is not yet finished.[1] It was replaced about 1734.[2]

> 1. *P.G.M.*, p. 118.
> 2. *V.E.*, pp. 137–138; R. Traquair and M. Barbeau, "The Church of Saint Jean," *McG.U.P.*, no. 23.

*circa* 1683   Saint-François, I.O., first chapel. Noted in the 1683 report as "a chapel built in wood, 30 feet long and 20 feet wide, without a presbytery . . . dedicated to Saint-François-de-Sales."[1] Replaced by the first church in 1707.[2]

> 1. *P.G.M.*, p. 117.
> 2. *V.E.*, pp. 159–162; R. Traquair and M. Barbeau, "The Church of St. François," *McG.U.P.*, no. 14.

1683   Grondines, first chapel. The report of 1683 says of Grondines, "a chapel has been begun, which the *habitants* have promised to finish."[1] Replaced by the first church, begun in 1715.

> 1. *P.G.M.*, p. 122.

1683   Cap Saint-Ignace, first chapel. In 1685 Mgr de Saint-Vallier wrote, "I saw the new building of a chapel which they are putting up at la Pointe-à-la-Caille [i.e., Saint-Thomas de Montmagny]; . . . it will be served by the same missionary who is at Cap Saint-Ignace, where the church, although only in wood, is handsome enough, but as poor as the others, although it is in the most populated part of the mission. . . ."[1] The date of construction is presumed from a deed giving land for the church of Cap Saint-Ignace in 1683.[2] Replaced by a church begun *c.* 1690.

> 1. Quoted by N.-J. Sirois, *Monographie de St-Ignace du Cap St-Ignace*, Lévis, 1903, pp. 10, 61.
> 2. "Acte d'acceptation par Mgr. de Laval d'une terre offerte par le sieur Gamache pour l'érection d'une église au Cap Saint-Ignace . . . 2 mars 1683," *B.R.H.*, XXXV, 1929, p. 186.

1683     Châteauguay, first chapel. Dedicated to Saint-Joachim. Replaced by the
         church begun in 1735.[1]

>    1. *V.E.*, p. 227.

1684     Sault-au-Récollet, Jesuit chapel for the Indians. Apparently replacing a
         primitive *cabane d'écorce,* its construction is described in the *Jesuit Rela-
         tions,* where the dimensions are given as 60 feet long and 25 feet wide.[1] It
         was rebuilt in stone by the Sulpicians in 1691.[2]

>    1. R. G. Thwaites (ed.), *The Jesuit Relations,* LXIII, Cleveland, 1900, p. 233.
>    2. *M.H.:S.-S.,* p. 205 f.

1684–    Quebec, rebuilding of the Cathedral. Notre-Dame-de-la-Paix was elevated
1687     to the rank of a cathedral church by Clement X's bull dated October 1,
         1674. Laval was naturally anxious to embellish the church, but work did
         not begin until 1684, the year he left for France. Between 1684 and 1687
         a tower with a clocher was added to the façade, and the church lengthened
         50 feet by the choir, thus making to all intents and purposes a new church
         of it.[1] This work was under the general direction of the architect Claude
         Baillif,[2] but in 1688 Saint-Vallier sent to Quebec a "skilled and clever
         building contractor called Larivière, along with six masons and three
         carpenters, to work on Our cathedral and succursal church";[3] Larivière
         seems to have finished the job. In 1697 the façade was altered again; in
         1705 a sacristy was added to the south side, and in 1732 another on the
         north side. The church never seems to have been too highly regarded
         architecturally, however; Charlevoix's comments are savage.[4] The cathedral
         underwent another major alteration in 1744.[5]

>    1. *V.E.,* p. 1 f.
>    2. *A.N.F.,* pp. 127–128.
>    3. The quotation is from a letter written from Paris to officials in New
> France by Saint-Vallier, dated February 22, 1688. "Inventaire des documents
> concernant l'Eglise du Canada," *Rapport de l'Archiviste de la Province de
> Québec pour 1939–40,* p. 283 f. Born in 1639, "notaire, arpenteur et architecte,"
> Larivière died at Quebec in 1729. *D.G.F.C.,* p. 44.
>    4. Charlevoix in a letter to the Duchesse de Lesdiguières, dated at Quebec,
> October 28, 1720, declares: "The Cathedral would not be worthy of a good
> parish in one of the smallest towns of France. . . . Its architecture, its choir, its
> high altar, its chapels—all are exactly like the architecture of a country church.
> The most tolerable feature is a rather high tower, solidly built, which is fairly
> presentable from a distance." R. P. de Charlevoix, *Journal d'un voyage fait par
> ordre du roi dans l'Amérique septentrionale,* III, p. 73, quoted in *B.R.H.,*
> XXIX, 1923, p. 259. Charlevoix's comments are to be interpreted with care,
> however, since he seems to have had some private dislike for the Church in
> New France. Cf. P.-G. Roy, "L'Historien Charlevoix à Québec," *V.d.Q.,* II,
> pp. 31–32, which is a *précis* from J.-Edmond Roy, *Essai sur Charlevoix.*
>    5. See further, Paul-V. Charland, "Les Ruines de Notre-Dame," *Le Terroir,*
> September, October, November, 1924; Auguste Gosselin, *Henri de Bernières,*
> Quebec, 1902, chap. XIII, p. 158 f.

*circa*    Baie-du-Febvre, first chapel. A very primitive structure, replaced by the first
1685     church built in 1703.[1]

1. J.-E. Bellemare, *Histoire de la Baie-Saint-Antoine dite Baie-du-Febvre, 1683–1911*, Montreal, 1911, p. 8.

1685    Saint-Thomas de Montmagny, second chapel. Replacing the first chapel of 1679, it was built in *bois équarris*; Mgr de Saint-Vallier in 1685 noted that "I saw the new building of another chapel which is being built at la Pointe-à-la-Caille, and which they have to furnish with everything necessary. . . ."[1] He was able to consecrate the new building on April 21, 1686. Replaced by a stone church begun in 1715.

    1. F.-E.-J. Casault, *Notes historiques sur la paroisse de Saint-Thomas de Montmagny*, Quebec, 1906, pp. 19 f., 37 f.

1685    Rivière-Ouelle, first chapel, dedicated to Notre-Dame de Liesse. Begun late in 1684, it was opened for worship in 1685.[1] In 1750 the church was lengthened by the façade; in 1758 transepts in cut stone were built; the clocher was rebuilt in 1768. The church was completely reconstructed in 1792.[2]

    1. H.-E. Casgrain, *Une Paroisse canadienne au dix-septième siècle*, Quebec, 1880, p. 76 f.
    2. Information from the *Livre de Comptes*, transmitted to Gérard Morisset by curé Alphonse Têtu (1945), in the files of the Inventaire des Œuvres d'Art de la Province de Québec.

1685–    Saint-Joachim de Montmorency, first church. Begun in the summer of 1685
1686    and consecrated July 7, 1686. Burnt and completely destroyed by Wolfe's army in 1759.[1]

    1. *V.E.*, p. 231; *L'Abeille* (Quebec), July 9, October 23, 1849.

1686    Montreal, chapel of the second Hôtel-Dieu. A new building, replacing the 1644 structure, was designed for the Hôtel-Dieu in 1686. This edifice, including the chapel, was 130 feet long and 31 feet wide, and was designed by Abbé Guillaume Bailly.[1] It was apparently gutted by fire in 1695.[2] Rebuilt by Louis Geoffroy in 1702, it stood until 1721, when, along with most of the old city of Montreal, it was wiped out in a great conflagration.[3]

    1. Bailly arrived in Montreal in 1666. He was confessor and Superior of the Sœurs de la Congrégation from 1685 to 1691. In 1691 he returned to France where he died the same year. *M.E.A.*, pp. 140–141.
    2. E.-Z. Massicotte, "Les Incendies à Montréal sous le régime français," *B.R.H.*, XXV, 1919, p. 216. His information is drawn from *A.V.M.*, I, pp. 60, 350.
    3. June 12, 1721. E.-Z. Massicotte, "L'Incendie du vieux Montréal en 1721," *B.R.H.*, XXXII, 1926, p. 583 f.

*circa*    Saint-Louis au bout de l'Isle (Montreal), first chapel. The date, somewhat
1686    disputed, is that of Girouard.[1] It was built by the Sulpician missionary priest d'Urfé. The settlement was wiped out during the Indian wars beginning in 1688, and until 1713 no church existed on the site. In the latter year, the name was changed to Sainte-Anne du bout de l'Isle; a church was begun in 1714.

1. Désiré Girouard, *Lake St. Louis, Old and New*, Montreal, 1893, p. 146 f. A date of 1674 for the chapel was proposed by Bourgeault in *L'Echo du cabinet de lecture paroissial*, 1866, p. 226 f., who also maintained that the building was used as a parish church until 1714. Girouard's evidence would seem ample to modify both statements.

*circa* 1687      Laprairie, second chapel. Like the first chapel of *c.* 1668 which it replaced, it was also of wood. Replaced by the first church built in 1704.[1]

1. Jos. Chevalier, *Laprairie, notes historiques*, Montreal, 1941, p. 49 f.

1688      Quebec, church of Notre-Dame-des-Victoires (Plate XIII). Already in 1682 Bishop Laval was writing to M. de Seignelay in Paris, "There will soon be space to construct a chapel, of which the Lower Town stands in great need."[1] The corner-stone of the church, however, was not laid until 1688.[2] Originally dedicated to l'Enfant-Jésus, the name was changed to Notre-Dame-de-la-Victoire to commemorate the failure of Phips' attack on Quebec in 1690. In 1711 the name was changed to Notre-Dame-des-Victoires, and the façade rebuilt by popular subscription, following the fiasco of Walker's expedition against Quebec, wrecked in the Gulf of St. Lawrence. During the siege of 1759 the church was gutted by fire; Short's drawing shows its condition in 1760. Restored and re-opened for worship in 1765, it has since undergone considerable alteration. The interior was extensively restored in 1817. Three times during the nineteenth century it narrowly escaped destruction by fire.[3] Most of the exterior undoubtedly dates from between 1830 and 1860.[4] There was another restoration in 1888. The extant masonry probably dates from 1688 in good part.

1. P.-G. Roy, "Quelques Lettres de Mgr de Laval," *B.R.H.*, XLVI, 1940, p. 66 f.
2. *V.E.*, pp. 47–51. The inscription, in Latin, reads: "The Year of Our Lord 1688, Innocent XI being Supreme Pontiff, François de Laval first Bishop of Quebec, Louis XIV the Great reigning in France, the first stone of the succursal church of the Lower Town of Quebec, dedicated to l'Enfant-Jésus, was laid by the . . . Marquis de Denonville, Viceroy of New France."
3. Viz., April 30, 1836; September 12, 1840; August 15, 1854. *V.d.Q.*, I, pp. 483–484.
4. The treatment of façade and clocher is especially close to that of the Quebec school of this period. Compare, e.g., these features with those of Saint-Charles-Borromée, Bellechasse, rebuilt in 1828.

*circa* 1688      Rivière-des-Prairies, first chapel. The parish register here opens in 1688.[1]

1. Cyprien Tanguay, "Table chronologique des paroisses et missions . . . tenant registres, de 1621 à 1871," *D.G.F.C.*, p. 601.

1689– 1695      Sainte-Anne de Beaupré, third church (Plate VII). In 1689 the church of Sainte-Anne dating from *c.* 1676 was in need of repairs, and Claude Baillif, architect of the rebuilding of the Cathedral of Quebec dating from 1684, of Notre-Dame-des-Victoires, and later of Mgr de Saint-Vallier's Episcopal Palace, was called in to supervise them. He enlarged the church, and rebuilt the façade, creating to all intents and purposes a new building.[1] He designed the clocher (Plate VIII), which was built in 1696 by the carpenters R. Leclaire and Jean Marchand.[2] In 1787 parts of this church were rebuilt, but on the same design. It was replaced in 1878 by the fourth church, and upon its demolition certain parts of it were incorporated into the extant commemorative chapel, notably the clocher, the retable made by Jacques Leblond *dit* Latour about 1700, and the *tombeau* made by Thomas Baillargé, 1827.[3]

1. The foregoing information, which is substantially contradictory to earlier ideas, was obtained from M. Gérard Morisset, the director of the Inventaire des Œuvres d'Art de la Province de Québec.
2. *D.G.F.C.*, p. 409, lists a Jean Marchand, *charpentier*, baptized in 1646 in the bishopric of La Rochelle, who married Marie Hayot in Quebec in 1681, and had a numerous progeny. There is no mention of Leclaire.
3. J.-T. Nadeau, "La Vieille Eglise de Sainte-Anne-de-Beaupré," *L'Almanach de l'Action Sociale Catholique*, 1919, p. 120.

*circa* 1690     Cap Saint-Ignace, first church. Built in stone, replacing the chapel of 1683. This church, built on the river bank, collapsed into the river owing to erosion of the bank in 1744, and was totally destroyed.[1]

1. P.-G. Roy, "Un Episode de l'histoire du Cap Saint-Ignace," *B.R.H.*, XXXI, 1925, p. 321; N.-J. Sirois, *Monographie de St-Ignace du Cap St-Ignace*, Lévis, 1903, p. 60 f.

1691     Sault-au-Récollet, second chapel. Built by the Sulpicians, replacing the Jesuit chapel of 1684. Beaubien[1] says this chapel was in wood, with a bell-tower, but it is more probable that it was in stone, as the Sulpicians planned to use it for the Indian mission which had been centred in their "Fort des Sauvages" at the foot of the Côte des Neiges, built in 1680. The mission was not moved until 1696;[2] this may indicate an interval during which a stone chapel was being finished. In 1721 the Indians moved again, this time to Lac des Deux-Montagnes. Repaired in 1736 for the use of French settlers at the Sault, the chapel was demolished in 1749.[3]

1. C.-P. Beaubien, *Le Sault-au-Récollet*, Montreal, 1898, pp. 143–144, 149.
2. *M.H.:S.-S.*, p. 205 f.
3. Beaubien, *Le Sault-au-Récollet*.

*circa* 1692     Montreal, first Récollet residence and chapel. The Récollets established themselves in Montreal in 1692, under the leadership of Father Joseph Denys de la Ronde, a Canadian by birth.[1] Their first chapel was replaced by a more ambitious structure begun in 1706.

1. "Les Supérieurs ou Gardiens des Récollets à Montréal, 1692–1813," *B.R.H.*, XXXIV, 1928, p. 19.

*circa* 1692     Montreal, first Jesuit residence and church. The Jesuits taught in Montreal from 1694 on; Huguet-Latour would place their first residence and chapel in Montreal about 1692.[1] Their chapel, while never a parish church, served for public worship on special occasions.[2] Presumably replaced by the second church begun in 1719.[3]

1. *A.V.M.*, I, p. 209.
2. C. Bertrand, *Histoire de Montréal*, I, Montreal, 1935, pp. 180–181.
3. A drawing by James Duncan, in the "Album de Jacques Viger," represents this church as it appeared in 1837. It forms a right-angle with the body of the Jesuits' residence. At the opposite end, forming a kind of balancing wing, is another building which looks like a chapel; I suspect it may be the one built *c.* 1692.

1692    Varennes, first church. Replaced by the second church in 1718.[1]

> 1. Gérard Morisset, *Les Eglises et le trésor de Varennes*, Quebec, 1943, *passim.*

1693–    Montreal, chapel of Notre-Dame-de-Pitié, attached to the convent of the
1694     Sœurs de la Congrégation Notre-Dame. This order was founded at Montreal in 1658 by Mère Marguerite Bourgeoys.[1] Their first convent, located on the south side of St. Paul Street, opposite the Hôtel-Dieu, was destroyed by fire December 6–7, 1683.[2] It was rebuilt during the same decade. A chapel beside the new convent was begun late in 1693; funds were provided largely by Mlle Jeanne Le Ber and other members of her family.[3] This chapel was 54 feet long and 26 feet wide; the architect was probably Dollier de Casson, who consecrated it August 6, 1695.[4] The stonemason was Pierre Gay.[5] This chapel was destroyed by fire April 11, 1768.

> 1. "Les Congrégations de femmes au Canada," *B.R.H.*, L, 1944, p. 1.
> 2. E.-Z. Massicotte, "Les Incendies à Montréal sous le régime français," *B.R.H.*, XXV, 1919, p. 216.
> 3. Mlle Le Ber, who died October 3, 1714, at the age of fifty-two, lived the last nineteen years of her life as a recluse in a cell behind the altar of this church. "Notice chronologique sur la Congrégation de Notre-Dame à Ville-Marie," *A.V.M.*, I, p. 147 f.
> 4. *Ibid.* E.-Z. Massicotte, *M.E.A.*, p. 141, says the architect was Abbé Guillaume Bailly, who designed the new building for the Hôtel-Dieu in 1686. He probably refers to the rebuilding of the convent, since in the same article, pp. 140–141, he points out that Bailly died in France in 1691.
> 5. Massicotte, *M.E.A.*, p. 137, quoting an item from Abbé Faillon's *Vie de Mlle Jeanne Le Ber*, that in 1694 one Pierre Gay, "tailleur de pierre et maçon," contracted to construct a church 54 feet long and 26 feet wide, beside the convent of the Sœurs de la Congrégation.

*circa*    Lotbinière, first chapel. Mgr de Saint-Vallier spoke of a church in existence
1693     here at this date, but evidently he was in error; services were actually conducted in the house of Ignace Lemay, which was also used as a presbytery, until construction of a church proper, in 1717.[1]

> 1. *Edits et ordonnances des Intendants*, Ordinance of December 24, 1715.

1693    Quebec, third Récollet church (Plates XIX, XX). The Récollets, whose residence and church of Notre-Dame-des-Anges had been rebuilt in 1671 on the site occupied by them since 1621, felt the need of moving nearer to the centre of the city. In 1681 they acquired a plot of ground near the Château Saint-Louis and built on it a little *hospice* named, from its location, the "Couvent du Château."[1] It was not until 1693, however, after the sale of their establishment of Notre-Dame-des-Anges to Mgr de

Saint-Vallier for use as a hospital, that they "through the intercession of Count *Frontenac,* obtain'd leave of the King to build a little Chappel (which I call a Church;) notwithstanding the Remonstrances of Mr. *de Laval* our Bishop, who, in concert with the Jesuits, us'd his utmost Efforts for ten years together to hinder it."[2] Workmen excavating in the Place d'Armes in Quebec in 1824 uncovered two lead plaques which marked the first stone of this chapel, laid July 14, 1693.[3] Morisset believes the architect to have been Juconde Drué, Récollet, a pupil of Frère Luc, the designer of the Seminary of Quebec.[4] The new church and residence were built contiguous to the first *hospice,* forming with it a square which enclosed a spacious court. We know them well from engravings; they were considered one of the architectural features of the city. Charlevoix, writing in 1720, declared: "Les Pères Récollets ont une grande & belle Eglise, & qui leur feroit honneur à Versailles."[5] In the Récollet church were buried Governors Frontenac, Callières, Vaudreuil, and La Jonquière.[6] In 1759 the Récollet church was badly damaged; following the cession, the Récollets were forbidden to recruit, and their numbers rapidly dwindled from death and emigration to France. The church, repaired in 1760, was used for a time for Anglican services.[7] It was destroyed by fire September 6, 1796, and since the Récollet Order in Canada was practically extinct by this time the Récollet property was acquired by the government. The Anglican Cathedral of Quebec, begun in 1804, stands partly on this land.

1. *V.d.Q.,* I, pp. 529–530.
2. R. G. Thwaites (ed.), *Lahontan's New Voyages to North America,* Chicago, 1905, letter III, p. 39 f.
3. Odoric-M. Jouve, *Les Frères Mineurs à Québec, 1615–1905,* Quebec, 1906, p. 30.
4. *C.O.A.,* p. 14.
5. Père F.-X. de Charlevoix, *Histoire et description générale de la Nouvelle-France,* Paris, 1744, III, pp. 74–75.
6. *V.d.Q.,* I, pp. 529–530.
7. P.-G. Roy, "Le Lieu de réunion des Anglicains à Québec, de 1759 à 1804," *B.R.H.,* XLII, 1936, p. 231.

*circa* **Quebec, the "Chapelle du Petit-Hermitage," sometimes called the "Chapelle
1694** Saint-Roch."** In the 1692 contract of sale of the Récollet establishment of Notre-Dame-des-Anges, it is specified that since the Récollet land in the Upper Town, where their "Couvent du Château" was located, is too small for a garden, the Récollets shall have four acres of land on the other side of the St. Charles on which to grow vegetables and root crops, and on which to build a little retreat.[1] Following the completion of their new church in the city, they began to build a little chapel on this site; the act granting permission to build is dated November 4, 1693.[2] In 1697 it is recorded that Father Juconde Drué, the architect of the Récollet church in Quebec, was living in this little chapel while acting as chaplain of the Hôpital-Général; probably he designed the building. The chapel is indicated on a plan of Quebec drawn up in 1720 by Chaussegros de Léry, and in 1747 it is mentioned as a place for the instruction of Christianized Iroquois. Abandoned in 1759, it soon disappeared.

1. J.-Charles Gamache, *Histoire de Saint-Roch de Québec*, Quebec, 1929, pp. 24–25.
2. *V.d.Q.*, I, pp. 539–540.

1694    Saint-Augustin, Portneuf, first chapel. The chapel was moved in 1713 along with its cemetery to the Anse-à-Maheut site, to make it more conveniently accessible. Replaced in 1719 by a stone church.[1]

1. A. Béchard, *Histoire de la paroisse de Saint-Augustin, Portneuf*, Quebec, 1885, p. 19 f.

1694    Quebec, chapel in the Episcopal Palace (Plate XII). The contract for the building of an Episcopal Palace was given by Mgr de Saint-Vallier, second Bishop of Quebec, to Claude Baillif on January 10, 1693.[1] The first stone, however, was not laid until 1694. The building was substantially finished in 1697 when the Bishop returned from a trip to France. Lapotherie in 1700 described it as "a large building of cut stone; the main body of it, with the chapel making up the central section, faces the channel. It has a wing 72 feet long, with a pavilion at the end, forming an *avantcorps* on the east side. . . . The chapel is 60 feet long; its façade is of the composite order, built of fine cut stone, which is a sort of rough marble. Its interior is magnificent, by reason of its altar retable, the ornaments of which are a *raccourci* of that in the Val-de-Grâce. There would be few episcopal palaces in France which could rival it, if it were finished."[2] Occupied by the successive bishops of Quebec until 1759, it was ruined during the siege; Bishop Pontbriand wrote in 1759, "The Episcopal Palace is practically destroyed; there is not one livable apartment in it."[3] Known from Short's drawings of the ruins in 1759, it was subsequently transformed into the first Parliament Building of Quebec, in 1831.[4]

1. *V.d.Q.*, I, pp. 533–534.
2. Quoted by Roy, *ibid*. Cf. *B.R.H.*, XXXII, 1926, p. 291.
3. H. Têtu and C.-O. Gagnon, *Mandements des évêques de Québec*, II, Quebec, 1888, p. 6 f., "Description imparfaite de la misère au Canada."
4. H. Têtu, *Histoire du palais épiscopal de Québec*, Quebec, 1896, *passim*.

1694    Beaumont, first church. Served by the Récollets,[1] it was in wood, as we know from Intendant Bégon's directive in 1721, authorizing repairs and reconstruction in stone. This directive was apparently not acted upon immediately, since the second church was not built until 1727.[2]

1. J.-E. Roy, "Saint-Etienne de Beaumont," *B.R.H.*, XIX, 1913, p. 210 f.
2. *V.E.*, pp. 127–130; J.-E. Roy, "Saint-Etienne de Beaumont," *B.R.H.*, I, 1895, pp. 129–133; J.-T. Nadeau, "Beaumont, une vieille paroisse," *L'Almanach de l'Action Sociale Catholique*, 1934, pp. 65–78.

1694–   Quebec, chapel in the second Hôtel-Dieu. The first Hôtel-Dieu, finished in
1696    1644, was replaced in 1696 by a new building begun in 1694 by François de Lajoue. It was destroyed by fire on June 7, 1755.[1]

1. *V.d.Q.*, I, pp. 159–160. Roy's source here is primarily *Histoire de l'Hôtel-Dieu de Québec* (attributed to Mère Jeanne-Françoise Juchereau de Saint-Ignace), Montauban, 1751.

1694    Montreal, chapel in the Institut des Frères Charron (Hôpital-Général). The Institut des Frères Charron was designed primarily as a home for the aged; classes in arts and manufactures were also held there. The building was in three storeys, 90 feet long and 30 feet wide, probably designed by Pierre Le Ber.[1] The Institut, however, fell into financial difficulties, and in 1747 was taken over by the seigniors of Montreal, owing debts of more than two thousand *livres*. Mme d'Youville and the Grey Nuns thereupon made the building into the Hôpital-Général of Montreal. Most of the buildings were destroyed by a fire in 1765,[2] but parts still survive.

> 1. C. Bertrand, *Histoire de Montréal*, I, Montreal, 1935, pp. 179–180. Le Ber, a native of Montreal (1669–1707), was best known as a painter, particularly for his portrait of Marguerite Bourgeoys, made in 1700.
> 2. N. Bosworth, *Hochelaga Depicta*, Montreal, 1839, p. 137; *A.V.M.*, II, p. 34 f.

*circa*  Montreal, rebuilding of the Sulpician fort, foot of the Côte des Neiges. The
1695    first building, dating from *c.* 1680, was destroyed by fire in 1694. It was rebuilt in stone by Vachon de Belmont,[1] and thenceforth known as the "Fort des Messieurs." The chapel is described by Lapotherie as "de 50 pieds de long sur 25 de large, dont les murailles sont revêtus d'un lambris sur lequel il y a quelques ornements, comme d'urnes, de niches, de pilastres et de piédestaux, en façon de marbre rouge veiné de blanc."[2] With the rebuilding of 1796 in part altering its appearance, it survived into the twentieth century.[3]

> 1. *M.H.:S.-S.*, p. 23 f.
> 2. P.-G. Roy, "Le Fort des Messieurs à Montréal," *Vieux Manoirs, Vieilles Maisons*, Quebec, 1927, p. 5.
> 3. See the illustration by Roy. For an illustration of its appearance in the early nineteenth century, cf. N. Bosworth, *Hochelaga Depicta*, Montreal, 1839, p. 122; see further O. Maurault, *Le Fort des Messieurs, Montréal*, Montreal, 1925, *passim*.

1695    Saint-Laurent, I.O., first church (Plates VI, XLIX). Originally 55 feet long and 22 feet wide, it was lengthened by 20 feet in 1708 by the architect Jean Maillou, who built the church at Charlesbourg in 1695. The clocher was constructed in 1709 by Joseph Chabot, master carpenter of Quebec. This building served as parish church until September 26, 1864, when the second church was consecrated; it was subsequently demolished except for the clocher, which was taken down intact and at some later date (as yet undetermined) donated to the mission of Mont-Tremblant, a hundred miles north of Montreal. Here a replica of the old church of Saint-Laurent, at least in general lines, was erected in wood, and capped by the original clocher; this is still extant (Plate IX).[1]

> 1. Information furnished by Gérard Morisset from the Inventaire des Œuvres d'Art de la Province de Québec, based on the *Livre de Comptes* of Saint-Laurent. See also David Gosselin, *Histoire de la paroisse de Saint-Laurent, I.O.*, Quebec, 1904.

1695    Charlesbourg, first church, replacing the 1670 chapel. Its date is fixed by an entry in the *Livre de Comptes* for 1695, recording the payment to architect Jean Maillou of 198 *livres,* "pour le travail de Léglise."[1] Damaged in 1759, it was restored, and existed until its replacement by the second church begun in 1827.

1. Charles Trudelle, *La Paroisse de Charlesbourg*, Quebec, 1887, *passim.*

1696    Saint-Nicolas (Lévis), first chapel. Replaced by the first church begun in 1728.[1]

1. J.-E. Roy, *Histoire de la seigneurie de Lauzon*, I, Lévis, 1897, p. 435 f.; II, Lévis, 1898, pp. 38–39.

1696    Neuville, first church (Plate III), replacing the 1679 chapel. Neuville is sometimes referred to under its old name of La Pointe-aux-Trembles, not to be confused with Pointe-aux-Trembles near Montreal. The first church, which was not completely finished until 1715, was 75 feet long and 40 feet wide. Most of the interior decoration dates from the régime of Abbé Charles-François Bailly de Messein, curé from 1777 to 1794.[1] In 1845 the present nave was built. A complete rebuilding had been planned, but the parishioners objected to the destruction of the old apse, which still remains intact. This alteration in plan, sparing the old apse, resulted in the strange angle which it makes with the new nave.[2]

1. *V.E.*, pp. 65–66. Morisset suggests that the famous baldachin was designed by Augustin Quintal, Récollet (1683–1776), in 1766, and executed by his sculptor Gilles Bolvin (1711–1776), and others who made up the "Trois-Rivières school" of eighteenth-century sculpture. *C.O.A.*, pp. 30–31.
2. P.-G. Roy, "Saint-François de Sales de la Pointe-aux-Trembles," *B.R.H.*, III, 1897, p. 129 f.; J.-T. Nadeau, "La Pointe-aux-Trembles," *L'Almanach de l'Action Sociale Catholique*, 1921, pp. 69–72.

1696    Batiscan, the old presbytery. A wooden chapel, built about 1680 and mentioned in the 1683 report, was the first church building at Batiscan. A stone presbytery was built in 1696, and part of it was used for services until 1755, when a parish church proper was built. Such an arrangement was typical of many localities. Restorations in 1734, 1836, and 1855 have altered the internal woodwork and the roof of the old presbytery, but the walls remain from 1696, giving evidence of the general appearance of this type of presbytery-chapel. In 1876 the building became a farmhouse; it is now a summer cottage.[1]

1. R. Traquair, *The Old Architecture of Quebec*, Toronto, 1947, pp. 45–46.

1697    Montreal, devotional chapel to Sainte-Anne. Erected by Pierre Le Ber as a personal place of devotion, it later became a pilgrimage site. It was built in stone by François Charon.[1] After the Cession it was abandoned, but its ruins were still visible in 1823.[2]

1. E.-Z. Massicotte, "La Première Chapelle de Sainte-Anne à Montréal," *B.R.H.*, XLVIII, 1942, p. 51.
2. *A.V.M.*, I, pp. 350–351.

1697 Trois-Rivières, chapel in the Ursuline convent. This convent was founded in Trois-Rivières with the assistance of Mgr de Laval.[1] It was destroyed by fire in 1792.[2]

> 1. Auguste Gosselin, *Vie de Mgr de Laval*, Quebec, 1890, II, p. 497 f.
> 2. R. Traquair, *The Old Architecture of Quebec*, Toronto, 1947, p. 33.

1697 Champlain, first church. Replacing the chapel mentioned in the 1683 report, it was designed by Louis Geoffroy, Sulpician.[1] Repaced by the second church in 1808. According to Cloutier, the plans for the 1697 church were given by Geoffroy, although the act deeding land for the church, dated February 8, 1684, was witnessed by the architect Claude Baillif;[2] it is quite possible that he may have had a hand in it. Other names preserved in the *Livre de Comptes* of Champlain are Pépin, mason; Du Tremble, carpenter; Giasson, wood-worker.

> 1. Geoffroy was born in Paris about 1661; in Canada, he was successively curé of Laprairie, Champlain, Contrecœur, and Boucherville. He was actively interested in architecture and design. See further *M.E.A.*, p. 141; Prosper Cloutier, *Histoire de la paroisse de Champlain*, Trois-Rivières, 1915–1917, p. 170 f.
> 2. Cloutier; Eddie Hamelin, "Pages trifluviennes—Champlain," *Le Bien Public*, August 15–25, 1933.

1698 Sainte-Foy, first church. Replacing the Jesuit chapel built for the Indians in 1669, which the French settlers had been using since the mission was moved to Ancienne-Lorette. Destroyed by Murray during the campaign of 1760.[1]

> 1. H.-A. Scott, "La Paroisse de Sainte-Foy," *L'Almanach de l'Action Sociale Catholique*, 1919, pp. 68–70.

1698 Montreal, chapel of the Ferme Saint-Gabriel. This residence for the Sœurs de la Congrégation Notre-Dame was built to replace an earlier wooden structure of 1668 which burned in 1694. Wings added in 1726 and 1728.[1]

> 1. *V.E.*, pp. 103–104; *A.N.F.*, Figure 37; R. Traquair, *The Old Architecture of Quebec*, Toronto, 1947, p. 38 f.

*circa* 1699 Saint-François-du-Lac, first chapel. It served until 1734, when the first church, begun in 1731, was finished.[1]

> 1. Benjamin Sulte, *Histoire de la paroisse de Saint-Francois-du-Lac*, Montreal, 1886, p. 95.

1699 Ile-aux-Tourtes, first chapel. Built in connection with a Sulpician mission to the Indians. Replaced by a church in 1709.[1]

> 1. *M.H.:S.-S.*, p. 155 f.

1700–1760 (CHAPTER IV)

*circa*
1700
Cap Santé, first chapel. A Récollet, Father Guillaume Beaudoin, signed the first parish act here in 1693.[1] The first church dates about 1715; the chapel was actually the presbytery and *salle des habitants.*[2]

> 1. J.-E. Roy, "Saint-Etienne de Beaumont," *B.R.H.*, XIX, 1913, p. 217.
> 2. Gérard Morisset, *Le Cap Santé: ses églises et son trésor*, Quebec, 1944, pp. 11–12.

*circa*
1700
Chicoutimi, first chapel. Built by Jesuit missionaries, dedicated to Saint-François-Xavier. Replaced in 1727.[1]

> 1. "Chicoutimi, la reine du Nord," *B.R.H.*, XIX, 1913, p. 361.

*circa*
1700
Rimouski, first chapel. Built by Récollet missionaries, dedicated to Saint-Germain. Not extant after 1760.[1]

> 1. P. Hugolin, "Les Registres paroissiaux de Rimouski," *B.R.H.*, XVIII, 1912, pp. 129–130.

1700
L'Islet, first chapel. Built by Récollet missionaries, it measured 25 feet long by 20 feet wide, and contained only eleven pews. Replaced by the first church, begun in 1721.[1]

> 1. *V.E.*, pp. 213–214.

*circa*
1700
Jeune-Lorette (Loretteville), first chapel. The Huron mission at Ancienne-Lorette was moved to a new site, Jeune-Lorette, in the 1690's. There is considerable uncertainty about the date of the first chapel at Jeune-Lorette; but we know that in a letter of February 13, 1698, Mgr de Saint-Vallier announces his intention of giving 150 *écus* towards the building of a chapel at Jeune-Lorette, and in 1700 Father de Couvert, in charge of the mission, writes that "the ruins of the chapel [at Ancienne-Lorette] will serve to build the new one [at Jeune-Lorette]."[1] This first building was used until 1722, when the Jesuit Fathers' presbytery was consecrated as a chapel. From 1722 to 1730 the presbytery served as both priests' residence and chapel, as was not uncommon; in 1730 the second chapel was built.

> 1. "La Chapelle des Hurons à la Jeune-Lorette," *B.R.H.*, XXXI, 1925, p. 351 f. For further bibliography, see under the second chapter at Jeune-Lorette, 1730.

*circa*
1700
Bécancour, first chapel. Built by the Jesuits as an Indian mission. Replaced by the second chapel, *c.* 1735.[1]

> 1. "Notes sur les premiers temps de la colonisation à Bécancour," *B.R.H.*, VIII, 1902, p. 42.

1700–
1702
Saint-Antoine de Tilly, first chapel. In wood, built by the seignior Pierre-Noël Le Gardeur, Sieur de Tilly, who bought the seigniory in 1700 from a Carignan-Salières lieutenant, and served by the Récollets. It collapsed in 1721 and was replaced by a stone church.[1]

> 1. *V.E.*, p. 285 f.; A. Leclaire, *Le Saint-Laurent historique*, Quebec, 1906, pp. 71–72; P.-G. Roy, "Saint-Antoine de Tilly," *B.R.H.*, VIII, 1902, p. 321 f.

1702–
1703
Lachine, first church (Plate XXIX). Replacing the chapel of 1676, it was built by the mason-contractor Michel Lefebvre. It measured 60 feet long and 30 feet wide, and was opened for worship in 1703. It received a new roof in 1717, and the clocher was rebuilt in 1718. A new church was begun at Lachine in 1865, and the last Mass in the old church was celebrated November 26, 1865. Demolished in 1869.[1]

1. Désiré Girouard, *Lake St. Louis, Old and New*, Montreal, 1893, p. 45 f.; line drawing p. 50.

1703
Baie-du-Febvre, first church. Replacing the chapel of *c.* 1685, it existed until 1753 when it was replaced by the second church.[1]

1. J.-E. Bellemare, *Histoire de la Baie-Saint-Antoine dite Baie-du-Febvre, 1683–1911*, Montreal, 1911, p. 29 f.

1703–
1714
Sainte-Anne du bout de l'Isle, first chapel. The first chapel on this site was that dedicated to Saint-Louis, built in 1686, and destroyed during the Iroquois wars. No register was kept from 1688 to 1703, indicating a complete abeyance of religious activity here. In 1703 a stone chapel was begun, but it seems to have overtaxed the resources of the place, and was not entirely complete when, in 1714, it was decided to abandon this project and build on a larger scale. This first chapel, according to Girouard, was so small that it had no windows, being lit only from the roof.[1]

1. This probably means it was some kind of basement. Désiré Girouard, *Lake St. Louis, Old and New*, Montreal, 1893, p. 153 f.

*circa*
1704
Ile-Dupas, first chapel. The archives of the parish are fragmentary, but a wooden chapel, about 40 feet long, was certainly in existence by 1706. Replaced by a church begun in 1751.[1]

1. *A.V.M.*, I, pp. 1 f., 15.
2. "Les Archives Paroissiales de l'Ile-Dupas," *B.R.H.*, XXXII, 1926, pp. 241–242.

1704
Laprairie, first church. Replacing the chapel of *c.* 1687, it was built in stone by the Jesuits, and dedicated in 1705. It was roughly 80 feet long, 30 feet wide, and 20 feet high. It became the church of the parish when the Jesuit mission for the Indians was moved to Caughnawaga in 1716.[1] In 1769 the tower on the church was rebuilt, and in 1783 there was some damage from lightning, but the church stood until 1841, when the second church was completed.[2]

1. C. Bertrand, *Histoire de Montréal*, I, Montreal, 1935, pp. 245–246.
2. Jos. Chevalier, *Laprairie, notes historiques*, Montreal, 1941, pp. 62 f., 78 f., 120 f.

*circa*
1705
Vaudreuil, first chapel. Built as a Sulpician mission, dedicated to Saint-Michel. Replaced by the first church, *c.* 1728.[1]

1. E. R. Adair, "The Church of Saint-Michel de Vaudreuil," *B.R.H.*, XLIX, 1943, pp. 38–49, 75–89.

1705– Pointe-aux-Trembles (Montreal), second church (Plates XXX, XXXI). Re-
1709  placing the first wooden church begun in 1674. This church, which existed
   until its destruction by fire February 21, 1937,[1] provided a *coup d'œil* of
   the Montreal trends in church architecture and decorative sculpture over
   two centuries. The first stone, laid in June, 1705, was consecrated by
   Vachon de Belmont.[2] The church was finished in 1709. The tabernacle,
   dating from 1726, and probably the interior as well, was the work of
   Pierre-Noël Levasseur.[3] In 1740 the church was lengthened and side
   chapels added by the mason La Rose, this alteration giving it a cruciform
   plan.[4] The additions were decorated by Antoine Cirier, native of the
   parish, on the interior; this work was carried out between 1740 and 1747,
   under the direction of the Sulpician curé, Joseph Dargent.[5] The main
   façade was restored in 1792, and a new roof added in 1797. The clocher
   was rebuilt in 1799; a new clocher was put up in 1818, and this was
   restored in 1857. A sacristy was added in 1802, and a new vault put in
   between 1806 and 1809. Between 1818 and 1828 a major work of restoration on the interior was carried out by Urbain Brien *dit* Desrochers. In
   1823 the façade was again remodelled, and a *jubé* built. In the years
   1869 and 1870 the interior was "modernized."[6] It is thus obvious that this
   church, while of great interest in the details, hardly presents a coherent
   stylistic picture from any one era.

    1. See the account of the fire in *Le Canada* (Montreal), February 22, 1937.
    2. *Q.v.*, Notre-Dame, Montreal, 1672.
    3. Born in 1690, he died in 1770. Cf. Gérard Morisset, "La Dynastie des
   Levasseur," *C.O.A.*, p. 27 f.
    4. The main sources of information about this church are: *V.E.*, pp. 73–74,
   all of which information is drawn from *A.V.M.*, II, pp. 211–234; E. R. Adair,
   "The Church of L'Enfant-Jésus, Pointe-aux-Trembles," *B.R.H.*, XLII, 1936,
   411 f., which contains additional information drawn from the *Livres de
   Comptes.*
    5. C. Tanguay, *Répertoire général*, Quebec, 1868, p. 100, and *A.V.M.* say
   Dargent was a skilled architect and drew up the plans for the enlargement; but
   Adair, with good reason, is inclined to disagree.
    6. Of the existing photographs of this church, none that I know antedate
   this restoration.

1706– Montreal, first Récollet church (Plate XXIII). Replacing the chapel of
1713  *c.* 1692, it was begun in 1706.[1] In 1712 Pierre Janson *dit* Lapalme, mason,[2]
   contracted to finish the façade of the church by August 15, 1713, in
   "bonnes et loyales pierres," as well as other necessary works on the
   building.[3] Surviving the Cession, the church became the property of the
   government following the extinction of the Récollet order in Canada at
   the end of the eighteenth century. In 1818 it was sold to the *fabrique* of
   Notre-Dame. Repairs were begun, which lasted eighty years; from 1825
   on it was used by the Irish Catholic congregation of Montreal.[4] In 1830,
   following the completion of the new parish church of Notre-Dame,
   permission was asked and granted to transfer the façade from the old
   Notre-Dame (1722–1725) which was about to be demolished, to the
   Récollet church, along with its other fittings. The church, however, proved
   too small, despite enlargements, for the growing Irish congregation, and in

1843 a new church, St. Patrick's, was begun to accommodate it. The new church was opened in 1847, but the old Récollet church survived until its demolition in 1867.

1. S. Lesage, "Les Récollets au Canada," *La Revue canadienne*, IV, 1867, p. 304.
2. He was born in Paris, and died in Montreal in 1743. A well-known mason, other works by him include the clocher of Notre-Dame, Montreal (demolished 1843), the façade of the Jesuit church of Montreal (1719), and the third church of Varennes (1718). *M.E.A.*, p. 136.
3. E.-Z. Massicotte, "Edifices transplantés," *B.R.H.*, XLVII, 1941, pp. 202 f., 324 f.
4. *M.H.:M.*, p. 149 f.

1706    Saint-Sulpice, first church. Built by the Sulpicians, and served by them until 1776.[1] Presumably in wood, since the Intendant ordered a new stone church built in 1723.

1. A. Leclaire, *Le Saint-Laurent historique*, Quebec, 1906, p. 20.

1707    Saint-François, I.O., second chapel. Like the first, *c.* 1683, in wood. Various additions and repairs were made in succeeding years, but in 1730 the archdeacon Chartier de Lotbinière found that the building was "toute pourrie" and "menaçait ruine," and ordered the assembling of materials for a stone church, which was built in 1734.[1]

1. *V.E.*, pp. 159–163; R. Traquair and M. Barbeau, "The Church of St. François," *McG.U.P.*, no. 14.

1708    Sorel, first church. Replacing the chapel of *c.* 1680, it was built in 1708 by Louis Geoffroy, Sulpician.[1] Replaced by the second church begun 1732.[2]

1. *M.H.:S.-S.*, p. 201.
2. A. Couillard-Després, *Histoire de Sorel*, Montreal, 1926, p. 175 f.

1709–    Ile-aux-Tourtes, second chapel. Replacing the 1699 chapel, it was begun in
1711    1709 and finished in 1711 under René-Charles de Breslay, Sulpician,[1] as a mission for the Indians. Following the transfer of the Indian mission to Oka (Lac des Deux-Montagnes) in 1721, the mission was abandoned in 1726, and the chapel fell into decrepitude.[2] It was razed by Arnold in 1776.

1. He was born at Mons in 1658. *M.H.:S.-S.*, p. 155 f.
2. Désiré Girouard, *Lake St. Louis, Old and New*, Montreal, 1893, pp. 170–171.

1709    Kamouraska, first church. Built in wood. Guillaume Paradis was paid 25 *livres* in the autumn of 1709 "pour l'accommodement de la chapelle." A clocher was built in 1713, and in 1719 a tabernacle put in. Replaced by a second church begun in 1727.[1]

1. Gérard Morisset, "Les Eglises de Kamouraska," *Kamouraska* (A. Paradis, ed.), Quebec, 1948, p. 317 f.

*circa*    Trois-Pistoles, Récollet chapel. Date of construction uncertain, probably
1710    before 1760.[1]

1. P. Hugolin, "Les Registres paroissiaux de . . . Trois-Pistoles," *B.R.H.*, XVIII, 1912, p. 181 f.

*circa*   Yamachiche, first chapel, probably served by the Récollets. Replaced by a
1710      church built *c.* 1730.[1]

> 1. N. Caron, *Histoire de la paroisse d'Yamachiche*, Trois-Rivières, 1892,
> p. 60 f.

*circa*   Nicolet, first church. Bellemare says it was a stone church,[1] but a more
1710      probable tradition describes it as "bâtie en bois ronds, plus tard lambrissée
          en planches, et couverte en chaume."[2] Replaced by the second church
          begun in 1734.

> 1. J.-E. Bellemare, *Histoire de Nicolet, 1669–1924*, Arthabaska, 1924, p. 363.
> 2. "Les Trois Premières Eglises de Nicolet," *B.R.H.*, XXXII, 1926, p. 15 f.;
> this article is based upon notes made by the Rev. M. Moïse Proulx, Superior of
> the Seminary of Nicolet, about 1860. The description was made by Proulx on
> the basis of reminiscences of the oldest members of the parish at that time, of
> the accounts of the first church given by their grandparents.

1710–     Trois-Rivières, third parish church (Plates XXV, XXXII, XXXIII). Re-
          placing the 1682 church; the first stone was laid July 11, 1710. Elaborately
          planned, the church took some time to complete; the main interior decor-
          ating programme did not begin until 1730. Morisset suggests that the
          architect may have been Juconde Drué, Récollet.[1] The interior was de-
          signed by Augustin Quintal, Récollet, and executed by Gilles Bolvin.[2]
          The façade and clocher were rebuilt after the Cession.[3] The church was
          destroyed by fire in June, 1908.

> 1. The same who built the Récollet church in Quebec in 1693, *q.v.* Cf. *C.O.A.*,
> p. 15 f.
> 2. Quintal and Bolvin were the leading figures in the Trois-Rivières school
> of sculpture. Cf. Morisset, *C.O.A.*, p. 30 f., and O.-M. Jouve, *Les Franciscains
> et le Canada: Aux Trois-Rivières*, Paris, 1934, p. 135. The photographs of the
> now-destroyed interior of this church, which have been preserved in the
> Inventaire des Œuvres d'Art de la Province de Québec, justify Morisset's
> description of the sculptures as "dans le style des portes de la chapelle de
> Versailles," and Sulte's characterization of the interior as "du bon style Louis
> XV." "Nous avons ici le modèle même, l'art original, l'article non falsifié, et
> c'est rare, surtout de notre côté de l'océan." His footnote comments: "Le style
> Louis XV y brillait en effet dans toute la beauté de ses fantaisies." Benjamin
> Sulte, "L'Eglise paroissiale," *Mélanges historiques*, XIX, 1932, p. 28 f., and
> also the appendix to this volume by Gérard Malchelosse, pp. 82–83. Sulte's
> article was first published in *Le Trifluvien*, May 12, 1905; an English translation
> appeared in the *Catholic Record* (London, Ont.), May 27, 1905; see also
> *Canadian Antiquarian*, 1889, p. 87.
> 3. Sulte says 1773–1775, and is followed in this by Morisset.

1710      Chambly, chapel in the fort. The 1665 buildings of the fort were rebuilt in
          stone between 1710 and 1712 on the plans of Josué Boisberthelot de
          Beaucours under his personal direction.[1] Burnt by the Americans in 1775,
          the fort was restored in 1777. Abandoned 1847.[2]

> 1. Boisberthelot de Beaucours was born in 1662 and came to New France
> in 1688. From 1712 to 1715 he was again *ingénieur en chef* of the colony,
> after his work (1707) on the fortifications of Quebec. Successively Governor of
> Trois-Rivières and of Montreal, he died at Montreal May 9, 1750.
> 2. F.-A. Baillargé, "Le Fort de Chambly," *B.R.H.*, XV, 1909, p. 32.

**1711**     Contrecœur, first church. Like the 1675 chapel, in wood. Replaced by the second church in 1726.[1]

> 1. Mathieu-A. Bernard, "Sainte-Trinité de Contrecœur," *B.R.H.*, IV, 1898, p. 193; F.-J. Audet, *Contrecœur*, Montreal, 1940, p. 87.

**1712**     Boucherville, second church. Replacing the 1670 wooden church, it was in stone, the largest stone church between Montreal and Trois-Rivières.[1] The first stone was laid by Vachon de Belmont.[2] It is therefore possible that he may have had a hand in the plans. Apparently this church was without lateral chapels, since a project to add them was considered in 1786; eventually, however, it was decided to rebuild completely, and a new church was begun in 1801.

> 1. L. Lalande, *Une Vieille Seigneurie—Boucherville*, Montreal, 1890.
> 2. *A.V.M.*, I, p. 279 f.

**1713**     Pointe-Claire, first church. In stone, 60 feet long and 30 feet wide.[1] Erroneously attributed to Boisberthelot de Beaucours.[2] Replaced by the second church c. 1750.

> 1. Désiré Girouard, *Lake St. Louis, Old and New*, Montreal, 1893, p. 186 f.
> 2. By Massicotte, *M.E.A.*, pp. 136–137. In commenting on a passage in the *Mémoires* of Franquet, Beaucours' successor as chief engineer of the colony, Massicotte mistook a reference to Sainte-Anne de Bellevue (Sainte-Anne du bout de l'Isle) for Pointe-Claire. Cf. "Voyages et mémoires de Franquet," *Annuaire de l'Institut Canadien de Québec*, 1889, p. 69, August 3, 1752: "Embarked at 5 a.m. at Pointe-Claire, with the curé of Lachine. . . . . . . Arrived opposite the church of Sainte-Anne, where there is a little rapid. . . . . . The distance from Pointe-Claire to Sainte-Anne is estimated at 3 *lieues*. Having lunched with the curé of this village [i.e., *Sainte-Anne* not Pointe-Claire, as Massicotte took it], entered the church, more properly a chapel than a parish church; it was built on the plans of Mr. de Beaucourt, formerly engineer and Governor of Montreal. . . ." This error has been pointed out by Gérard Morisset.

*circa*      Deschambault, first chapel. The parish registers here open in 1713.[1]
**1713**

> 1. *D.G.F.C.*, p. 601.

*circa*      Saint-Vallier (Bellechasse), first church. The date of construction may be
**1713**     surmised from the opening of the parish register;[1] the church was demolished in 1904. Photographs of it are in existence, showing the clocher as reconstructed in the early decades of the nineteenth century.[2]

> 1. *D.G.F.C.*, p. 601.
> 2. *A.N.F.*, Plate 56b.

*circa*      Sainte-Anne du bout de l'Isle (Sainte-Anne de Bellevue), first church. The
**1714**     enlargement of the 1703 chapel was carried out on the plans of Boisberthelot de Beaucours.[1] In 1820 the church was again enlarged by about a third. Destroyed c. 1900.[2]

> 1. See note 2 on Pointe-Claire, first church, 1713.
> 2. Désiré Girouard, *Lake St. Louis, Old and New*, Montreal, 1893, p. 153 f.

1714–
1715
Cap-de-la-Madeleine, first church (Plate XXXIV). Now a chapel attached to the pilgrimage church. Replacing the 1661 chapel, it was begun in 1714 and finished in 1715.[1] As to what remains today from this early period, Arthur Joyal's statement is instructive: "De fait, au cours de ses deux siècles d'existence, en dépit de certaines réparations au clocher, dans la façade, à la couverture, dans la voûte, les boiseries ou le plancher, leur œuvre, dans ses grandes lignes, est demeurée parfaitement la même. . . . une porte a été pratiquée en arrière du maître-autel et l'on a élargi un châssis du côté sud. . . ."[2] The *flèche,* completed in 1719, was rebuilt in 1796; an attempt was made to reproduce the original form, however, and the same thing was true of a general restoration of the building which took place in 1904. Thus the church as it stands today probably looks not too unlike the original.

> 1. "Notes sur le Cap-de-la-Madeleine," *B.R.H.*, XXXIII, 1927, pp. 96–97.
> 2. Quoted by P.-G. Roy, *V.E.*, pp. 57–60.

*circa*
1715
Cap Santé, first church. Replacing a Récollet mission chapel built *c.* 1700. Morisset suggests that a plan by Jean Maillou in the archives of the Seminary of Quebec may be for this building.[1] Replaced by the second church, 1754.[2]

> 1. Gérard Morisset, *Le Cap Santé: ses églises et son trésor,* Quebec, 1944, p. 13 f.
> 2. Two histories of Cap Santé were published before Morisset's, by Abbés Gatien and David Gosselin, appearing at Quebec in 1884 and 1899 respectively.

1715–
1716
Grondines, first church, replacing the chapel of 1683. Begun in 1715, it was finished in 1716.[1] Replaced by the 1837 church designed by Thomas Baillargé.

> 1. *Livre de Comptes de la Fabrique de Grondines,* from the Inventaire des Œuvres d'Art de la Province de Québec.

*circa*
1715–
1719
Saint-Thomas de Montmagny, first church. Replacing earlier chapels of 1679 and 1685, it was begun either in 1715 or in 1716, and was consecrated July 23, 1719. This church had lateral chapels forming a transept, as we know from a contract assigning pews in them. In 1736 one Jean Michon contracted to do interior woodwork, and in the same year he and Pierre Bélanger contracted to repair the roof and clocher. "A l'égard du clocher," it is interesting to note, "s'obligent les dits Bélanger et Michon le mettre à l'épreuve de la pluie et de la neige et empêcher les goutières, soit en y appliquant du mastic d'avoine, soit en mettant des bardeaux en dehors, faire une écoutille au pont du dit clocher, mettre sur le dit pont un prélart de toile goudronnée, y faire, en un mot, au dit clocher et à la dite couverture, les réparations nécessaires."[1] This church was built on the same site as its predecessors, i.e., on the Pointe-à-la-Caille; about 1770 a new church was constructed on the present site of the church of Saint-Thomas, and the old one was abandoned in 1771. The change in site was necessitated by the erosion of the river bank on which the old church stood; it was not until 1837, however, that it collapsed into the water, and until

late in the nineteenth century its ruins were still visible, overrun twice daily by the tide. The second church was begun in 1768.

> 1. F.-E.-J. Casault, *Notes historiques sur la paroisse de Saint-Thomas de Montmagny*, Quebec, 1906, pp. 43 f., 80 f.

1716    Sainte-Anne de la Pérade, first church. This church was hardly finished when it began to deteriorate badly, and it was patched up continuously until its replacement by the second church in 1771. The retable of the altar was made around 1748 by Gilles Bolvin, "sculpteur des Trois-Rivières." Apparently this work was retained for the new church in 1771, being refurbished at this time. For gilding it, "M. Levasseur" received 387 *livres*.[1]

> 1. Chanoine Rhéault, *Autrefois et aujourd'hui à Sainte-Anne-de-Lapérade*, Trois-Rivières, 1895, pp. 42–43.

1716    Sainte-Anne de la Pocatière, first chapel. Built under missionary curé Lesclaches, in wood. Replaced by a church in 1735.[1]

> 1. N.-E. Dionne, *Sainte-Anne-de-la-Pocatière et l'Ile-aux-Oies*, Quebec, 1910.

1717    Caughnawaga, first chapel. The Jesuits, who had been conducting an Indian mission at Laprairie (*q.v.*, chapels of *c.* 1680 and 1687), moved it from Laprairie to Caughnawaga in 1716. The King granted them 2000 *livres* for the construction of a stone fort and chapel there.[1] This chapel was constructed in stone in 1717; it was replaced by a church, in 1845.[2]

> 1. C. Bertrand, *Histoire de Montréal*, I, Montreal, 1935, pp. 245–246.
> 2. J. G. Forbes, "Saint-François-Xavier de Caughnawaga," *B.R.H.*, V, 1899, p. 131 f.

1717    Lotbinière, first church, called the Domaine church. Built in the same area as the 1693 chapel. This 1693 chapel was replaced by the second church of Lotbinière in 1750, called the Sault-à-la-Biche church; thus on the *Carte générale des paroisses* made shortly after 1750 (*q.v.*), the 1717 church appears as the "old" church of Lotbinière. Both churches were replaced by the third, begun in 1818.[1]

> 1. Louis-C. Paradis, *Annales de Lotbinière*, Quebec, 1933, p. 34.

*circa*    Saint-Pierre, I.O., second church. Replacing the first church of *c.* 1676, it
1717–    was begun either in 1717 or 1718.[1] Most of the work that we see today
1719     dates from the first half of the nineteenth century; the eighteenth-century work is carefully listed in the monograph by Traquair and Barbeau.[2] In broad lines, however, the church preserves much of its old form. An enlargement of the choir was made about 1850, and between 1855 and 1857 there was a general renovation.[3]

> 1. 1717 is the commonly accepted date. On October 24, 1917, the parish celebrated its second centenary. Cf. David Gosselin, *A travers Saint-Pierre, I.O.*, Quebec, 1923. Barbeau notes that in 1717 one Guillaume Laberge received payment for "les soins de l'église neuve."
> 2. "The Church of Saint Pierre," *McG.U.P.*, no. 22.
> 3. *V.E.*, pp. 79–89.

1718     Montreal, chapel of Notre-Dame-de-la-Victoire. The convent of the Sœurs
         de la Congrégation, as rebuilt *c.* 1685, with its chapel of Notre-Dame-de-
         Pitié (1693), attached, was rebuilt farther up the Island in 1702, by Louis
         Geoffroy, Sulpician.[1] Apparently the chapel of Notre-Dame-de-Pitié was
         left standing in its old location, however. In 1718 a new chapel, closer to
         the rebuilt convent, was begun by the Sœurs, and dedicated to Notre-Dame-
         de-la-Victoire.[2] Both chapels, along with the convent, were destroyed by
         fire April 11, 1768.[3] The chapel of Notre-Dame-de-la-Victoire was rebuilt
         in the same year, the first Mass being said in the reconstructed chapel
         building on December 7, 1768.

> 1. *M.E.A.,* p. 141.
> 2. *A.V.M.,* I, p. 15; C. Bertrand, *Histoire de Montréal,* I, Montreal 1935,
> p. 201.
> 3. "Notice chronologique sur la congrégation de Notre-Dame à Ville-Marie,"
> *A.V.M.,* I, p. 147 f.

1718     Varennes, second church. The builder was the master-mason Pierre Janson-
         Lapalme.[1] The clocher was built in 1719; the main door by Noël Levasseur
         in 1726. Interior decoration included a pulpit stair by Caron, carpenter of
         Montreal, and a retable by Paul Jourdain *dit* Labrosse (1697–1773).
         Replaced by the third church, 1780.[2]

> 1. Janson-Lapalme came from Montreal. He was in Varennes by February,
> 1718, cutting stones, assisted by his son Christopher. See further *A.N.F.,* p. 133.
> 2. Gérard Morisset, *Les Eglises et le trésor de Varennes,* Quebec, 1943,
> p. 19 f.

1719     Saint-Augustin, Portneuf, first church. A contract for the building of this
         church with the mason Jean Ayde *dit* Criquy is cited by Béchard.[1] It
         describes in considerable detail a stone church 80 feet long by 38 feet
         wide, the walls 20 feet high to the eaves. The clocher is described in a
         separate document. (See above, chap. IV, nn. 77, 78.) Replaced by the
         second church begun 1809.

> 1. A. Béchard, *Histoire de la paroisse de Saint-Augustin, Portneuf,* Quebec,
> 1885, p. 43f. Jean Ayde *dit* Criquy was born in 1661 in the bishopric of La
> Rochelle; he lived at Neuville (Pointe-aux-Trembles), where he died December
> 12, 1726. *D.G.F.C.,* p. 2.

1719     Montreal, second Jesuit church, built by Pierre Janson-Lapalme.[1] It measured
         92 feet long and 30 feet wide. Partially destroyed by fire in 1754 and
         restored in 1756, it was confiscated by the government after the Cession.[2]
         The Jesuits returned to Montreal in 1842 and in 1863 began a new church.

> 1. *M.E.A.,* p. 136; *B.R.H.,* XLVII, 1941, p. 324.
> 2. C. Bertrand, *Histoire de Montréal,* I, Montreal, 1935, pp. 180–181, II,
> pp. 256–257; J. Douglas Borthwick, *Montreal: Its History,* Montreal, 1875,
> Plate p. 74, text p. 134 f.

1720–    Beauport, second church. Replacing the first church of 1672. First stone laid
1723     1720; completed 1722. Replaced by the third church in 1849.[1]

> 1. "Nos Eglises: Beauport," *L'Action Catholique* (Quebec), February 10,
> 1923.

*circa*     Saint-François-de-Sales (Montreal), first church. Built upon the erection of
1720     the parish, September 20, 1720.[1]

> 1. Elie-J. Auclair, "Saint-Vincent-de-Paul," *Mémoires de la Société Royale du Canada,* 3e série, 1932, Section I, p. 141; Auclair, *Sainte-Rose de Laval,* Montreal, 1940, p. 23.

1720     Quebec, chapel in the second Ursuline convent (Plate XXIV). The first convent, dating from 1641, was rebuilt following the fire of 1650; the reconstruction of the chapel went on from 1656 to 1667. In 1686 the convent was destroyed by a second fire. This time reconstruction was even slower. A new chapel was finally begun in 1720 and opened for worship in 1722. Its designer was François de Lajoue, a native of Paris,[1] who was popularly supposed to have modelled it on the chapel of the College of Louis le Grand in the capital.[2] The mason was J.-B. Boucher-Belleville.[2] The decoration of the chapel was done between 1734 and 1739 by Noël Levasseur (1680–1740), assisted by his cousin Pierre-Noël (1690–1770).[3] Not seriously damaged in the siege of 1759, the chapel existed relatively intact until a restoration in 1902. Photographs are extant of the original condition.[4]

> 1. *Les Ursulines de Québec, depuis leur établissement jusqu'à nos jours,* Quebec, 1863, II, pp. 108–112. François de Lajoue was baptized in Paris in 1656. He was married in Quebec in 1689. *D.G.F.C.,* p. 300.
> 2. This chapel includes a large retable, still extant, which evidently served Lajoue as his model. There is a drawing of it in the possession of M. Gérard Morisset, in the Inventaire des Œuvres d'Art.
> 3. Pierre-Noël married one of Lajoue's daughters in 1719.
> 4. *V.E.,* pp. 146–157.

*circa*     Trois-Rivières, Récollet chapel, now the Anglican church. In 1749 Peter
1720     Kalm noted that in Trois-Rivières there were "two churches of stone."[1] One of these was the parish church begun in 1710; the other, a Récollet chapel begun at some time subsequent. Unfortunately, there is no certain information about the latter. A lot in Trois-Rivières was deeded to the Récollets by Count Frontenac in 1692. It is possible that a chapel in wood was begun on this property at that time; in 1699 Frère Didace Pelletier was recorded as working on the "Récollet church of Trois-Rivières."[2] Since the 1682 church in Trois-Rivières was also known as the "Récollet church,"[3] it cannot be determined whether the Récollets had a separate building there in the seventeenth century. But in 1871 a stone was revealed during a restoration of the Anglican church in Trois-Rivières which bore the date 1720; this, it is presumed, was the keystone of a stone Récollet chapel begun in Trois-Rivières in that year. This chapel was appropriated by the government after the Cession, and became an Anglican church in 1762, after the Récollets had removed from it practically all furnishings. Enlarged in 1830 and repaired in 1871, it is still extant, although it is highly doubtful if anything beyond the walls survives from the 1720 building.[4]

> 1. *P.K.T.,* p. 419.
> 2. *V.E.,* p. 91 f.
> 3. Odoric-M. Jouve, *Les Franciscains et le Canada: Aux Trois-Rivières,* Paris,

1934, p. 32 f. He assumes that Didace Pelletier was related to the René Pelletier who contracted to build the church in Trois-Rivières in 1682. But, according to D.G.F.C., the two belonged to separate families.

4. S. Lesage, "Les Récollets au Canada," *La Revue canadienne*, IV, 1867, p. 303 f.

1721　　Saint-Antoine de Tilly, first church. In stone, replacing the chapel of 1700–2. Replaced by the second church in 1788.[1]

1. A. Leclaire, *Le Saint-Laurent historique*, Quebec, 1906, pp. 71–72; *V.E.*, p. 268; P.-G. Roy, "Saint-Antoine de Tilly," *B.R.H.*, VIII, 1902, p. 321 f.

1721　　L'Islet, first church, replacing the chapel of 1700. It was 72 feet long and 25 feet wide, with forty-one pews. Demolished in 1768.[1]

1. *V.E.*, p. 213.

1721　　Oka (Lac des Deux-Montagnes), Sulpician fort and chapel for the Indians. Both buildings were in stone. This was the Sulpician mission to the Indians which had been moved successively from the Côte des Neiges and Sault-au-Récollet locations (*q.v.*, 1691). Destroyed by fire in 1877.[1]

1. *M.H.:S.–S.*, pp. 165 f., 205 f.

1721　　Lauzon, second church of Saint-Joseph de la Pointe de Lévy. The first church, built *c.* 1675, was being completely rebuilt when the agent Collet came to the spot in 1721 while making his survey preliminary to the delimitation of the parishes. Built in cut stone by Guillaume Couture, the façade had five niches with statues. The completed church cost 4545 *livres*; a clocher was built in 1723 costing 563 *livres*. Of this amount the King gave 150 *livres*. Replaced by the third church begun in 1830.[1]

1. J.-E. Roy, *Histoire de la seigneurie de Lauzon*, I, Lévis, 1897, p. 273; II, Lévis, 1898, p. 96 f.

1722–　　Berthier-en-Haut, first church. Built in stone by the seignior, Pierre de
1724　　l'Estage, it had only forty-five pews.[1] Replaced by the second church in 1782.[2]

1. *V.E.*, p. 267.
2. S.-A. Moreau, *Précis de l'histoire de Berthier*, Berthier, 1889, p. 70 f.

1722　　Ancienne-Lorette, first church. The ruins of the 1674 Jesuit chapel at Ancienne-Lorette having presumably been used for the construction of the new Jesuit chapel at Jeune-Lorette, *c.* 1700 (q.v.), this site remained without a church from 1700 to 1722. On March 23 of the latter year Laurent Dubeau, builder, of the parish of Saint-Augustin, contracted with the *fabrique* of Ancienne-Lorette to build a church.[1] This was replaced by the second church begun 1837.

1. P.-G. Roy, *Inventaire des ordonnances des Intendants*, I, Beauceville, 1919, p. 217.

1722　　Montreal, rebuilding of the third parish church. This church, begun in 1672, was the most important in the colony after the cathedral church of Quebec.

In 1708 it had been enlarged by Vachon de Belmont. The extensive alterations begun in 1722, while utilizing the old structure to some extent, made a new church of it to all intents and purposes. The major work begun was on the façade.[1] Final plans for the design were drawn up by Chaussegros de Léry,[2] and on February 24, 1723, a contract for the masonry was signed with Paul Jourdain *dit* Labrosse.[3] The pilasters and gable of the façade were finished first; then, apparently, the *fabrique* ran into difficulties; for, on June 10, 1725, "on the evidence that rain and bad weather were damaging the tower which was begun, and in view of the fact that it cannot be finished before the beginning of winter, owing to the lack of funds, it is decided that money will be borrowed to finish it."[4] Not until 1728, however, was a bell ordered from Pierre Latour, *fondeur*.

Rapid increase of population in Montreal soon made it apparent that a completely new and larger church must be built for the parish; the church was widened in 1731 by three chapels inserted between the projecting transept and the right tower of the façade, and in 1734 the same thing was done on the left side; in 1742 a contract was signed with Dominique Janson-Lapalme for work of some sort on these extra bays, costing 100 *francs* per bay.[5] In 1757 it was definitely decided to build a new church. The new structure was to be 300 feet long, and the church wardens were authorized to acquire land for it. The war, and the subsequent cession, put an end to these plans. Repairs were urgently needed, however; in 1766 it was noted that both walls and woodwork of the old church were in ruinous condition. The roof was repaired in that year, and in 1767 the mason Jacques Beaucens contracted to repair the façade for 100 *livres* "attendant on its reconstruction." On February 16, 1777, it is reported that a clocher should be built, and MM. Lepailleur, Auger, Lemoyne *père,* and Poudret have been named to prepare plans for this work. I think this may refer to the long-deferred second clocher of de Léry's façade plan. However, this work does not seem to have been carried out; in 1787 Mgr Hubert, coadjutor of Quebec and deputy of the Bishop of Quebec, exhorts the church wardens to spend as little as possible on the old church, in anticipation of a new building; apparently this is what they have been doing. As early as 1794 plans were made to cover the church roof with tin, but in 1801 we learn that the wardens sold fifty cases of tin and the boards earmarked for this work, and in the same year the Governor's permission was asked for the building of a new church on the Place d'Armes. However, on May 22, 1803, it was resolved to cover the old church immediately with tin, since the college had just burned down, fired by sparks on the roof, and a similar disaster was feared for the old church. This work was carried out in 1804 by F.-X. Davelui, mason, and P. Saint-Amour, master-carpenter. In 1809, the vault and cornice were rebuilt, and the clocher repaired. Further work on the interior was carried out by Louis Quévillon, who received 5040 *livres* 19 *schillings* for his efforts in 1813.

This would seem to have been the last work done on the old church. Ten years later the vast new neo-Gothic church of Notre-Dame was begun. Upon its completion in 1830 demolition of the old structure was started.

However, the history of the old building was not yet over. The tower was left standing in the Place d'Armes until 1843. The façade was dismantled in 1830 and added to the Récollet church of Montreal, which had been begun in 1706 (*q.v.*). Here it remained, along with the interior fittings of the church, which were likewise taken over, until 1867, when the old Récollet church, used by the Irish congregation of Montreal from 1825 on, was finally demolished.[6]

1. For an account of this stage of the work, see chap. IV, pp. 78–79 and n. 67.

2. Chaussegros de Léry was born at Toulon in 1682; he came to New France in 1716 as Royal Engineer, and died at Quebec in 1756. J. Daniel, *Le Vicomte Chaussegros de Léry et sa famille,* Montreal, 1867, *passim; M.E.A.,* p. 138.

3. Paul Jourdain *dit* Labrosse was born in 1697; he belongs to a family of artisans better known as sculptors. In 1721 he made an organ-case for Notre-Dame; he died in 1773. *C.O.A.,* pp. 18, 111, 160.

4. *A.V.M.,* I, p. 345 f. All the remaining factual references to the architectural history of Notre-Dame cited here are from this source.

5. Dominique Janson-Lapalme was born at Quebec in 1701, the son of Pierre Janson-Lapalme. For some time he was Royal Architect at Quebec, where he died in 1762. *A.N.F.,* p. 133. It was following this work that Peter Kalm commented so favourably upon the parish church of Montreal: ". . . by far the finest, both in regard to its outward and inward ornaments, not only in this place, but in all Canada." Kalm was writing in 1749. *P.K.T.,* p. 412.

6. *M.H.:M.,* p. 149 f. The monograph on Notre-Dame by Olivier Maurault, *La Paroisse,* Montreal, 1929, deals mainly with the new church of Notre-Dame, finished in 1829, but in the early parts of the book treats of the 1672 and 1722 epochs. It is the best single modern study on this church. See also E.-Z. Massicotte, "Edifices transplantés," *B.R.H.,* XLVII, 1941, pp. 202, 324.

*circa* 1723   Saint-Sulpice, second church. Replacing the church of 1706, it was ordered by the Intendant in 1723.[1] Demolished in 1830.[2]

1. P.-G. Roy, *Inventaire des ordonnances des Intendants,* Beauceville, 1919, I, p. 248; quoted by Antoine Roy, *L.S.A.,* p. 153, n. 5.

2. A. Leclaire, *Le Saint-Laurent historique,* Quebec, 1906, p. 20.

*circa* 1723   Sainte-Geneviève, Batiscan, first church. A decree of March 15, 1723, accords permission to the inhabitants of this parish to build a church. The date of construction is not certain, but in 1727 an altar was finished for the church. Replaced by the second church *c.* 1755.[1]

1. E.-Z. Massicotte, "Sainte-Geneviève de Batiscan," *B.R.H.,* XL, 1934, p. 492 f.

1723   Montreal, chapel of the third Hôtel-Dieu. The 1686 building, rebuilt after the fire of 1695, was again destroyed by fire in 1721. Rebuilding began in 1723. The third building was destroyed in its turn, on April 10, 1734, again by fire.[1]

1. *A.V.M.,* I, pp. 60–61.

1724   Longueuil, first church. Replacing in function the chapel of *c.* 1682, it was not finished until 1727. Replaced by the second church in 1811.[1]

1. A. Jodoin and J.-L. Vincent, *History of Longueuil,* Montreal, 1889, p. 316.

1724    Lachenaie, first church (Plates XXXV, XXXVI). Planned in 1723, construction was not begun until 1724. The monograph by Traquair and Neilson gives complete details of the subsequent alterations, which were quite minor in character.[1] The church had a splendid tabernacle, the work of Gilles Bolvin on plans by Augustin Quintal (Plate XXXVI). Demolished 1883.

    1. R. Traquair and G. Neilson, "The Old Church of St. Charles de Lachenaie," *McG.U.P.*, no. 38.

*circa* 1724    Verchères, first church. The Intendant's order to build a church in stone in this parish is dated 1724.[1] Replaced by the second church in 1799.

    1. P.-G. Roy, *Inventaire des ordonnances des Intendants,* Beauceville, 1919, I, p. 264. Cf. *L.S.A.*, p. 158, n. 5.

1725    Repentigny, second church, replacing the 1679 building (Plates XXXIX, XL). In general outlines the church remains as it was from this time; actually, however, only the apse and roof remain from the 1725 building. About 1850 it was lengthened and widened, exactly how much is difficult to say.[1] The clochers were built between 1737 and 1749, and restored in the years 1838 and 1839. The original interior design was by Antoine Cirier in the years 1735–1756; a new vault was put in by Quévillon in 1819, but thoroughgoing repairs on the interior by one Querrete de Latulippe in 1850 and further nineteenth-century work have rendered the interior substantially late nineteenth century. The transept, main door, and *œil de bouc* were rehandled in 1806.[2]

    1. *V.E.*, pp. 97–98.
    2. Documentary information from the *Livre de Comptes,* and from the files of the Inventaire des Œuvres d'Art de la Province de Québec.

*circa* 1725    Saint-Roch des Aulnaies, first church. Land for this church was acquired in 1717, but in 1724 Bishop Saint-Vallier had to write to the parishioners of this new parish, created in 1722, urging them to put their project for a stone church into execution. This they apparently did soon after. This first church was replaced by a second church finished in 1777.[1]

    1. Henri Têtu, *Notice biographique: L'Abbé David-Henri Têtu, curé de Saint-Roch-des-Aulnaies,* Quebec, 1898, p. 12 f. This parish was originally known as Saint-Roch-des-Aulnets.

1726    Contrecœur, second church, replacing the first of 1711. In stone, 80 feet long and 40 feet wide. Replaced by the third church finished in 1817.[1]

    1. M.-A. Bernard, "Sainte-Trinité de Contrecœur," *B.R.H.*, IV, 1898, p. 193; A. Leclaire, *Le Saint-Laurent historique,* Quebec, 1906, pp. 21–22.

1727    Chicoutimi, second chapel. Replacing the first chapel of *c.* 1700. A stone church was built in the 1840's, but the old chapel existed until the end of the nineteenth century.[1]

    1. "Chicoutimi, la reine du Nord," *B.R.H.*, XIX, 1913, p. 361.

1727–   Longue-Pointe, first church. Owing to charges of fraud against the contractor,
1730    the construction of this church was unduly prolonged. Local workmen were
        responsible for most of the construction: Jacques Lefebvre roofed the
        church; Toussaint Périnau of Montreal did the masonry. The interior was
        mainly the work of Antoine Cirier; he contracted to do the vault in 1731,
        along with a pulpit which was to have a "twisting stairway like that in the
        Récollet church of Ville-Marie [Montreal]."[1] The sacristy behind the
        apse was built in 1798 by Nicolas Brisson, mason, of Sault-au-Récollet. In
        1834 the outside of the church and the towers were refurbished; the nave
        was re-roofed in 1845, and a crypt added in 1847.[2] The church was gutted
        by fire June 10, 1893. It was rebuilt along the old lines, with an interior
        entirely of plaster and a heavy neo-Romanesque clocher; this state of the
        church is seen in Leclaire's line drawing.[3] This rebuilt church was totally
        destroyed by fire November 7, 1907.

    1. A. Bellay, "L'Eglise de Saint-François d'Assise de la Longue-Pointe," *La
    Revue canadienne,* XXIX, 1893, p. 423 f.
    2. Olivier Maurault, *Saint-François d'Assise de la Longue-Pointe,* Montreal,
    1924, p. 5 f.
    3. A. Leclaire, *Le Saint-Laurent historique,* Quebec, 1906, p. 24 f.

1727    Beaumont, second church. The ordinance of Intendant Bégon in 1721,
        authorizing construction of a new church to replace the 1694 structure,[1]
        was apparently acted on at the time only to the extent of some repairs.
        Not until 1727 was the second church of Beaumont built. The building was
        damaged successively by Wolfe in 1759 and Montgomery in 1775, but
        apparently the church was not too badly harmed either time. The major
        alterations which have transfigured the church did not begin until 1870,
        when Ferdinand Peachy rebuilt the clocher. There followed a major
        rebuilding in 1894; in 1922 the façade was restored by Lorenzo Auger,
        and in 1933 the interior was repaired.[2]

    1. *V.E.,* pp. 128–129, quotes the document at some length.
    2. J.-E. Roy, "Saint-Etienne de Beaumont," *B.R.H.,* I, 1895, p. 129 f., and
    XIX, 1913, p. 238 f.

1727–   Kamouraska, second church. Replacing the first church of 1709, it was built
1736    in stone, the first stone being laid July 15, 1727. Work went very slowly,
        however. By 1732 only the crossing had been constructed. The façade
        was built in 1735, the vault in 1736. Considerably later the belfry of the
        clocher was erected. In 1789 the church was partially ruined by an earth-
        quake, and a new church was begun in 1791. Demolition of the second
        church began in 1801.[1]

    1. Gérard Morisset, "Les Eglises de Kamouraska," *Kamouraska* (A. Paradis,
    ed.), Quebec, 1948, p. 317 f. Cf. the drawing by Morisset of the second church
    on p. 86 of this book.

1728    Vaudreuil, first church. Replacing the chapel of *c.* 1705, it was also used by
        the people of Soulanges until 1780, when the church of Les Cèdres was
        built. Replaced by the 1773 church.[1]

    1. E. R. Adair, "The Church of Saint-Michel de Vaudreuil," *B.R.H.,* XLIX,

1943, p. 39; E.-J. Auclair, *Saint-Joseph de Soulanges ou Les Cèdres,* Montreal, 1927, pp. 24, 28–29.

1728    Saint-Nicolas (Lévis), first church. The Intendant's order to replace the chapel of 1696 was issued in 1721.[1] A start on the work was made at this time by the seignior Stephen Charet, and it is possible that the design was by Juconde Drué, Récollet.[2] The interior was built mainly over the walls of the old chapel, and it was planned to have a façade with five niches containing statues.[3] It was soon decided, however, to have a completely new church instead of a rebuilding. The first stone of the new edifice was laid July 9, 1728. Replaced by the 1821 church.[4]

    1. P.-G. Roy, *Inventaire des ordonnances des Intendants,* Beauceville, 1919, I, p. 201.
    2. He served at Saint-Nicolas from November, 1718, to September, 1720, according to J.-E. Roy, *Histoire de la seigneurie de Lauzon,* II, Lévis, 1898, p. 96 f.
    3. Cf. the church of Saint-Joseph, Lauzon, 1721. I think it quite possible that while at Saint-Nicolas Drué supplied designs for both churches.
    4. J.-E. Roy supplies this and further detailed information on the church.

1730    Jeune-Lorette (Loretteville), second chapel. The first chapel here, built for the Hurons *c.* 1700 upon their removal from Ancienne-Lorette, served until 1722, when Mgr de Saint-Vallier consecrated the presbytery of the Jesuit Fathers as a chapel. In 1730 a new chapel was begun, under the direction of Jesuit Father Richer. It would seem that in both the chapels at Jeune-Lorette the Jesuits tried to perpetuate the idea of the original Huron chapel at Ancienne-Lorette (1674), i.e., an imitation of the Santa Casa at Loretto in honour of Marie, patron saint of the Hurons; when he visited Jeune-Lorette in 1749 Peter Kalm recorded that: "There is a fine little church here, with a steeple and bell. The steeple is raised pretty high and covered with white tin plates. They claim that there is some similarity between this church in its shape and plan and the Santa Casa at Loretto in Italy. . . ."[1] A fire on June 10, 1862, destroyed the 1730 church but it was restored on substantially the original lines and still stands.[2]

    1. *P.K.T.,* p. 462.
    2. *V.E.,* p. 107 f. Cf. also L. St-G. Lindsay, *Notre-Dame de la Jeune-Lorette en la Nouvelle-France,* Montreal, 1900. The most complete study of the chapel is by Ramsay Traquair, "The Huron Mission Church . . . of Notre Dame de la Jeune Lorette," *McG.U.P.,* no. 28.

*circa*    Yamachiche, first church, replacing the chapel of *c.* 1710. Destroyed by fire
1730    March 19, 1780.[1] Morisset suggests as architect Augustin Quintal, Récollet.[2]

    1. N. Caron, *Histoire de la paroisse d'Yamachiche,* Trois-Rivières, 1892, p. 70 f.
    2. *C.O.A.,* p. 15, and *A.N.F.,* pp. 137–138. If Quintal were the architect the date of *c.* 1730 is preferable to the one suggested by Caron (*c.* 1735).

1731    Saint-François-du-Lac, first church. It had a tabernacle made by Jacques Leblond *dit* Latour.[1] Replaced by the second church begun in 1845.[2]

1. O.-M. Jouve, *Les Franciscains et le Canada: Aux Trois-Rivières,* Paris, 1934, pp. 76–77. For Leblond *dit* Latour (1670–1715), see *C.O.A.,* pp. 15, 26, 27, 50, 161.

2. Benjamin Sulte, "Saint-François-du-Lac," *La Revue canadienne,* 1886, p. 129 f.; 1887, p. 147 f.

1732–
1735

Saint-Laurent (Montreal), first church. Consecrated in 1735, it was built almost entirely at the expense of the Seminary of Saint-Sulpice. Repaired at various times, it existed until 1836.[1]

1. Armand Grou, "Les Origines de la paroisse Saint-Laurent," *La Revue canadienne,* VII, 1870, p. 721 f.

*circa*
1732

Lanoraie, first church. From 1724 on, Lanoraie was developed into a flourishing seigniory by Sieur J.-B. Neveu. The parish registers open in 1732 with the appointment of a curé; presumably the first church dates from around this time. Replaced by the second church, 1744.[1]

1. "Notes historiques sur Lanoraie," *B.R.H.,* XXVI, 1920, p. 337 f.; A. Leclaire, *Le Saint-Laurent historique,* Quebec, 1906, pp. 23–24.

1732–
1744

Sorel, second church, replacing the 1708 building. Although construction dragged on until 1744, the building was never satisfactory, and it was replaced in 1750 by a third church.[1]

1. A. Couillard-Després, *Histoire de Sorel,* Montreal, 1926, p. 180 f.

1733

Saint-François de Montmagny, first church. Variously repaired, it survived well into the nineteenth century. A new façade was built in 1866, and in 1870 F.-X. Berlinguet built the second church.[1]

1. *Livres de Comptes de la Fabrique de Saint-François,* in the files of the Inventaire des Œuvres d'Art de la Province de Québec.

1734

Terrebonne, first church. Begun in 1734, the church was consecrated in October, 1735. The tower was added in 1784; whether this was a rebuilding is difficult to say. In 1795 the roof was repaired and the sanctuary painted white. Lightning which struck the roof in 1831 necessitated another repair. It would seem that at some time, probably in the mid-nineteenth century, the cut-stone door-frames were added. In 1877 the first stone of the new church was laid, and the old one was demolished in 1885.[1]

1. C.-A. Gareau, *Aperçu historique de Terrebonne,* Terrebonne, 1927, p. 26 f.

1734–
1736

Saint-François, I.O., first church (Plate XXXVIII). Replacing the chapel of 1707, its construction was planned from 1730 on. Between 1731 and 1734 there are records of payment for cut stone to Thomas Allard, mason, of Quebec; in 1734 some one, perhaps Allard, is paid for making the plans. In 1759 the church was used by English troops as a barracks, and the interior woodwork destroyed. This was gradually replaced in the following years. André Paquet did most of the present interior between 1835 and 1844. The clocher was twice rebuilt, in 1821, and again in 1864 by François Gosselin of Saint-Laurent, I.O.[1]

1. *V.E.,* p. 159 f.; R. Traquair and M. Barbeau, "The Church of St. François de Sales," *McG.U.P.,* no. 14.

1734     Nicolet, second church. Replacing the first church, it was finished in 1740. The first stone was laid July 28, 1734. The third church was begun in 1781, and upon its completion the second was demolished, in 1787, and the stone sold to Yamachiche.[1]

> 1. J.-E. Bellemare, *Histoire de Nicolet, 1669–1924*, Arthabaska, 1924, p. 363 f.

*circa*
1734     Saint-Jean, I.O., second church. According to Barbeau, popular tradition alone sets the date of this church, which replaced the first church of c. 1683.[1] Popular tradition also has it that curé René-Philippe Robineau de Portneuf left the parish when the inhabitants refused to build according to his ideas, on a large cruciform plan. Additions and renovations to the church, which is still extant, include the clocher, rebuilt between 1775 and 1777 "à la forme des Récollets,"[2] and again completely rebuilt along with the façade, by Berlinguet between 1852 and 1853; the interior, done by Louis-Basile David about 1812; frescoing of the vault about 1815; a *jubé* built in 1813, rebuilt 1836, demolished 1853 and replaced by two new *jubés*.

> 1. R. Traquair and M. Barbeau, "The Church of Saint Jean," *McG.U.P.*, no. 23.
> 2. *V.E.*, p. 137 f.

1734     Sainte-Croix, Lotbinière, first church. According to Leclaire, it replaced a wooden missionary chapel of c. 1722. This locality was served for its first fifty-two years by the Récollets. Replaced by the 1836 church.[1]

> 1. A. Leclaire, *Le Saint-Laurent historique*, Quebec, 1906, p. 70.

*circa*
1735     Bécancour, second Indian chapel. Peter Kalm in 1749 made note of the settlement at Bécancour "wholly inhabited by Abenakee [Algonquin] Indians who have been converted to the Roman Catholic religion, and have Jesuits among them."[1] Measuring 30 feet wide and 60 feet long, it was burned in 1757.[2]

> 1. *P.K.T.*, p. 422.
> 2. "Notes sur les premiers temps de la colonisation à Bécancour," *B.R.H.*, VIII, 1902, p. 42.

*circa*
1735     Neuville, processional chapel (Plate XXI). Extant.[1]

> 1. *A.N.F.*, p. 65 and Figure 73.

*circa*
1735     Beaumont, processional chapel in cut stone. Built, according to tradition, in the 1730's; but Morisset is inclined to doubt this date.[1]

> 1. *A.N.F.*, p. 65 and Figure 74.

*circa*
1735     Forges-Saint-Maurice (Trois-Rivières), chapel. A chapel was in existence here in 1740, built "en bois rond."[1] It appears on the *Carte générale* of c. 1750[2] as a very primitive construction. Antoine Roy remarks on it as an isolated example of wood construction in this late period of New France's history.[3]

> 1. Auguste Gosselin, *L'Eglise du Canada depuis Monseigneur de Laval*, III, Quebec, 1914, p. 160.

2. See further discussion under the date *c.* 1750.
3. *L.S.A.*, p. 154, n. 1.

**1735**    Châteauguay, first church. Replacing the chapel of 1683, it was apparently quite small. Replaced by the extant church in 1775.[1]

> 1. *V.E.*, p. 227; C. Auclair, *Histoire de Châteauguay*, Montreal, 1935, p. 170 f.; Benjamin Sulte, "Châteauguay," *Le Monde Illustré* (Montreal), XI, p. 543 f.

**1735**    Sainte-Anne de la Pocatière, first church. Replacing the chapel of 1716. Dionne[1] says it was in wood, but this is probably a slip, inasmuch as he points out that following its destruction by fire in 1766 it was rebuilt on the old walls. Interior work here was by Jean Baillargé in the years 1750 and 1751. Replaced by the second church begun in 1795.[1]

> 1. N.-E. Dionne, *Sainte-Anne-de-la-Pocatière*, Quebec, 1910.

*circa*
**1737**    Saint-Joseph de la Beauce, first church. Damaged in 1759 and repaired, it was replaced by a second church in 1790.[1]

> 1. J.-E. Roy, *Histoire de la seigneurie de Lauzon*, II, Lévis, 1898, pp. 198–199; J.-T. Nadeau, "Saint-Joseph-de-la-Beauce," *L'Almanach de l'Action Sociale Catholique*, 1923, p. 121 f.

*circa*
**1737**    Saint-Jean-Port-Joli, first chapel. There is no exact record of its construction, but a burial is recorded in the "chapel" on January 7, 1738.[1] Replaced by a second chapel in 1756.[2]

> 1. Gérard Ouellet, *Ma Paroisse*, Quebec, 1945, p. 29 f.
> 2. *V.E.*, p. 241 f.

*circa*
**1738**    Pointe-du-Lac, first church. Replaced by the second church in 1844.[1]

> 1. "Deux Cents Ans de vie paroissialle à la Pointe-du-Lac," *Pages trifluviennes*, A, no. 21, 1939, p. 21.

**1739**    Maskinongé, first church. In wood, it was falling to ruins by 1763. A second church was completed in 1766.[1]

> 1. Hermann Plante, *Saint-Justin*, Trois-Rivières, 1937, p. 16.

**1739**    Chambly, first church. Replacing the chapel in the fort as rebuilt in 1710, it was built and served by the Récollets. Destroyed by fire in 1806.[1]

> 1. Jacques Viger, *Archéologie religieuse du diocèse de Montréal*, Montreal, 1850, p. 9.

**1739**    Saint-Mathias, Rouville, first church. Built in wood (?), it was demolished in 1777 and replaced by a stone presbytery serving also as a chapel.[1]

> 1. P.-G. Roy, "Saint-Mathias de Rouville," *B.R.H.*, V, 1899, p. 201.

**1740**    Pointe-aux-Trembles, Montreal. Remodelling of the 1705 church into a cruciform plan, with transepts. *Q.v.*, 1705.

1740    Ile-Perrot, first church. The Bishop of Quebec found it too small and too remote from the inhabitants, and refused to consecrate it, although it was finished by 1743. By 1767 only four walls remained, and materials for a new church had been assembled at a different site.[1]

> 1. R. Traquair and E. R. Adair, "The Church of Ste. Jeanne . . . Ile Perrot," *McG.U.P.*, no. 35; T. Napoléon Lemoine, "Essai historique sur l'Ile-Perrot," *L'Opinion publique*, summer, 1882.

*circa* 1740    Oka, pilgrimage chapels. Built by Sulpician missionaries to the Indians who had come there in 1721 (*q.v.*), they are of interest as examples of chapel building.[1]

> 1. *V.E.*, p. 119 f.

1740    Saint-Denis-sur-Richelieu, first church. A small chapel, it had already depreciated badly by 1752, and a new church was considered, but the exigencies of the war years rendered this impossible, and in 1758 the church was renovated merely. Replaced by the second church, which also served as a presbytery, and was finished in 1767.[1]

> 1. J.-B.-A. Allaire, *Histoire de la paroisse de Saint-Denis-sur-Richelieu*, St. Hyacinthe, 1905, chapter xiii, *passim*.

1743    Montreal, chapel of the fourth Hôtel-Dieu. The third building was destroyed by fire in 1734. The new chapel was consecrated August 12, 1744. Repaired and altered in 1827, it was replaced by a church begun in 1860.[1]

> 1. *A.V.M.*, I, pp. 60–62.

1743– 1746    Sainte-Famille, I.O., second church (Plate XXXVII). Replacing the 1669 church, it was begun in 1743, and the walls and roof were completed in 1746. It was flanked by twin towers on either side of the façade.[1] In 1806 the clochers were rebuilt, and in 1843 the central clocher was added. The interior of the choir and the side-altars were decorated by Thomas Baillargé in the years 1820 to 1825. In 1868 there was a general restoration of the west façade. The stone cornice above the door was added in 1910.[2]

> 1. According to R. Traquair and M. Barbeau, "The Church of Sainte Famille," *McG.U.P.*, no. 13, these towers were added in 1806. But Morisset has proved that they were part of the original scheme, and that the work in 1806 was a rebuilding of the clochers only. Cf. *A.N.F.*, p. 50.
> 2. *V.E.*, p. 171 f.

1744    Quebec, rebuilding of the Cathedral. A long and costly rebuilding of the 1684 structure, about which Charlevoix commented so unfavourably in 1720 (*q.v.*), was undertaken in 1744 by Chaussegros de Léry. When Peter Kalm was in Quebec in 1749 he reported that "the people are at present employed on ornamenting it";[2] the main work was substantially finished by 1748. "On its west side," said Kalm, "was a round steeple of two storeys, the lower one of which contained bells. The pulpit and some other parts within the church were of gilt. The seats were excellent." We see from Richard Short's drawings, several of which depict the Cathedral, that it was very badly damaged during the siege; the interior was completely gutted, and the masonry of the walls heavily damaged. A full-scale restoration of the Cathedral was begun in 1768.[3]

1. *Q.v.*, the 1722 façade of Notre-Dame in Montreal, and the 1730 Jesuit church in Quebec.
2. *P.K.T.*, pp. 427–428.
3. *V.E.*, p. 1 f.; Paul- V. Charland, "Les Ruines de Notre-Dame," *Le Terroir*, September & October, 1924.

1744 Lanoraie, second church. Replacing the first church of *c.* 1732, it was built of cut stone, and measured 80 feet long by 40 feet wide. Apparently the clocher was built later, for the first bell was not installed until 1773. Replaced by the third church opened in 1864.[1]

1. "Le Sacré-Cœur de Lanoraie," *B.R.H.*, V, 1899, p. 163; "Notes historiques sur Lanoraie," *B.R.H.*, XXVI, 1920, p. 337 f.

1744 Saint-Vincent-de-Paul, first church. Not finished until 1748. Replaced by the second church begun in 1857.[1]

1. P.-G. Roy, "Saint-Vincent-de-Paul," *B.R.H.*, III, 1897, p. 115; *Journal de Québec,* June 23, 1857.

*circa* Cap Saint-Ignace, second church, replacing the church of *c.* 1690 which had
1745 crumbled into the river. The building of the second church dragged on for some time, owing to a dispute among the parishioners as to the new location for the church. It was not completed until *c.* 1750.[1] Serving the functions of both church and presbytery, it existed until its replacement by the third church in 1773.[2]

1. P.-G. Roy, "Un Episode de l'histoire du Cap Saint-Ignace," *B.R.H.*, XXXI, 1925, p. 321 f.
2. N.-J. Sirois, *Monographie de St-Ignace du Cap St-Ignace*, Lévis, 1903, p. 60 f.

1745 Sainte-Rose, Montreal, first church. A presbytery-chapel was constructed at Sainte-Rose in 1741; when a parish was formed here in 1745, a church was immediately built. This church was abandoned in 1768 when, owing to an altercation with the bishop, the parish was placed under an interdict. No services were held at Sainte-Rose until *c.* 1788, when the second church was built. A document of May 30, 1746, names Pierre Leclaire as contractor for the 1745 church.[1]

1. E.-J. Auclair, *Sainte-Rose de Laval,* Montreal, 1940, p. 23 f.

*circa* Sainte-Marie, Beauce, first church. An act deeding land for this church is
1746 extant, dated February 23, 1746.[1] Replaced by the second church, 1856.

1. "Contrat de concession d'un terrain pour l'église de Sainte-Marie, Nouvelle-Beauce," *B.R.H.*, XIII, 1907, p. 372.

1747– Tadoussac, second church (Plate XXII). Between 1664, when the 1661
1749 church was burned, and 1737, there was no church at Tadoussac. In 1747 a wooden chapel for the Indians was built.[1] Intendant Bigot donated 200

*livres* for the chapel in 1749 to aid in its completion. Although built of wood, it has survived, with necessary repairs, the vicissitudes of two hundred years, and is still extant. The stone steps were built in 1942 by Sylvio Brassard.[2]

    1. Ch. Rambure, "L'Art monumental au Canada français . . .," *Bulletin de la Société de Géographie de Québec*, VI, 1912, gives as the builder Father Coquart, Jesuit. He was followed in this by P.-G. Roy, *V.E.*, p. 179 f. Antoine Roy, *L.S.A.*, p. 225, produces evidence that the builder was Michel de la Voye, a lawyer-farmer living at Petite-Rivière between 1737 and 1772. Cf. J.-A. Lavoie, *La Famille Lavoie au Canada*, Quebec, 1922, pp. 35–36; P.-G. Roy, *Rapport de l'Archiviste de la Province de Québec pour 1921–22*, p. 46.
    2. See also "Antiquités," *Journal de Québec*, December 24, 1856.

1748    Ile-aux-Coudres, first chapel. The land for this chapel was set aside as early as 1730. Replaced by the first church, 1771.[1]

    1. Alexis Mailloux, *Histoire de l'Ile-aux-Coudres*, Montreal, 1879, p. 18.

1748    Bécancour, first parish church in stone. Replaced by the second church, *c.* 1808.[1]

    1. "Notes sur les premiers temps de la colonisation à Bécancour," *B.R.H.*, VIII, 1902, p. 42.

1749    Les Becquets, first church. Replaced by the second church, 1838.[1]

    1. *Livre de Comptes de la Fabrique des Becquets*, I, 1748, p. 2; I, 1749, p. 2.

1749–   Sault-au-Récollet, first church. Replacing the chapel of 1691, it was conse-
1751    crated in 1752. Charles Guilbaut was the mason, and Joseph Valade the carpenter. The interior is entirely the work of the Quévillon school of the early nineteenth century, mainly of David Fleury-David, who worked on it beween 1816 and 1881. The façade is the work of John Ostell in 1851.[1]

    1. R. Traquair and E. R. Adair, "The Church of the Visitation, Sault-au-Récollet," *McG.U.P.*, no. 18; *V.E.*, p. 195; *M.E.A.*, p. 140. According to Massicotte, Charles Guilbaut was active from 1727 to 1766. He died at the Sault June 15, 1766.

1750    Saint-Antoine-sur-Richelieu, first church. Begun October 3, 1750, it was replaced by a second church begun 1779.[1]

    1. "La Centenaire d'une église," *La Minerve* (Montreal), October 15, 1880.

1750    L'Assomption, first church. Replacing an earlier wooden chapel of uncertain date, it was enlarged *c.* 1820 and replaced by the second and present church in 1864.[1]

    1. *V.E.*, p. 189.

1750    Lotbinière, second church. Replaced by the third church, 1818. See Appendix, p. 137.

1750    Sorel, third church. Replacing the 1732 church, under the direction of curé Collet. In 1769 it was rebuilt by Sieur Lamothe *dit* Laramée; the walls were repaired and raised a foot, and a sacristy was added. The rebuilt church was opened for worship c. 1770. Replaced by the fourth church, begun in 1826.[1]

> 1. A. Couillard-Després, *Histoire de Sorel,* Montreal, 1926, p. 160 f.

**1750**      Rivière-Ouelle, rebuilding of the 1685 chapel. This rebuilding, in which the original structure was lengthened by the façade, was followed by the building of transepts in 1758, which essentially made a church out of the chapel. *Q.v.,* 1685.

*circa*      Ile-aux-Oies, chapel. Burned June 5, 1764, and not rebuilt.[1]
**1750**

> 1. N.-E. Dionne, *Sainte-Anne-de-la-Pocatière et l'Ile-aux-Oies,* Quebec, 1910, pt. II.

*circa*      Pointe-Claire, second church. Replacing the first church of 1713, it was
**1750**      destroyed by fire April 16, 1881.[1]

> 1. Désiré Girouard, *Lake St. Louis, Old and New,* Montreal, 1893, p. 186 f.

*circa*      Perhaps the best map in existence which shows the number and extent of the
**1750**      church buildings in eighteenth-century New France is the one titled *Carte générale des paroisses et missions établies des deux côtés du fleuve Saint-Laurent, depuis Rimouski en montant jusqu'au côteau des Cèdres* (Plate I). This map is found in A.-L. Pinart, *Recueil des cartes, . . ., 1651–1731,* n.p., 1893. Pinart dated it 1690–1700. Study of this map soon convinced me that such an early date was impossible, and I wrote to the Dominion Archivist, W. Kaye Lamb, who had kindly supplied me with a photostat of it, proposing instead a date of c. 1745. His reply to me, dated May 26, 1949, reads in part as follows: "Mr. Richardson, of the Map Division, informs me that he is now fully convinced that you are correct in your deductions. . . . We are altering the date in our index accordingly." After the time of our correspondence, I was interested to discover a reference to this map by J.-E. Bellemare, *Histoire de la Baie-Saint-Antoine dite Baie-du-Febvre, 1683–1911,* Montreal, 1911, p. 45. On almost the same premises as my deductions, he concludes: "Nous croyons qu'elle est notablement postérieure à cette époque [1690–1700], et qu'elle a été confectionnée vers 1740." Bellemare's use of the word "confectionnée" might seem to imply that he considers the map a fake; but there is nothing on it to indicate that the original draughtsman was intending to palm off his work as late seventeenth century. However, the draughtsman apparently had not visited all the churches he indicates, since their architectural features are in many cases inaccurate. But the map shows many buildings which indicate its authenticity. For example, according to P.-G. Roy, *V.E.,* p. 241 f., the first church building at Saint-Jean-Port-Joli was not built until 1756. But Gérard Ouellet, *Ma Paroisse,* Quebec, 1945, p. 29 f., presents evidence that there was a small chapel in existence on this site by 1738; the map does show a small chapel at Saint-Jean, and before Ouellet's evidence came to light, it had been doubted on this account. M. Gérard Morisset has lately pointed out (letter to the

writer, January, 1953) that the map also shows both the 1717 and 1750 churches of Lotbinière [*q.v.*]; on this account he proposes to date the map *c.* 1752–1753, and further suggests Abbé Jacrau, curé of Quebec, as its author. Assuming a date of *c.* 1750 and a high degree of accuracy for this map, it proves the existence of chapels, presumably small missions, concerning which documentary evidence is lacking. These are:

La Malbaie.
Les Eboulements.
Saint-Pierre, Montmagny.
Saint-Michel, Bellechasse.
Les Ecureuils.

1751    Ile-Dupas, first church. Replacing the chapel of 1704, it was finished late in 1752 or early in 1753. Measuring 72 feet long by 30 feet wide, it had no regular curé until 1831. Replaced by the second church begun 1851.[1]

    1. *A.V.M.*, I, p. 22 f.

1751    Pierrefonds (Sainte-Geneviève-de-Jacques-Cartier), first church. Consecrated in 1751, it measured 90 feet long and 33 feet wide, and was 17 feet high. Lateral chapels were built to enlarge the church in 1772, along with a tower, probably one of two planned, which survived until 1925, when it was demolished. Replaced by the second church, 1847.[1]

    1. J.-E. Roy, "Saint-Geneviève de Jacques-Cartier," *B.R.H.*, IV, 1898, p. 321; P.-G. Roy, "Sainte-Geneviève de Pierrefonds," *B.R.H.*, XLVI, 1940, pp. 378–379.

1751    Deschaillons, first church. The parish was established in 1744[1] and the church begun in 1751; it was finished in 1753. Replaced by the second church begun 1791.[2]

    1. "Deuxième Centenaire de la paroisse de Saint-Jean-Baptiste, Deschaillons," *Le Soleil* (Quebec), July 23, 1944, p. 7.
    2. Felix-L. Lemay, *Histoire de Saint-Jean-Baptiste de Deschaillons,* Quebec, 1934, pp. 96, 118.

*circa* 1752    Saint-Charles-Borromée, Bellechasse, first church. J.-E. Roy would date it 1749.[1] Replaced, to all intents and purposes, by the second church built 1828; the sanctuary walls, although left intact, were completely redecorated on the interior.[2]

    1. J.-E. Roy, *Histoire de la seigneurie de Lauzon*, II, Lévis, 1898, p. 231.
    2. Georges Côté, *La Centenaire de l'église Saint-Charles-Borromée, sur rivière Boyer,* n.p., 1928, *passim*; P.-G. Roy, "Saint-Charles de Bellechasse," *B.R.H.*, IV, 1898, p. 5. According to the latter, the church was not opened for worship until May 8, 1757. I am following here Côté's account.

1753    Trois-Rivières, chapel in the second Ursuline convent. The first convent of 1697 burned in 1752; rebuilt, it existed until 1806 when it was burned again.[1]

    1. Ramsay Traquair, *The Old Architecture of Quebec,* Toronto, 1947, p. 33.

1753    Saint-Ours, first church. Replaced by the second church in 1877.[1]

    1. A. Couillard-Després, *Histoire de la seigneurie . . . de Saint-Ours,* Montreal, 1920, p. 49.

1753     Baie-du-Febvre, second church. Replacing the first church of 1703, it stood
         until its replacement by the third church, designed by Thomas Baillargé
         and built by Alexis Milette, in 1836.[1]

> 1. J.-E. Bellemare, *Histoire de la Baie-Saint-Antoine* . . ., Montreal, 1911,
> p. 29 f.

1754     Cap Santé, second church (Plates XLI, XLIII). Replacing the first church
         of *c.* 1715, it was built as one of the largest parish churches in New France,
         under the inspiration of curé Joseph Fillion. It was designed as a twin-
         towered church. The stone-cutter was named in the records as Aide-
         Créquy of Neuville, presumably one or both of the sons of the man who
         designed the 1719 church of Saint-Augustin, Portneuf.[1] The mason was
         named Pierre Renaud.[2] The builders contracted to finish the church by
         1758, but the war intervened and the façade and towers were not complete
         until 1763. The final work was done by the mason Descarreaux, of Neuville,
         and the clochers built by the carpenter Bélisle. When finished, it was the
         most imposing church in New France, owing to the ruin of the great
         churches of Quebec and Montreal. It was widely imitated.[3] Various changes
         since this time have altered the appearance of Cap Santé, although not
         fundamentally; the most important comprised the rebuilding of the towers
         in the years after 1807; the imitation of stone and wood on the façade,
         covering the original fieldstone; and the little lean-tos on the towers built
         by David Ouellet in 1877. The interior was largely finished by 1773, in
         which year the 1715 church was demolished; the interior was refurbished
         in 1830 and in 1889 by Raphaël Giroux.

> 1. Gérard Morisset, *Le Cap Santé: ses églises et son trésor*, Quebec, 1944,
> *passim.* Morisset considers Renaud the designer, and does not mention the
> relationship of the "stone-cutter" Aide-Créquy to the builder of Saint-Augustin;
> it is quite probable, however. Tanquay, *D.G.F.C.*, p. 2, shows that Jean Aide-
> Créquy had two sons, Louis and Antoine, both of whom followed their father's
> profession. Louis died in February, 1755, so that it was probably Antoine who
> worked at Cap Santé.
> 2. *V.E.*, p. 219 f. Roy's main source here is the parochial monograph
> published by the Abbé Gatien, Quebec, 1884.
> 3. These influences are summarized by Morisset, p. 26 f.

1755     Sainte-Geneviève, Batiscan, second church. Replaced the first church of
         *c.* 1723. Its building, as was the case with most churches begun in the last
         decade of New France's history, extended over a long period. Land for
         the new church was acquired as early as 1746; the 1755 church was, how-
         ever, not complete until 1770. It was enlarged in 1822. Sainte-Geneviève
         de Batiscan was not erected canonically as a parish until 1833. The church
         was demolished in 1870.[1]

> 1. E.-Z. Massicotte, "Sainte-Geneviève de Batiscan," *B.R.H.*, XL, 1934,
> p. 492 f.

1756     Montreal, rebuilding of the Jesuit church of 1719. Restored following its
         damage during the 1760 campaign, in 1763, it was given to the Church of
         England in 1789 for use as a parish church, by Lord Dorchester. It was

partially destroyed by fire in 1803, and abandoned in 1810 when Christ Church was completed.[1]

1. C. Bertrand, *Histoire de Montréal,* I, Montreal, 1935, p. 181; II, p. 250.

1756    Saint-Jean-Port-Joli, first church. Replacing the chapel of 1737, it was built in wood by missionary father Dolbec on land given by the first seigneur of Port-Joli, Ignace-Philippe Aubert de Gaspé. Roy seems to believe this church was completed at this time,[1] but according to Ouellet[2] there was not much more than a reconstruction of the old chapel to accommodate the growing population. The present church, which we may call the second, of Saint-Jean-Port-Joli, was in use by 1779.

1. *V.E.,* p. 241 f.
2. Gérard Ouellet, *Ma Paroisse,* Quebec, 1948, p. 39 f.

# INDEX